Cherry's Jubilee

Singin' and Swingin' through Life
with Dino and Frank,
Arnie and Jack

Don Cherry
and
Neil T. Daniels

TRIUMPH
B O O K S
CHICAGO

Library of Congress Cataloging-in-Publication Data

Cherry, Don, 1924–
    Cherry's jubilee: singin' and swingin' through life with Dino and Frank, Arnie and Jack / Don Cherry and Neil T. Daniels.
        p. cm.
    Includes index.
    ISBN-13: 978-1-57243-834-7 (alk. paper)
    ISBN-10: 1-57243-834-7 (alk. paper)
    1. Cherry, Don, 1924– 2. Singers—United States—Biography. 3. Golfers—United States—Biography. I. Daniels, Neil T., 1953– II. Title.
    ML420.C47217A3 2006
    782.42164092—dc22

                                                                2006001053

This book is available in quantity at special discounts for your group or organization. For further information, contact:

Triumph Books
542 South Dearborn Street
Suite 750
Chicago, Illinois 60605
(312) 939-3330
Fax (312) 663-3557

Printed in U.S.A.
ISBN-13: 978-1-57243-834-7
ISBN-10: 1-57243-834-7
Design by Graffolio Book Design & Typesetting

Contents

||||||||||||||||||||||||||||||||||||||||||||||||||||||||||||||||||||||||||||||||||||||||||||||||||||||||||||||||

From the bus of Willie Nelson—

They said: "Well, if he'd put as much time into his singing career as he did golfing . . ." etc., etc. And then others said: "Well, his golfing is so great, he should give up singing." But enough about me—let's talk about Don Cherry, my friend who did it all with grace, glamour, and beauty. He don't drink or smoke—hell, what am I doing hanging out with him anyway? I have no idea! Except when I'm 75 years old, I want to be just like him, especially that sweet disposition.

—WILLIE NELSON

Foreword

by Dan Jenkins

I FIRST SAW DON CHERRY IN 1947 ON A GOLF COURSE in Breckenridge, Texas, when he drove a 350-yard par-4 with a 3 wood. I asked somebody in a tool dresser's hat who that was.

"That's Don Cherry, and you don't want to know him," the man said.

"Why not?" I asked.

"Because he's always pissed off," the man said, lighting a Camel and picking up his canvas golf bag.

I said it was obvious Don Cherry was pissed off, seeing how he could drive a damn ball 350 yards with a f*cking 3 wood.

We became friends anyhow, and I followed his career as an amateur golfer who blew the U.S. Open and U.S. Amateur on numerous occasions, mostly by being pissed off, and tried to blow his singing career, mostly by being pissed off.

Someone asked me one time if Don had always been cynical, and I said, "I don't know for sure, but the only time I ever saw him laugh out loud was when he heard that two school buses collided head-on."

Something I remember about him in his golfing prime was that every time I ever asked him about one of the great Texas amateurs—Billy Maxwell, Earl Stewart, Morris Williams Jr., Joe Conrad, Tony Holguin—his response was, "He never beat *me!*"

The only thing I know about him for sure is that he's the best golfer who could also sing and the best singer who could also play golf.

And I suppose if God hadn't invented him, I'm sure I would have—for a novel.

Preface

by Neil T. Daniels

MY FIRST ENCOUNTER WITH DON CHERRY was in the mid-1960s when, at the ripe old age of 15 (thanks to child labor laws), I had the good fortune of assisting a network television executive at NBC. Don had just finished his first of many appearances on *The Dean Martin Show.* Before I could tell him that he was my mom's favorite singer, he was whisked away down the hall by the NBC Sports department to do an interview about golf. It was then that I realized Don Cherry was living a double life. The secret agent craze was beginning to sweep the nation then, and to this teenager, Don Cherry seemed to fit the 007 image to a tee. On any given morning you might find him at a prestigious country club battling world champion opponents. By nightfall, looking impeccable in a Sy Devore tux, Cherry could be at the Riviera crooning with the likes of secret agent Matt Helm (also known as Dean Martin). His five best friends in the world partied around him, earning the reputation of martini-drinking playboys who liked their drinks *"shaken...not stirred,"* and just like James Bond or Napoleon Solo, Don Cherry was always surrounded by the world's most beautiful women. Cocktail waitresses to beauty queens saw through the terrible-tempered exterior he often displayed to find a shy, sometimes insecure little boy, often haunted by the voice of his strict mother's upbringing. Well-known country vocalist Larry Gatlin once wrote, "Don, you can be simultaneously the most exasperating (that means horse's ass) and ingratiating (that means angelic) person I've ever met. Through it all, you remain my dear friend and I love you." Did his dual careers lead to his dual personalities? Or was it the other way around? Hopefully, this book will help you decide. All I really know is that everybody who has ever met Don Cherry has been touched in a unique and genuine way, myself included. From Demaret to Crosby, Dino to Palmer, Nicklaus to Sinatra, or baseball great Mickey Mantle to former U.S. presidents, Don Cherry prowled around with the world's most intriguing and powerful names in the world, but unlike 007, his adventure is real and is not a fabrication of this writer's wild imagination.

During the past year and a half, I did extensive research to learn more about Don's career in our efforts to write an accurate and compelling book. From full-length articles to mentions in popular columns, it was amazing to find such a flurry of articles written about him. Almost daily, his name appeared in publications such as *Las Vegas Today*, *Las Vegas Review-Journal*, and *Las Vegas Sun*.

In the literally thousands of paragraphs written about Don during this period, I have struggled to find a single sentence that was demeaning or degrading about him. Honestly, not one bad word! I sort of went ballistic, telling Don that it couldn't be! The readers want to hear "dirt." They are not going to believe all the wonderful accolades without hearing the other side of the coin. Trouble was, there was no other side to the coin. Don had them fooled. It took me a while before it hit me—Don not only had two careers, he also had two separate personalities. One that reminded me of Walter Matthau in the movie *Grumpy Old Men*— stubborn, cantankerous, hot-tempered, and determined to achieve. He assumed little patience for mistakes and took solitude by exiting out the back door. Starting into his fifties, Don began to change. His "other" personality was now beginning to overtake him.

Don once told me that it took him 50 years before he felt comfortable performing in front of an audience. Now I understand what he meant. Up to this point, I think golfing was his number-one mind frame. Singing before audiences was tough on him. His nerves preyed upon his shyness, and singing was work. By 1985, I think golf was becoming more work, and singing was becoming more pleasurable. Maybe the word *pleasurable* isn't exactly right, but the more Don enjoyed singing, the better he was becoming.

I don't like to get too far ahead of myself, but Don Cherry can wrap his voice around the lyrics of a song with more grace, ease, and feeling today than he did in all the preceding decades. That's not a lie. As Don began to enjoy performing for the people who came to see him, he began this Doctor Jekyll switch into Mister Hyde. He became relaxed and more engaging for the people who paid to see him. Okay, Don's still as ornery as ever, but his tightfistedness is well placed into being resourceful and thankful for the gifts he still has today.

His travels have taken him to every corner of the world. Once even through those White Pearly Gates. Hanging on to life, Don lay in a deep dark coma for days. Unexpectedly he awoke to travel on and live a true rags-to-riches story. Don Cherry recalls *everything* as if it happened yesterday, and has a "good-ole-down-to-earth" way of looking at things. Yet, when it comes to talking about himself or others he feels might be offended, he immediately becomes very uncomfortable.

I realized that my job was to push his limits, to balance the colorful memories Don has with the tragedies and hidden secrets he has nestled away, never wanting to reveal. I know that I really pissed him off at times, but I wasn't going to stand for a candy-coated, half-assed written documentary because his shy, sensitive, and headstrong nature stood in the way. The facts are the facts—no one will ever come close to what Don Cherry has achieved in a dual lifetime that is *still* making history. Who would have ever imagined that 30-some years after that first encounter, I would be sitting by Don's side writing as fast as I can, enthralled with the story you have in your hands.

P.S. Don, I'm changing my phone number!

Preface and Acknowledgments

by Donald Ross Cherry

AS OF THIS WRITING TWO PEOPLE ARE MISSING: my mother, Ross Alma Cherry, and my closest friend, father figure, and one of the greatest golfers of all time, James Newton Demaret (better known as "Jimmy"). It was my original intention to dedicate this book to them. Now, there is a third I would like to acknowledge and include. Someone who is very special to me, and whom I love very much...my wife, Francine Bond Cherry.

I also want to mention my cowriter, Neil Daniels. Other than reading the *Dean Martin Fan Center* magazines he publishes, I had no idea how good this man was. Neil states (at the end of the book) how he and I are very much alike. It's true. We have the same feelings about many things. In life, that's a hard quality to find. As two human beings, Donald Ross Cherry and Neil Thomas Daniels love and respect each other very much.

As for what's between the covers that you are now holding, I have tried to describe some of the greatest memories I have. I guess what comes to mind as I begin is an article once written by legendary sports writer Jim Murray. I was playing golf by daylight in the Sahara Open tournament and in the evenings I was performing in the Sahara Hotel's packed showroom. Murray came to hear me on a Saturday night, which didn't end until 1:30 in the morning. The following day I went out and shot a 38 on the front nine with two 3-putt greens and 29 on the back for a 67.

By Monday, Jim had written a whole syndicated article about me and finished it with: "Hearing Don Cherry sing 'Green Green Grass of Home' on Saturday night and watching him shoot a 67 with two 3-putt greens (on Sunday), and if you don't get goose pimples, then you wouldn't be impressed if Caruso went three for four in the World Series in the afternoon, and brought down the house with *Pagliacci* at the Met that night."

Of course there were also bad reviews and articles I won't forget either. I have recorded a few inside. Knowing that it takes a little of everything to make a book interesting to the person reading it, I was advised by another very well-known sportswriter, Oscar Fraley, that you have to include sex in a book to have it sell. Well, here goes...I was involved with a well-known movie starlet. When it came to sex, being very shy and from Texas, my only thoughts were that all the lights had to be out and nobody was allowed to talk. After four days, she finally made a statement: "This has been very good, but there are *other* ways." Even as naïve as I was, I knew what she was referring to. When she asked, "Have you ever heard of oral sex?" I replied soberly, "Sure. He's a preacher in Tulsa!"

As you have gathered by now, some people believe I was my own worst enemy. Many of these people have become good friends whom I love and whose friendships I value greatly. Of course there were some who understandably would not put up with my temperamental personality. For the longest time I have agreed with them, but lately I have improved. To everyone mentioned or hinted at, this is written with good intentions and hopefully will not hurt anyone. I think writing this book helped me figure it out a little, too.

Prologue: Before the Curtain Rises

<hr/>

MY GIVEN NAME IS DONALD ROSS CHERRY. Many years ago a columnist gave me the title "The Golfer Who Sang His Way to the Top," a phrase that has followed me ever since. Other titles concerning my vivid personality were soon to follow. Some say that I probably signed in with a hard-fisted temper when officially entering the game of life. For the record, I didn't break anything when the doctor first slapped me, although I probably took a swing.

I was very lucky to have been given two talents in life, singing and golfing. Both delivered me on the road to many heights. I have been fortunate to grasp a mantle full of golf trophies and sell a pretty good share of records, earning me a bit of gold. Yet, passing through the bridges of time, a single question still haunts me more today than ever. Could I have made it to grander peaks if I had chosen one career over the other? Would my name be up there—King of the Hill, Top of the Heap, "A" Number One, as my dear friend Mr. Sinatra would shout about?

Many people played an important role in my ride through life. Some celebrities, some athletes, some politicians, and even distinguished heroes. I have stories to tell about many of them, and for the first time I will attempt to confess my own disdainful secret: I never played the game. I don't mean the game of golf—the game that went along with it.

Throughout the years I adhered to the rules as best I could, but every now and then I would stray out of bounds. As you know, that's a 2-shot penalty. It has been a wild ride, as I split my efforts equally.

Now as I approach the final hole, I think I have figured out what the game is all about.

Find your seats…I'm ready to sing!

Let's take it from the top…

First Act

Chipping through the First 18

DONALD ROSS CHERRY FIRST CAME INTO THE WORLD at ten o'clock on a cold Friday night, January 11, 1924. If you do your math, you'll probably lose count, but that was five years before the Great Depression arrived. It was a poor time in America...the poorest. Thousands of investors began losing large sums of money as the stock market tumbled, which in turn led the country into depression. Millions lost their jobs as businesses closed and unemployment rose. Many lost their homes and some even lost their lives. Fortunately, my mother had a skill that was much needed during this time period and the years that led up to it.

Her name is Ross Alma Cherry—that's where my middle name was derived. Born in Mahia, my mother was probably the most sought after seamstress in all of West Texas. She could take a linen tablecloth and make a form-fitted shirt out of it in a matter of minutes, Mom was that good. In fact, Neiman Marcus courted her to work for them, but she refused in order to remain at home and watch over her children. She was a wonderful human being, a hard worker, and very religious, attending the Church of Christ. It's ironic that I don't have as much to say about my father, since I was given his name.

My father, also 'Don Cherry, was a rig builder for the oil industry, which was prominent in the Wichita Falls area of Texas. That's where I was born and where we lived. I really didn't know my father, since he left at the start of the Depression, never to return home. I discovered that he was born on October 13, 1883, in Montague, Texas, a year after his parents, Leonna Johnson and Noel Cherry, were married. He later met and married my mother, growing up with her family name of Bosley.

Of course, a lot of folks could care less about a family tree or reading about one's early years of growing up. I quite understand. I must warn you, though, shedding a little light on my formative years, and elaborating about my own dear mother, might compel you to become an instant psychologist. See if you can analyze the root of my hot-natured temperament or why, to this day, I kick myself for not picking one course in life to follow. Was it in my own power, or was it imbedded in me by my mother's careful guidance? If you think you can solve the clues and come up with the answers that I have been wrestling with all my life, I'd love to hear your theories. Of course, if that doesn't interest you in the least, you always have the option of skipping this chapter now and beginning with chapter three.

The thought that my own father didn't like me much was a great burden to carry as a child. I came to believe that my father didn't think I was really his. As I grew older, I learned that my father consumed alcohol—a bit more than his share, and at times a bit more than that. My guess is that hard times fell prey upon him, and my strong-willed mother was more than he could handle. Other families experienced similar circumstances, but I think needing a father was much more important because my mother was so dominating. She did everything in her power to be both Mom and Dad to me, but that also made her a very strict woman who exercised authority over much of what I did as a child. I sort of assumed his place in line for her to control.

Actually, I was really a good kid. Mother made sure of that. As a seamstress, she owned many yardsticks for measuring and disciplining. She used them quite frequently for both. Mom also knew that I was afraid of the dark, and if I wasn't careful, she would wait until dusk to send me to Mr. Davis' grocery store for a needed item. I don't know what the world's record was in those days for the 880, but I must have set a new one every time she made me go.

Ross Alma was only 5'5", but weighed 240 pounds. That also helped her take command over me. I remember we had a next-door neighbor who worked all night at the dairy, and needed to sleep during the days. We were told to be quiet when playing outside, so we wouldn't wake up Mr. Moore. Well, one day I had heard this brand-new song called "Pistol Packin' Mama" by Bing Crosby and The Andrews Sisters that tickled my fancy, and I had to try it out at the top of my lungs. Of course, I had to belt it from atop the chinaberry tree in our front yard.

Mom flew out of that house as fast as a Texas tornado and told me to come down from that tree that instant. Realizing that she had a three-sided yardstick in her hand, and what it was gonna to be used for, I declined her request.

Knowing her parting words would do me more harm than that yardstick, my mother walked back inside and muttered, "It *will* get dark!"

\|\|\|\|\|\|\|\|\|\|\|\|\|\|\|\|\|\|\|\|\|\|

Never seeing paper money until I was five, I hunted empty milk bottles for the two cents each one could fetch. When my Aunt Vivian arrived one day and handed me two brand-new dollar bills, I thought the well had struck oil. I packed those crisp notes away and didn't spend them for nearly six years. That should give you a glimpse into how formidable times were.

To help supplement our income, we canned fruits and vegetables to sell, picked cotton, and took in washing. From the moment I can remember, I would help my mom hang up the clothes we had taken in to wash. The backyard had these long rows of clotheslines that stretched from end to end over the top of the vegetable garden we planted. There were three rows, then an aisle, and three more rows behind that. The poles themselves were made so one could raise and lower the lines. I would reach as high as I could to pin the wet items as straight as possible. The neater the shirts and dresses were hung, the easier it was for Ross Alma to press them after they dried. The butter beans, lettuce, and tomato plants would soak up whatever moisture dripped from above.

I can still picture that little house we lived in on 26th Street. It sat on the north side of the street and had a screened-in porch with two bedrooms. My mother's sewing machine and materials were set up on a four-foot round wooden table in the living room that sort of melted into the dining area. When ladies came to try on their dresses, I would have to go into the back bedroom and wait there until they were finished. Then, it never failed, Mom would insist that I come out and show them how I could sing. I'd sing one of her favorites, "The Irish Lullaby" or "The Whiffenpoof Song." I don't think she realized how shy I was and how it scared me each time. It was probably due to the fact that she was such the opposite. Her personality was so commanding and outgoing that I fell behind her presence. That feeling of being shy lasted a long time…would you believe about 50 years?

Much has been said and written about the special bond between mothers and daughters and even fathers and daughters. But to sons, moms are like guarded secrets. Rarely does one recall hearing a son elaborate on his mother in excessive detail. I can't ever recall a time another male has ever told me anything about his own mother. Men just seem to have a harder time communicating and expressing their feelings verbally. Believe me, I'm not an exception to that rule. I've now taken the time and allowed myself the rewards in recounting my memories of my mother. Ross Alma was very full of life and often had a good laugh watching the predicaments I would get myself into.

Take for instance the time I wandered outside to play. I looked all over the place for my old tattered and repaired softball. With no success, I finally gave up my search. Then I began looking for something else to do, and I spotted the chicken coop. After accidentally releasing our hens, I did the only thing I could think of, and ran to the neighbor's house to grab the bird he had caged up, to replace ours. Little did I realize that this wasn't your ordinary chicken, but a trained fighting cock—the meanest creature on two legs I had ever met. That cock tore me apart, clawing me from head to toe before I could get him back home and push him into the cage with the others I had captured.

There was also the time I escaped from home at the age of four. Somehow I managed to get the front door open and slip out onto the street. Wearing only underpants at the time, I instinctively made my way down the road and walked five blocks to the school that my brother Paul was attending. How I found my way there at that young age is very bewildering to me. Making my way inside the building and to the door of his classroom, I stood and called to my brother, "P-A-U-L!" He quickly escorted me back home, where my mother thought of a punishment while containing her laughter over the situation.

Years later, when I was old enough to attend the same school, I was assigned the same teacher, Mrs. Lewis, as Paul once had for history. On the first day of school, Mrs. Lewis told everyone to acknowledge their names when she called them. When she got to Don Cherry, I yelled, "Here!" Mrs. Lewis lowered her head to look over her glasses and snapped back, "I seem to remember that you've been here before!" She remembered.

In my mother's busy schedule of cleaning the house and making clothes to earn us a living, I guess I was a handful for her. I recall on a couple occasions (and long before it was considered "politically incorrect") she would tie one end of a rope to me, and the other end to the bed. It was her way of making sure that I wouldn't wander off or get hurt while she tended to the chores at hand. It's a funny analogy, but being tied to my bed like that might have been why I wandered from my bed during my early marriages. If I had one major downfall, that was it.

As for my childhood, I enjoyed it immensely, and my memories are good ones. I now understand why my mother had been so strict in raising me without a father. It was merely her way of bringing me up to have respect and gratitude for even the smallest things in life. She was such a delightful person and, in my opinion, a wonderful mother.

A turning point surely befell me on my eighth birthday. Mom had given me a complete set of golf clubs. She had gone to Zales and put a dollar down, agreeing to pay twenty-five cents a week for them. The set included a putter, driver, wedge, and 5 iron, and it came with the golf bag too! Little did she realize how far that $9 would take me in just a few more years down the road.

Although I was the youngest of three, I was actually raised much like an only child. My brother Paul was 13 years older than I, and he was out of the house when I was still little. Anna Lee, my sister, fell ill and passed away just as I reached my teens.

Anna Lee was such a beautiful girl and had a voice to match. She was so good, in fact, she became a teacher of voice and dramatics. Back then it was called "expression"—what a wonderful word that has lost its meaning over the decades of time.

As kids back then, we never fully realized how poor but lucky we were. Most of our neighbors were struggling along, too. On the eve of the Great Depression, in 1930, the population in Wichita Falls was 43,607. Most of the hundred or so industrial businesses around Wichita Falls either slowed down their production or closed up all together. It wasn't until I was 14 that a major oil discovery was made in the nearby town of Kamay that helped turn the economy around. Up 'til then, most people didn't have the money needed to see expensive doctors when they fell ill. So the U.S. government set up special low-cost training programs when families needed medical attention. They brought in interns, practicing what they learned on the live patients who needed care.

Mom took both Anna Lee and myself to the hospital when it was discovered they would remove our tonsils for free. It was basically a simple operation, and I came out just fine, but Anna Lee had complications. Displaying all the immediate signs of tuberculosis—fever, sickness, coughing, shortness of breath, etc.—she remained in the recovery room with pain for two days. After more tests, they eventually discovered what really occurred. Apparently Anna Lee had inhaled a small piece of her infected tonsil, which invaded her vital lungs. The interns treated her as they would their tuberculosis patients. Two days later, after her fever subsided, my sister was released to go home, while the practicing interns apologized for the outcome.

Mom made a special room for her in the house, where Anna Lee rested comfortably. To help her lungs heal, we kept the windows open for ventilation throughout the warm summer months. Nearly a whole year passed in my sister's life as she vigorously fought on. Anna Lee watched what she ate and fetched plenty of bed rest. Even throughout her horrible ordeal, Anna Lee unexpectedly found a gleam of happiness with a handsome-looking young man by the name of Melvin Stengel. They came to marry, and Melvin moved in with us to help take care of and look after my sister.

Late one warm summer evening in July, as misfortune would have it, a draft inadvertently blew through the open window in Anna Lee's room, sending a chill throughout her body. Loud coughing and choking woke everyone up. Knowing the gravity of the sounds, Mother scooped Anna Lee up and rushed her to the hospital. A few hours later, angels took my sister to rest. Shortly after, we lost her new husband, who had moved on and out after relinquishing his precious bride to the nemesis of life.

I'll never forget those blurred images burned into my consciousness at her funeral. In all my bereavement, I looked up in shock to find my father standing in the crowd on that final day. I hadn't seen him in so long, I was numb in disbelief. Then, before I knew it, he was gone. Vanished. As quick as he appeared, he disappeared. It was the very last time I saw him. Ever. Half the family I had known was expelled from my life at that point. You can't imagine the emotions rolling around in my 13-year-old head that day.

||||||||||||||||||||

My brother Paul was a handsome lad. Although 13 years older than I, we played golf together a lot growing up. Paul was very good at the game, and I usually acted as his caddie. One day Paul had bet three others a dime for every hole he could make, and promised to share 10 percent of his winnings with me if I caddied for him. I guess I was about nine or ten at the time, and probably wanted the money to buy more of my favorite treasured vice, "Delaware Punch," so I agreed with his proposition.

We started early, and by the time we arrived at the last hole and pressed our bets, my brother had amassed about $13. Then, on his last endeavor, Paul blew it with a wedge shot, sending the ball up and into the water. Total quiet took over the once chattering voices. I walked to the exact spot where the ball had landed, and placed the golf bag right on top of the water as Paul and the others watched it sink. That's the first time I realized that I had this temper caged up inside.

As a boy growing up in the northwest area of Texas, softball fields and golf courses were everywhere you looked. They were the two biggest sports, and I loved playing both. I was quick on my feet and could whiz around those bases like the Road Runner in those Saturday matinee cartoons.

Eventually I came to realize that in the game of softball, I had to share the responsibility with all the other members of the team, whereas in golf, there's no one around but yourself. Everything is in *your* control. It also fit into the structure that I was accustomed to. You would have to go from point A to point B, and do your best to get there in fewer moves than your opponent. If you could manage to do it in fewer moves than the average set for the course, you would score under par.

I guess I felt most comfortable conforming in structured settings—as you know by now, Mom's influence on me was pure discipline and structure. She constantly praised everything I did, but again, didn't allow me to stray too far outside of her command. Heck, I never went out on a date until I was 20 years old, and as shocking as this may sound, in more than 80 years, I have never drunk or smoked. Ever.

Reflecting back, I realize now that Ross Alma had the proper destination figured out in life. I absolutely knew she was right, too, but I often felt that she took a boarded-up boxcar on a straightaway train track to get there. I wanted to get to the same place by driving a convertible with the top down!

Quite often I struggled to show my mother, and mostly myself, that I could be successful without having to be so confined—sometimes to the point that the kettle inside me would boil. When steam needed to escape, and away from those I might hurt, I exploded. Unfortunately, it got worse, as you'll find out later.

Every Wednesday and Sunday, Mother and I would board the bus and take it into town. We would exit through a mixture of gas and heat from both the bus and many vehicles on the street, to attend the Church of Christ at 10th and Austin. Many times after an evening service we would go to see a movie at the local theater. The church we attended was large, seating seven or eight hundred. It displayed a great deal of charm when you entered its doors, and it usually took us a few minutes to find a seat. Everyone would stop Ross Alma to talk to her. My mother was well loved and respected, as I could gauge by the number of pats on the top of my head.

Inside the church, musical instruments were not to be found, since they were not mentioned in the good book. The congregation relied on the pure voices of its parish to harmonize God's praises.

I guess I was about six or seven when I first started to join in. It was strange because, many times, people would turn and stare at me. I asked Mom why they were looking, and she said, "They're staring because you sing better than they do!" So I just kept serenading. Many times, knowing that we were going to the movies afterwards, kept me from questioning it any further.

In those days, audiences went to the shows to make their Depression woes disappear, if only for a few hours. Newer movie theaters in New York and L.A. were being built to resemble palaces with their art-deco designs. Not so in Wichita Falls. We had the Majestic Theater, but it was only majestic in name. They would always have the current releases. The other theaters were much older and ordinary. You could see old Westerns at the Gem for a dime, or catch the "B" movies at the State for 15¢. Movie houses would change their marquees once a week, as the studios cranked out titles to meet the overwhelming demand. With three theaters to choose from, Mother could make our choices wisely.

It has been labeled "Hollywood's Golden Age," and there wasn't a rating system back then. The fear of sex, violence, and drugs never made it to the 30' screen, as it does in about everything that comes out today. Back then, you just went to see the new motion picture playing, knowing everything was safe. Mom spotted a movie in the paper called *The Big Pond*. It was about a Venetian tour guide who falls in love with an American tourist. We bought our tickets one Sunday evening following the Easter holiday in 1930. I really don't remember the movie or story much, but of course, I was only six. I do, however, recollect hearing that French actor Maurice Chevalier was nominated for an Oscar in the film. Apparently his highly praised role wasn't what impressed me the most. It was the song Chevalier sang in the film, "You Brought a New Kind of Love to Me."

After watching the movie only once, I came out of the theater singing most of the words to the song. I probably drove my mother nuts on the way home, reprising it over and over. "New Kind of Love" is my very first recollection of ever really singing a song, except maybe the hymns at church. Someone should have signed me to a contract then!

Attending Carrigan Elementary School, I was like most other kids, though maybe a bit more shy. Let me rephrase that, I was a *lot* more shy! When I started school, Dick and Jane were born. The book series was supposed to be the new innovative way to teach reading to kids. Remember the famous phrases like, "See Spot. See Spot Run"? Honestly, I don't remember either Dick, Jane, or Spot. I guess Dick and Jane's middle-class families didn't allow them to visit us in Wichita Falls.

Toward the end of my primary years, when the weather was warm, I would sometimes head down to where the floodgates were located. Usually traveling alone, I might recognize another kid from the neighborhood once I got there.

The floodgates resembled a small dam with tall retaining walls that had a couple of 18" metal tubes bored through them. Depending on if the hole openings were kept open or closed, the water would flow through them at really good speeds, dumping into the irrigation channels.

Already prepared, I would have on my swimming trunks and jump into the top end of the reservoir, holding my breath as the racing water carried me through the bored holes. Being fast and skinny and never giving it a thought, I'd swim like a tadpole born in water. That was until the time I got halfway through one of the tubes and my swimsuit caught on something. With the rushing water pounding all around me, I didn't have time to panic. I managed to free myself from my trunks, only to swim around and go back through to unhook and retrieve them. There was no way I was leaving buck naked without them. It is the one and only time I went swimming without clothes. That was in contrast to some of the other boys who shed their knickers about 700 yards to the north. In all their glory, and behind the trees, they would compare the size of their portfolios. The area was known as Holiday Creek, and the boys nicknamed themselves "Bankwalkers" after their game of equivalence.

I confess, I was never a Bankwalker. I kept my assets right in my own life savings trunk.

After sixth grade, I went onto Reagan Junior High. Nowadays some call it "middle school." I'd walk to school passing Golden Glow, where hamburgers piled mile high with the works cost six for a quarter. Farther down came the aroma of the fried pies from the donut shop on Holiday Street. They came in all sorts of flavors—cherry, apple, lemon, and my favorite, peach. Three for a dime—an irresistible offer, and I figured out how to get them for free. I'd buy three and quickly eat one down on the way to school. Then, being the salesman I was, I'd sell the other two for five cents each. Voilà! I kept that same dime for three years. My math skills were sharp.

My books were something that I never carried out past the school steps. I didn't have the time to open them at home. It's amazing that I got through school by just winging it. When my classes ended each day, I'd hightail it over to the golf course to see if anyone needed a caddie. On Monday mornings, they would allow all the caddies, like me, to play on the course. There were many famous faces of golf that passed through those gates and those early years of mine. At age 13, I had caddied for Dave Marr Sr. in the Texas PGA, not knowing what history he was about to make. At age 14, I caddied for Tommy Bolt, affectionately known as "Terrible Tommy Bolt." But before I start talking about golf, I need to graduate...

Wichita Falls High. I entered in the year of 1938. By now I had abandoned the bike that Aunt Vivian had given me when I turned eight for a brand-new Silver-King Mom had bought for me at one dollar and twenty-five cents a week. My wondrous and trusted new bicycle would assist me on my new job.

At the grand old age of 15, I got a job working for Western Union. It fit well into my schedule. I would get up and make it to school at 8:00 in the morning, get out at 3:20, and rush over to the Wichita Falls Municipal Course to see if I could caddie. Sometimes I did, sometimes I didn't. Then my shift at Western Union would begin at 6:00 in the evening, and would end at midnight. Here is where I got my first taste of show business (though I must admit I never felt comfortable with the term "show business").

Western Union had what was called "singing telegrams" in those days. To determine the best singer the company had, Western Union held a competition. I don't have to tell you who won. My pay was 25¢ for performing each telegram I could manage in a night. Whatever money I made, by the end of the week I'd hand it all to Mom.

To add excitement to the job, ASCAP, the union that protects songwriters and publishers, declared that Western Union was not paying a royalty fee each time one of us sang "Happy Birthday" to the recipient. It sounded silly, but Western Union was bound to oblige, and so stopped using it. I guess lawyers were as hungry then as they are today.

Delivering birthday greetings to their customers without being able to sing that wistful tune presented a problem, so some bigwig came up with the idea of putting words to a melody already classified as public domain, thus avoiding being sued by ASCAP. From here on, to the tune of "Yankee Doodle," I had to sing;

> *Congratulations so-and-so (name),*
> *A happy, happy birthday,*
> *The best of health and happiness,*
> *A happy, happy birthday.*

Exciting? Not as exciting as the evening I had to deliver a telegram to a room at the Holt Hotel in downtown Wichita Falls. The Holt, as it was called, was a neoclassical structure built about a decade before I was born. The likes of many dignitaries passed through its doors—Eleanor Roosevelt, Babe Ruth, and Will Rogers, to name a few. Many, though, were just weary travelers. I remember a lot of nice-looking ladies stayed there, too. Fashion models, I assumed.

I had delivered telegrams to the Holt before, and this one night didn't seem any different. Hopping off my bike, I ran up the stairs, found the right door, and I delivered what I thought was a bang-up birthday greeting. When I had serenaded women in the past, very often they would render some change to show their gratitude. This time, when the lady in the doorway brought up the subject of a tip, she implied a different method of payment.

I must have turned 15 shades of red as the swelling in my head took over. "No . . . ma'am . . . thank you," I stammered in embarrassment as I ran for my bike and sped off into the cold night air. I learned very quickly and was a bit more cautious about my Yankee Doodlin' from then on. Fashion model my ass!

It was soon after that I quit the Western Union. Working and playing at the golf course now devoured the better part of my off hours. My job caddying a game of 18 holes would earn me 55¢ (a nickel of which went to the caddie master). Some of the wealthier players who had money might even tip an extra three bits or a buck every so often.

It was sometime around my 17th birthday that I caddied for a man who informed me I could make a lot more money working at Sheppard Air Corps training center, now Sheppard Air Force Base (AFB). The man told me he had a friend by the name of Wilburn Page who was head of Special Services, and that I should pay him a visit. Having recently graduated from Wichita Falls High, and not leaving any stone unturned, I did just that.

Sheppard was located just north of the city limits. It proclaimed the only glider school in the country and was set up as a series of flight-training facilities established by the United States Army Air Corps in 1940. The government had determined the area was perfect. The location was glamorous, centrally located, and serviceable by the nearby railroads. It also possessed a pastureland terrain that made it easy to build upon. Lo and behold, the U.S. government persuaded J. S. Birdwell, the original land owner, to sell 300 acres to them. In turn, they paid the cattle rancher one dollar for the property deed.

Construction of the base began June 12, 1941, and was completed on October 17. Five hundred additional acres were added later, and within two months, 300 troops began arriving. The area was named Sheppard Field in honor of Texas Senator John Morris Sheppard.

I was immediately hired in as a runner, carrying papers and delivering messages between offices. Sometimes I got to do a little filing, too. The pay was now $66 a month—quite a nice advance over what I had been earning before.

Working at Sheppard Field didn't exclude me from the game of golf. In fact, I had extra time to play and even entered the Wichita Falls Junior Golf Championship. It was my first tournament, and I was delighted!

The excitement soon passed, though, when all hell broke loose on December 7, 1941, and Pearl Harbor was attacked. The following day the United States declared war on Japan. Just 816 hours later, on my 18th birthday, I was eligible for the draft.

D-Day

UNCLE SAM SHIPPED ME 150 MILES SOUTHWEST to the town of Abilene, where I received basic training. Little did I know at the time how Wilburn Page, the man who hired me in at Sheppard, would become a big influence on the rest of my life.

Unbeknownst to me, Mr. Page made a couple calls while I was away and requested that I be sent back to Sheppard. Six weeks later, after basic training, I arrived back home with my old job in place again. That lasted about six months until the others found out I was quite a good golfer.

Sheppard Field had a golf squad and wanted good players to represent them, so they put me on their team. That entailed my transfer over to the 62nd Air Base, which was in control of all incoming and outgoing flights. I was still on the same base, only in a different building located a small jaunt away. It took me a while, but I finally got the hang of my new position.

Making my stay even better, they assigned me to a patterned rotation. I would work a 24-hour shift, dispatching planes to and from the field, then be off for 48 hours. The days I didn't have duty would give me plenty of time to play golf. I was also able to pick up a little money on the side with a bit of show business experience. Whoops, there's that "showbiz" word again!

Mr. Solon Featherston was sole owner of the Wichita Falls Country Club, where I would practice my golf game. He knew that I could carry a tune and so made me an offer to sing on Sundays for the crowd of people who came to enjoy the club's buffet. Featherston also made sure that the entire golf team had complete access to the club at all times. I really couldn't refuse. It seemed so perfect.

During the time I was to sing, a woman would accompany me on the piano. She and I would try and find songs we both knew to keep up the atmosphere while guests dined during that hour and a half. Rumor had it that Mr. Featherston paid $50,000 for the country club and golf course. I received $1.50 for my part. *Showbiz.*

In 1991, five decades later, I performed a show from that very same stage with a 14-piece orchestra. All of the people I had known most of my life were there in attendance. It was the 50-year reunion of my high school graduating class. From the stage I stated to my friends and classmates, "As most of you know, I used to sing here on Sunday afternoons for a buck and a half. You can see how my career has progressed. My pay here tonight is zero!"

My aging audience went wild with laughter, which got me laughing, too, about what I had said. That night turned out to be one of the most exciting of my career, thanks to the reception that I received.

Back on base, I was accepted and well liked by everyone who knew me. When an Army-sponsored show had been scheduled for the servicemen at Sheppard, my buddies sent a message to the officer in charge. They requested that I be called up on stage to sing during the event. When the moment arrived, it marked the first time that I ever performed with a microphone. I canoodled it well.

My singing wasn't the only thing that stood out among the squadron of other soldiers. I dressed better than the rest of them. I wouldn't always tell them the secret, but my mother had made all of my clothes. Don't forget, she was an expert seamstress, and in my mind, the best there was. Whether I was in a uniform or in a pair of fatigues, I looked like a Wall Street giant even on $17 a month.

I also drew separate rations, amounting to an extra $8. Except for the six weeks in basic training, I never spent one night in the barracks that they assigned to me. Home was always on 26th Street, and I would retreat there every night. When I wasn't golfing with my Army Airforce team, I was spending most of my extra time competing in other off-base events. In the middle of my tour of duty, I competed and took the top spot title the 1943 Lubbock Invitational, which was my first real amateur crown since winning the local Junior Golf Championship before entering the service. An article, "Files of the Times," dated September 6, 1945, reported, "Sunburned Don Cherry, who corporals at Sheppard Field when he is not swatting a golf ball, set a blistering pace to defeat Jack Laxton of Brownwood to win the 18th annual Country Club Invitational crown and his second tournament title of the summer." Golf was really becoming a natural part of me. I seemed to live and breathe the game, and always had a set of clubs over my shoulder wherever I would go.

Those clubs had accompanied me on one of my first real dates. Martha Jean Keel was her name, and it was actually a double date. Man, she was eager, if you know what I mean, but I guess my strict upbringing and mind-set on golf kept me from doing anything rash. One day Martha Jean's parents came by the house to visit my mother. They informed her that while I was a 19-year-old serviceman, Martha was a mere 15, and she should stop her son from making passes at her. Mother listened, and when they finished what they had to say, she looked both of them dead in the eyes and enlightened them. "Your daughter's no saint. Take another look . . . it's Martha Jean who's making the passes!" And she returned to her weekly Saturday morning house-cleaning chores.

While back on base, my "on-duty" teammates and I traveled the country in an AT-7 aircraft, which flew all of us to our various assigned golf matches. It's unbelievable that I can still remember their names. According to rank, there was Chuck Hyatt (Captain and All-American basketball player), Maurice Pishlou (First Lt.), Johnny Stammers (Tech Sergeant and Oklahoma State Amateur Golf Champion), Warren "Kid" Brown (Sergeant and a Native American from Oklahoma), and Johnny Whitten (PFC from Arkansas who had more moves than a mongoose). Not to brag, but I had a couple of moves myself.

Sheppard had a foot race officially called "The 300-Yard Shuttle." They would place two markers 60 yards apart. You would then have to run around them five times, which gave you the 300 yards. Quite shocking to the others, I set the record for their game in 42 seconds the first time I ran it. I don't think that score was ever broken.

Another move was the time it took me to run the obstacle course they had. You have to picture what I looked like. I weighed in at 135 pounds, and that was soaking wet. I never lost a fight because nobody could ever catch me. Their obstacle course was duck soup.

Now "flight planning" was far more interesting. Since we usually prepared the planes for the servicemen who flew in and out, it was a bit more engaging when an order came in for a private citizen or someone else. It even turned eventful one time when a real Hollywood movie star showed up. Born right in the state of Texas and known the world over as the original singing cowboy, Gene Autry's visit rivaled that of any president. Everyone imaginable came out to greet Autry when he arrived.

Major Drum was the person in charge who did everything possible for our golf team. I don't ever remember us losing a single match. There was another in charge of the base itself, Colonel Claggett. Toward the end of the war, we received a flight plan for six P-47s. They were the last fighter planes made at that time. When the aircraft and their flyers arrived, Claggett was given the news. He got in his car and drove to the operations office to welcome them, along with just about every ranking officer there. Funny how I never saw Colonel Claggett in the operations office until that day.

The thought of using women as pilots had been suggested as early as 1930, but the Chief of the Air Corps at the time scoffed, saying that the possibility was "utterly unfeasible" due to women being "too high strung for wartime flying." Ten years later, the Air Corps Plans Division favored the use of experienced women pilots to fly AAF aircraft within the US. The women flyers were nicknamed "WASPs," which stood for Women's Airforce Service Pilots.

With only about 100 of these pilots in the air, no one at Sheppard had ever seen a woman flyer. Except for a few officers who knew ahead of time (and couldn't wait to welcome them), there wasn't even a clue for the rest of us that a few of these women were going to be landing one day.

The first woman pilot pulled up, stopped, slid back the cover to the cockpit, and stood up. You heard the gasps from everywhere, "My God, look! It's a woman!"

As she stood up, it was made known that she was wearing only a skimpy top and a very revealing brassiere. Needless to say, there was, should I say, some confusion. Colonel Claggett cleared his throat, hit his right boot with his little whip, saluted, and, not knowing how to react, turned around and hurried away. I think the entire base took a much keener interest in who and what was flying in and out from that point on.

When I think back upon all this, I sometimes feel a bit guilty. I think about what happened to all those young men and women during that time. No doubt I was one of the lucky ones.

Singin' in the Clubs

FOUR YEARS LATER, AFTER BEING DISCHARGED FROM THE SERVICE, I found myself pondering my future. I never had the father I needed to teach me an occupation or a trade, nor did I have a family business to walk into. Without having a clue, I took the Army Air Force (as it was called in those days) up on its offer to pay for schooling, and enrolled at Midwestern University.

I signed up for courses that were prerequisites, getting the college required classes done first. Joe Garland was my assigned physics professor. After attending school for about nine or ten weeks, Professor Garland took me aside to make a proposition.

"Don, if you would sing 'The House I Live In' in front of the entire class, I'll give you a B+ for the course, and you won't have to come back to finish the semester out," he said with a serious tone. Even though Professor Garland was a physics teacher, the song must have made a personal impact on him, as it did a huge portion of the population in 1945.

Singer Frank Sinatra had presented "The House I Live In" in an 11-minute-long movie by the same name. Produced by Frank Ross, the film's message was meant to oppose anti-Semitism and acceptance of people's differences at the end of World War II. It made such a strong statement that the following year it was awarded a Golden Globe and an honorary Oscar. With nothing to lose, I took Garland up on his offer and sang in front of the entire class. Glancing over, I saw my professor wipe a tear from his eye before dismissing the class and giving me my B+.

The following week, another of my teachers heard about what had happened in Mr. Garland's class and offered me the same deal. Professor Carolyn Ferguson, my psychology professor, wanted to see her students' reaction to my effect on the girls in the class by singing to them. She decided on a popular love tune at the time called "Sweet Sixteen." Once again, I took up her offer. Actually, I had it in my mind that it probably wasn't the students she wanted me to sing it for. When the day arrived, I gave it my all, ending my vocal presentation with the lines "When You were Sweet Sixteen" much in the style of Perry Como.

I waited until she dismissed the class, when I approached her. Professor Ferguson was only about a year older than I and wasn't too hard on the eyes, either. Politely, I asked her if she would like to accompany me to the country club that evening. Professor Ferguson graciously replied with a "No," and said that she couldn't date one of her students. At that point I had passed the class anyway, and realized that I was no longer one of her students. I guess my singing hadn't been a good enough test on *her*. That was it for my lesson and for my schooling. Singing carried me through my nine-week higher education experience. I attended all of half a semester, never to return to school again.

The two futures I knew anything about involved singing or golfing. Both seemed to be what I had a knack for, and I liked the fact that they could be managed at opposite ends of the day.

The Wichita Falls Country Club played a very important part in my life at this point. While in the service, and immediately following, I began competing in many of the amateur golf tournaments in the West Texas area. Amazingly, I was on a hot streak. Playing in some of the most popular events, mainly in West Texas, I probably won six out of the 10 I competed in. Of course, this only helped fuel the fire for me to continue. When the spring of 1947 rolled around, I entered and won the Southwest Open (Pro-Am) and I was on my way.

There was also a great lesson to be learned by competing in all of these events. Something that only competing in tournament play after tournament play would teach: the art of discipline. Many people are born with it, and others can acquire it, but in the short amount of time that skill is needed to win, concentration and focus are just as essential. I learned quickly that no one else is in control except yourself, and other people, distractions, and elements have to be shuttered out to give it your full control. The encyclopedia defines discipline as "a model of polite restraint." Many who knew me, saw my skills in concentration hone, but as for polite restraint, I worked hard at it, but both words "polite" and "restraint" didn't mesh with my internal gift for lambasting myself and bending clubs around trees. My game seemed to be on target, but my personality still needed work. Thank goodness I was afforded many opportunities to improve.

In between all of this, I had been dating a girl for a while now by the name of Betty Mims White. A young lady golfer herself, Betty had won the Texas State Amateur and, in 1946, qualified for the Women's National Amateur that was to be played at Pebble Beach that year. After only the second day, Betty called me on the phone and was very excited about meeting the legendary Bing Crosby on the course. The thought crossed my mind that it was *Bing* who was probably the one most excited in meeting *Betty*! Betty was considerably pretty, yet a bit naïve about things. She was very shy and had no idea how she appealed to most men sexually. If you knew anything about Bing Crosby, well, I didn't say anything to Betty.

Lo and behold, Betty made it to the semifinals of the tournament. She called me on Thursday, the night before her semifinal match, and confessed that she had told Bing all about me and how well I could sing. Bing told her that when she got back to Dallas, she should have me go in and record a couple of songs, then send the recordings to him.

When she returned, I did just that, only one better—I recorded both "White Christmas" and "Don't Fence Me In." I thought Bing would be familiar with both songs, after all, they were two of his biggest sellers, right? I heard nothing back, and nearly forgot about it until four years later, and I'll tell you about that in a little bit.

Through the grapevine, I was told that I had the musical ability and the look of what Hollywood producers might be searching for, so when I heard that a couple of friends were going to drive out to the West Coast, I asked if I could tag along. Once I made my way into Hollywood, I had a meeting with a studio executive at Columbia Pictures, which lasted all of about 30 minutes. I guess I wasn't what they wanted at the time. Within the week, I was back home. I didn't think twice about it, and enrolled as a match play competitor in the West Texas Golf Tournament that was taking place at the Wichita Falls Country Club the following weekend.

I played a good game during the competition hours and returned that evening to entertain the guests, as I had been paid to do many times in the past. Usually I would perform three songs with whatever musicians also were playing there at the time. This night, because of the tournament, they brought in a bigger name band to perform: the popular Jan Garber Orchestra.

Jan Garber's orchestra had been around since the 1920s, and was very well known in the nation. They had gained popularity each decade, as Garber would make musical transitions and drastic changes in personnel to fit the time period. By the 1940s, Jan Garber was known as the "Idol of the Air Lanes," and was blessed with a string of popular vocalists such as Tommy Traynor and Tim Reardon. Alan Copeland and his Twintones singing group, later changing their name to the Meltones with leader Mel Torme, were also popular members of Garber's musical family. As the big band sound emerged during the prewar years, Garber had pioneered the one-night-stand concept among dance orchestras. This particular Sunday night in Wichita Falls in 1947 was no different—people were swaying on the dance floor, serenaded by Garber and his orchestra.

After a few hours of dancing, some of the people attending began dispersing. I thought it would be a good opportunity to hop up on the stage and sing while the band was still there. Hoping they would fill in the melody behind my warbling, I chose the song "Guilty." The band and I fell in naturally together, and the people there seemed to enjoy it and asked for another. I can remember the two songs that I followed "Guilty" with as clearly as a bell, "The Anniversary Waltz" and "Till the End of Time," both deeply romantic songs.

I ended my short set and decided to stay around the dance hall for what was left of the evening. I was certainly glad that I did because shortly after, Jan Garber himself approached me with an offer. He asked me if I could go out on the road with the orchestra and become his new lead singer. I would be paid a salary of $125 a week, and of course the cost of traveling figured in, since we were to travel by bus.

I hadn't any real training in music and was a bit apprehensive, depending on the band to lead with a melody to get me started. Garber seemed to understand and actually fired his lead singer, Roy Cordell, on the spot that evening to open the position for me. It was a bit awkward for the rest of that evening.

A day and a half later we started out, traveling east toward New York. A betting man, Garber had already known about my golfing skills and began arranging matches for anyone who wanted to go up against "the kid." Everyone he suckered in thought I was just the kid singer, not an up-and-coming amateur golfer. He would make a fast $400 betting on me before we left town for the next city. Then he'd hand me my share of the winnings . . . a mere $25.

Pushing on again from city to city each day, I became increasingly uncomfortable. By the time the bus reached New York, we stopped to make a two-song recording of "Apple Blossom Wedding" and "You Do." It was my first recorded transcription. I did manage to make $200 for my singing on those recordings, which gave me a big lift. Still, the fast pace, changing crowds, and different faces proved too much for me. Outwardly, no one saw it, but inside I was fighting the insecurities of shyness. I became nervous from the lack of experience and what I was ill-prepared for. Quite frankly, I was exasperated. It took some doing, but after only 17 days on the road, I expressed my concerns to Jan Garber. Disappointed but understanding, Garber paid me what money I had earned and suggested that I take the next plane back home.

Left with little money in my pocket and thinking that I could save a few bucks, I headed back to Texas by bus. I probably would have done better if I bought that plane ticket in the first place. At 23, that entire experience was a huge learning lesson.

Upon returning to Texas, and with no money in my pockets, I decided to seek fame and fortune in Dallas. I immediately took employment at the Wilson Sporting Goods store. My job consisted of keeping the merchandise in order and taking care of the stock in the warehouse.

I was paid $28 a week and worked mainly on the second floor. Right away, they had me in charge of organizing the golf equipment, and once in a while helping customers out with any questions they might have. Those first few months, I was able to share a room with another friend I had met, Kenneth Stowe.

Kenneth and I split the cost of the rent, which was $12 a week for a room in this woman's house near where I began singing in the evenings. We would only use the back door, and had to keep as quiet as possible when we came and went. It was somewhat cramped, but I could walk to work and save money on transportation. During the spring months of May and June, I took a job appearing on Billy Mayo's 15-minute radio show, broadcasted over WFAA back in the Dallas area. It helped pay the rent and kept me in the limelight for a couple more months.

While in Dallas playing at the Tennison Park Golf Course, I immediately met and became friends with another fellow named Fred Kadane. Having to find a more permanent place to stay, Fred told me that I could come and stay in the front room at his house. I took him up on his offer and bunked there for a while. Fred was a heck of a nice guy, but he also had his mother living there, which created much mayhem. Fred's mother would often get up and go into the only bathroom in the house and close the door. Sometimes it would be hours before she'd come back out. I can remember Fred marching into the bathroom to force his soaking mother out of the bath. When all else failed, he would actually start spitting in her bathwater to make her get out. It's a funny story now, but at the time it was utter havoc.

Another friend of mine I met at Tennison offered me a place to stay at his house. His name was Carroll Shelby. At least with Carroll, I could go to the bathroom when I needed. Carroll was to become known as America's top road racing star 10 years later. He went on to win the famed LeMans Racing Event along with gathering many other top racing titles. He even earned a second SCCA crown before creating and designing his—and America's—ultimate dream car, the Ford (Shelby) Cobra 427. Shelby is one of the most famous car designers in history to this day.

Carroll's sense of humor was a little different from most, I must say. While staying at his house, I was offered a one-night singing job at a place between Dallas and Forth Worth called the Bagdad Club. It was known to be operated by some very shady people. The guy who hired me went by the name of Souchak, which I learned to be a nickname. Souchak offered me $15 to sing on a Saturday night. Since I had no transportation, Shelby said that I could borrow his truck that evening. There was one catch, though. To get the truck started, you had to either get a push or have it on a hill and let it start to roll while turning the key. Shelby gave me the first push, the truck started, and I was on my way. The place was about 15 miles away, and about five minutes after I had started to drive, Shelby proceeded to call the police and tell them that his truck had been stolen.

The police quickly found me behind the wheel and turned on their lights. My first thought was to pull over and stop, but I realized that if I didn't stop on a hill, I wouldn't be able to get the truck started again. If you have ever been to Dallas, you know that there aren't many hills around.

Right away I remembered that the Bagdad Club was built up on a hill, so I figured that as soon as I got there, I would pull over and stop. All the while the police kept on my tail. I kept wondering why they didn't pull in front of me and force me to stop. Finally, I got to the Bagdad and parked on the downhill side. As the cops got out of the car, I recognized that one of them was a good friend of Shelby's and mine by the name of Andy Sword.

Andy was laughing so hard that he could hardly stand up. He knew all about the truck and knew I was looking frantically for a hill to stop on top of. They just wanted to get my blood pressure pumping. You can now see what I mean about Shelby's sense of humor. I guess I can understand it; after all, we were both born on the same exact day and at the same exact time (January 11 at 10:20 PM) in Texas. Let the astrologers have a field day with that one!

Then one late October evening after work at Wilson Sporting Goods, Carroll and Fred decided they would take me to a little nightclub called The Chalet. When we arrived, we took a table up front and sat for a while. Carroll had arranged for the owner to ask me if I would get up and sing a song. "Yeah, sure," I replied, trying to figure out what song to sing. It must have been a wise choice because the owner came back over to me as soon as I finished. He introduced himself as Joe Blackwell, and offered me $5 a night for six nights a week if I would sing there on a permanent basis.

It was a charming place to work, and it was especially gratifying that a good deal of the people who frequented The Chalet liked the way I sang. I had learned a lot about performing to small crowds of 80 to 100, and grew comfortable with musicians, such as the Leonard Olson Trio who played with gusto behind me every night during the year and a half or so I worked there. Joe Blackwell, the club's owner, was one of the nicest souls I had ever met.

The weekly regulars who attended The Chalet wanted to send me to New York to audition for the popular *Arthur Godfrey Television Show*. Knowing that I didn't have enough money, they took up a collection between themselves and surprised me beyond belief. To have those generous people give of themselves was totally mind-boggling. It occurred to me then that I must have had some sort of talent for a gesture that grand. Either that, or they wanted to get rid of me.

I flew to New York for the very first time in 1950 and rented a room at the Henry Hudson Hotel for $11 a week. A fellow by the name of Howard Phillips, one of the higher-ups at NBC, set up the audition and the chance for me to record an audition tape. When the time arrived at the audition, I sang two songs for them, "That Old Black Magic" and "Guilty." Funny how that same song, "Guilty," keeps popping up—it must have been a state of mind!

The woman who was conducting the audition in New York noticed that I had quite a good singing voice, but my movements were not polished. Looking me square in the eyes, she asked, "Are you an amateur?"

I thought she was talking about *golf*, so I (wrongly) answered, "Yes, ma'am!"

Needless to say, I didn't get the *Godfrey Show* opportunity and returned back to Dallas, but not before recording a quick audition tape for both RCA and Decca Records.

Barely making it back to register in the Western Amateur Golf Tournament at the Dallas Country Club, I received a call from Howard

Phillips. Howard stated that Manny Sachs, the head of RCA Records, wanted to sign me to their label. I was very excited for about eight hours, when Howard called again. "Don," he said, "I'm afraid I have some more news for you." I only focused on the word "afraid," as he continued, "A man by the name of Milton Blackstone has brought in a young man named Eddie Fisher to audition for RCA and promised to spend $150,000 on publicity for him."

As we all know, Eddie Fisher was a good singer. I hung up the phone disappointed that the record contract had fallen through, and focused my attention back on the game I was preparing to start in. Qualifying for play consisted of 36 holes. With my full attention on the bout now, I shot a 67 and was tied for the lead after the first day. Everyone finished in the early afternoon, and, when I got in, a message was waiting for me to call Howard back again.

I waited a few moments before picking up the phone, prepared for more bad news when an elated Howard told me, "Morty Palitz at Decca Records has listened to your tape and wants you to come back to New York and record with Victor Young." Stunned for a moment, absorbing what Howard was telling me, I had had to shift my focus back and forth between singing and golfing so many times that day. It was a dizzying transition, but luckily I had realized that it was the moment I had been waiting for. To this day, I am so thankful for having a very close and dear friend, Mr. Bob French. He was the one who financed my trip back to New York. I withdrew from the tournament immediately and got back on a plane to New York that afternoon.

The following Tuesday, they prepared "Mona Lisa," "The Third Man Theme," and two songs written by Victor Young himself, "Mad About You" and "Our Very Own." The next morning after recording those four songs, Marty Palitz at Decca called song publisher Howard Richmond, and within the week he became my manager for recordings and public appearances.

While sitting in Marty Palitz's office two days later (he was Decca's Artists and Repertoire [A&R] man), one of his secretaries rushed in screaming, "Bing Crosby is in the building!" Noise levels dropped, and all six floors of people came to attention. Marty told me to wait in his office and he would bring Bing up to meet me. When he returned with Bing, I jumped to my feet to greet him. Even before I could say hello, Marty blabbed that I had just finished recording with Victor Young, and that he had very high hopes for me. Then he turned and introduced me: "Bing, this is Don Cherry."

Crosby replied, "I feel I already know Don. You see, Marty, I have his first recordings."

Holy shit, after four years of silence, Bing Crosby had remembered my demos! We immediately became very good and lasting friends because of singing and golf, a passion Crosby also shared.

Soon after Bing left, Marty also graced me with more news—I was hired to sing at the prestigious Hotel Pierre in New York by Stanley Melba, who was overseeing singer Uma Sumac at the time. Sumac, an alleged Incan princess, had an incredible vocal range spread over four octaves and had just signed with Capitol Records herself.

The Hotel Pierre, a tall, splendid, and delicate 1920s-deco design, was built in 1929. It greeted the public with two huge revolving doors facing 61st Street with a large canopied entrance also on Fifth Avenue. The huge lobby was inlaid with expensive Italian marble flooring, and you would pass the round tearoom to find the entrance enclosing the main ballroom. A very upscale room, it was unaccustomed to this plainspoken, wet-behind-the-ears, empty-pocketed young man from Boomtown. It happened *fast!*

I would sing two or three numbers in each set that Stanley Melba's Rooftop Orchestra would play each hour for the posh crowds who attended. Performers hired to entertain at the Hotel Pierre were usually sophisticated and well polished, so I guess I had them fooled. It was so far out of the norm when Pierre booked a young actor/comic with a common folk's view of things named George. He would stand on the stage with his guitar and tell jokes like, "College is a place to keep warm between high school and an early marriage," and, "My uncle was so mean, he used to kick little chickens in the creek," then sing a song with more humorous country-like punch lines.

The refined members of the audience sometimes couldn't grasp his down-home humor (or didn't want to acknowledge it). Quite often during the absolutely quiet moments, when nobody in the audience comprehended the joke he'd tell, the silence would be broken by the sound of my thunderous laughing from backstage. George and I became good friends, and a few years later, Lonesome George, as he came to be known, would have his own TV show on NBC. Even Eddie Fisher turned out to be one of his regulars during the six-year run. By then, George Gobel had even won over the sophisticated set.

My break into television finally came too. It happened during my singing engagement at the Pierre, when a man named Lester Lewis came in to see Uma Sumac. Listening to *Art Ford's Milkman's Matinee* on WNEW the night before, Lewis had heard my recording of "Mona Lisa." Following our one meeting, Lester Lewis had become my manager for television. Lester's two biggest other clients at the time were famous sports announcer Bill Stern and singer/entertainer Betty Furness.

Bill Stern had a radio show that originated from the rooftop of the Astor Hotel. During his half hour weekly broadcast, Stern would invite an actor or singer from the entertainment field to be his special guest. Because of Lester Lewis and the admiration of Bill Stern, I would appear on his show quite often. Stern mixed both sports talk and singing together on his shows, which made it a natural for me. I remember meeting this wonderfully talented teenage girl singer from the Bronx during one of Stern's shows. It turned out her voice grabbed the attention of Steve Allen, who signed her to his new *Tonight Show.* Eydie Gorme soon began a string of hit songs and caught the eye of her TV singing partner, Steve Lawrence. In 1957 they began singing concert dates as a newly married duo.

Lester Lewis' other big client, Betty Furness, was raised in upper-class fashion by a Park Avenue family. At a young age, she modeled for the Powers Agency in New York, and by the end of high school she appeared in her first motion picture when her family moved to Hollywood. Betty went on to appear in more than 30 movies, most of them for RKO, and unfortunately most of them forgettable. Wanting to return to New York after bearing a daughter and going through a failed marriage, Betty came back just in time to latch onto the new medium of television. In 1950 she hosted *ABC Showcase*, one of the very first variety shows on TV, and soon took to the air with *Penthouse Party* later that same year.

One time while appearing on her show, I had seated myself down on a sofa arm, prepared to sing a romantic ballad. Before the cameras came up from the commercial, Betty strolled over and told me, "You need to stand up and move your hands out when you sing. Move around a bit!" and she tried her best to animate me for television. Politely, I replied, "I'd feel more comfortable singing right here from the edge of this sofa." Betty walked away, never knowing that it was my extreme shyness that held me back from moving. I felt more comfortable keeping still, blending in. I mean, Perry Como managed to avoid much movement, right? Apparently the audience embraced me, even if I didn't exert my subtle nature. After that, I began appearing on the show regularly, transforming myself into a showbiz personality little by little.

Betty became a bigger celebrity after the show ran its course by evolving into a commercial spokesperson, pitching products with the catch phrase "You can be sure if it's Westinghouse." Westinghouse even sponsored Betty with her own daily talk show before she moved on to doing guest appearances in shows like *What's My Line* and *I've Got a Secret*. It was during Lyndon B. Johnson's presidential term that she was appointed Special Assistant for Consumer Affairs. Some of you might remember Betty following that as the co-host of the famed *Today Show*, sandwiched between the terms of Barbara Walters and Jane Pauley.

I met a lot of people during those *Penthouse Party* shows. It seemed everybody from Bob Hope and John Wayne to Gary Cooper and The Andrews Sisters would drop by. Just singing a duet of the popular song "The Thing" with Broadway and motion picture star Yul Brynner was a fabulous thrill. He was such a wonderful man.

Returning back to New York, I had found a close friend in a fellow named Martin Mills. Marty's father, Irving Mills, had started Mills Music, which soon became the foremost independent music publishing company in the world.

Mills Music was located at 1619 Broadway, in the heart of New York's music district. The building, originally built and owned by the Brill Brothers in 1931, housed their family clothing business and retail stores. When the Depression forced an imminent need for income, the brothers relented to renting out a couple of floors to the Mills Publishing Company. Soon, other publishers would move in, and the Brill Building grew to become legendary, housing more than 165 various music-related businesses.

One could accomplish everything in one place. Checking in with the songwriters to see what they had written overnight, you could take the song to an arranger across the hall, then have a lead sheet made and hire waiting musicians to make a demo, all within the same day. More talented songwriters, musicians, arrangers, producers, publishers, agents, and singers have passed through its doors over the decades. I spent countless hours in the Brill Building, listening to the various pitches and demos of new songs. Just a few of the famous names that came from the Brill Building were Carole King, Neil Sedaka, Jeff Barry, Neil Diamond, Tony Orlando, Burt Bacharach, Don Kirshner, Phil Spector, and Bobby Darin.

Stepping off the elevator on the second floor, I met Martin Mills walking the halls in front of Mills Publishing. His sense of humor clicked with me right away, and we became friends. His personality was also outgoing, which helped since I was so shy.

Because of our busy schedules, Marty and I decided to share a place right across the street from the Henry Hudson Hotel at 400 West 57th. Here, we shared the rent, the utilities, and took turns sleeping on the Murphy bed that folded up into the wall of the apartment. We had a lot of fun during those times.

Marty would also take me along with him to a place affectionately known as Birdland. It had recently opened a few years earlier, in late 1949, and was given its nickname because of its headliner, jazz great Charlie Parker. Located on Broadway, just a few blocks west of 52nd Street, the admission price was $1.50 for the whole evening, which sometimes lasted for five or six hours.

I have to admit that, at first, the kind of music they played there was a bit foreign to me. The more times I went with him, the more I understood and liked the place. As a result, I became friends with a lot of great jazz musicians. One in particular was Dizzy Gillespie. When

Gillespie was appearing, I would always go to Birdland to see him. He always had a milk bottle under his music stand, and the minute I would walk in, he would put the milk bottle on top of the stand, place a small Texas flag in it, and start to play "The Eyes of Texas." Then he would announce out loud, "This is for Dawn Cherries." Jazz music had a big influence on me from that moment on.

By now, Decca had me back in their studios on a regular basis. "Mona Lisa," my first record with Victor Young, had become a number one hit for Nat King Cole. Back then, there were only five major recording companies and when anyone had a hit almost every record company covered it. When "Mona Lisa" was released, my name was not on the record. Art Ford kept playing the song over and over one night on his radio show. He finally announced over the air, "If anyone knows who the singer on the record was, would you please call in to the station here at WNEW."

Some executive from Decca Records was listening and called in. As Ford was conversing with the executive on the phone, he asserted his voice and stated, "Even though this is Victor Young's record, the least you guys can do is put the vocal artist's name on the label." As people starting buying the record, and more had to be pressed up, Decca listed under Victor Young's name, "Vocal by Don Cherry."

My contract with Decca called for eight sides at a whopping $35 a side. That wasn't much for a hit record. I was told that Bing Crosby and Dick Haymes signed the same contract when they both started. If you believe that, I also have a graphite-shafted driver made in 1946 for sale.

Even though Victor Young's record sold a lot of copies, Morty Palitz and the people at Decca were not sure whether the success of it was due to Young's orchestra or to my singing. They decided to find out by recording me on my own. So for my fifth recording a song written by Bert Kalmar and Harry Ruby was chosen. They contracted David Street to arrange the piece, and in late 1950 "Thinking of You" came out, selling over 700,000 copies. They handed me another check for $35.

I actually made quite a bit of money on the side from "Thinking of You," but mostly as a result of nightclub and television appearances. Finally, after requesting a few meetings, a better contract was negotiated on my part. For the first time, I was making a little bit of money that I could send home to Mother to help out.

Eddie Fisher recorded the same song for his record label, RCA. A bit of satisfaction came my way when I was told by the trade magazines that I outsold his version two to one. A special party was held on the roof of the Astor that year. The industry's best-known disc jockeys and biggest producers were all invited. This gave the various record companies a chance to showcase their talented roster of stars. When we arrived, Eddie Fisher immediately found me. After saying "Hi" and looking around the room, Eddie leaned over and said, "You sing 'Thinking of You.' After all, you sold more copies than I did!" A very nice fellow, I have to say.

iiiiiiiiiiiiiiiiiiiii

Back during the onslaught of war in 1941, *Time* magazine stated, "The United States means skyscrapers, Clark Gable and Artie Shaw." Shaw was best known for his Big Band Orchestra that he led with that famous clarinet sound he conceived. Many people didn't know that Artie studied the great works of symphonic composers, such as Stravinsky, Bartok, and Ravel. That influence would soon surface in the late 1930s and, with his formal classical training, he would compose interludes and pieces that have become known as third-stream music.

Dubbed the King of Swing after such hits as "Begin the Beguine," "Frenesi," and "Stardust," Shaw was not only commanding large sums of money but also respect. Performing numerous chamber music recitals with string quartets at various colleges and universities, including the famed Carnegie Hall, Artie took a bit of time away to become my next mentor.

It was my seventh recording session when I met the great Artie Shaw at Decca. I felt so humble and somewhat embarrassed when we finally began to record a great Neapolitan song called "Just Say I Love Her." Right away I ran into trouble.

Because the song had to be translated into English, there were changes in the bridge that didn't fit well with the original. Artie had everyone take a break and took me aside into the empty studio next door. Here he proceeded to spend time working with me to figure out a melody change that would work. Imagine, the great Artie Shaw took the time with this young lad who never had a singing lesson in his life! He was so kind and gracious that everything fell right into place.

To this day, I consider Artie Shaw one of the 10 most brilliant men I have ever met. Our song turned out quite pleasant and unique, and another that we recorded later that day, "Don't Worry About Me," was featured as another A-side on one of Decca's soon-to-be releases.

When I next showed up at Decca, another great name was waiting for me, Tommy Dorsey. Actually, I had met Tommy earlier on the golf course and had been fortunate enough to play a couple times in the past with him.

Dorsey had been the force behind such vocalists as Connie Haynes, Jo Stafford, and the Pied Pipers. He also propelled a little known fellow named Frank Sinatra into stardom when he featured these different artists as lead vocalists in his orchestra. Dorsey was, by far, the most popular band leader of the swing era, and I didn't think anything was going to top meeting him. The company that my name was keeping time with on those record labels was astounding, to say the least. The next two recordings, "Strangers" and "Music Maestro Please" with Tommy Dorsey, did much to place my name in the history books, and I am sure kept me noticed among my peers and the public, for which I am forever grateful.

Decca Records had their own recording studios, but often contracted this huge old church to produce records in. Those days, before overdubbing (a process of recording your own voice, then recording another track with it as harmony) became common, a process called "reverb" was invented. Reverb would make a person's voice seem to vibrate a bit more, and also sound more powerful and robust. Everybody was experimenting with the new technique, but that was long before electronic synthesizers and computerized reverberation came into use.

The orchestra, which might have as many as 40 or 45 members, were all seated in the main part of the church building. With their chairs and music stands all strategically placed, a huge Telefunken microphone dangled high above to pick up the collective sound.

They usually placed me in a different room across from them, where the sound of my voice could be adjusted separately. The engineers would then run sets of wire and cables up over the stairwells and through the men's room, across the floor to the recording consoles.

The echoing effect off the walls was the sound they wanted to capture, much like singing in the shower. As people listened to the warm romantic ballads on those records, I don't think they pictured me standing in a church building filled with pews, crosses, and statues. Show business!

Later that year, musician Les Paul would invent multitrack recordings by laying down different chords on top of each other, at the same time combining vocals. The magnificent days of full orchestrations with only one take were soon to be history.

It was tough competition when I recorded a beautiful song written by Guy Woods and arranged by Sy Oliver, one of the greatest arrangers of all time. The name of the song was "Vanity." That same month, Les Paul and his wife Mary Ford's new tune "How High the Moon" would zoom up the charts to become one of the top 300 selling songs of all time. Still, my recording of "Vanity" became a huge hit itself, entering the *Your Hit Parade* charts with a bullet. It was the third time a song of mine was featured on the *Hit Parade* charts, thereby granting a great deal of attention on the radio. "Vanity" was also one of the most requested songs of 1951 according to the National Coin-Op Association. Quite a nice accomplishment.

The Jukebox companies—Rockola, Seeburg, and Wurlitzer—would install counters inside their brightly lit music machines. Every week they tallied up the selections that were played the most (i.e., making the most money), and replaced the nonproductive platters with the current new releases. Those zillions of nickels sure added up fast, since jukeboxes were in almost every bar, diner, and dance hall in the country. Even to this day, I have a classic, restored jukebox in my living room at home, filled with all my favorites. Those mesmerizing mechanical record players are a piece of Americana that I sorely miss today. In case you're wondering, among the others I have loaded inside my precious nickelodeon, you just might find a few Don Cherry songs. Vanity you say? The word actually means "a feeling of excessive pride." And, yep, my "Vanity" is in there, too.

The whirlwind continued. After the success of that song, I recorded my first duet record with popular Broadway actress and singer Eileen Wilson. Eileen had been appearing in the stage production of *Call Me Madame*, and scored a big hit called "My Foolish Heart," backed by the great Gordon Jenkins Orchestra. It seemed ironic that right after we recorded our duet, Eileen was chosen to star in the TV version of *Your Hit Parade* for CBS. I'd say that our duet of "Far, Far Away" did okay, but it never charted well enough to be featured in the top seven songs of the week in Lucky Strike's *Hit Parade*. A couple of my earlier hits did make the list, and Eileen was singing *my* solo hits, while I was being paired up at Decca with the great Sonny Burke, one of the big band leaders and arrangers of the 1940s.

Decca quickly acquired Burke to arrange charts and conduct music for many of their best singers. A couple years down the road, he would work with the light of my life, Peggy Lee. As 1960s rolled around, Sonny had been credited as arranger and producer on many of Sinatra's most successful albums. I learned a lot from Sonny. His style intertwined a bit of jazz and a hint of blues into an ordinary standard arrangement, something I wasn't accustomed to, but enjoyed very much.

Two weeks later, still in 1951, I met my newest composer, arranger, and mentor, Tutti Camarata, at Decca. Just say "Tutti" to anyone in the business, and his legacy is obviously well known. Acting simultaneously as an A&R representative for Decca, Tutti would take time with each of his engineers, musicians, and singers. I was no exception. Tutti greeted me first when I arrived at Decca's studio to see what selections were waiting for me. He had a few songs in mind, and we immediately went to work on them.

The orchestra pretty much had the melody down since they had been studying the material for a while. We started with a song called "I Will Never Change," then came "The Sweetheart Waltz." Before long, we recorded a few more. "While We're Young" and "Maybe It's Because" wound up becoming the cream of the crop, and Decca released them almost overnight. They were good-selling records and earned me more experience under my belt.

You may have seen Tutti's name on all those kids' Disneyland records. In 1955, when Walt Disney was scoring well on TV with *The Mickey Mouse Club*, he made a deal with Tutti to head Disney's newly formed record division. One of his first jobs was to record a blossoming teenager named Annette Funicello. Her records sold in the millions, as Tutti earned Disney huge revenues from the soundtrack and record sales he provided. Tutti later went on to start and own the famed Sunset Studios in Hollywood. Every major artist in the world has recorded there, such as Bob Dylan, The Rolling Stones, John Lennon, Elton John, Sheryl Crow, The Doors, and Prince.

Our big selling single, "Maybe It's Because," was actually written by legendary songwriter Irving Berlin. Berlin was best known for penning more than 900 popular standards, including "There's No Business Like Show Business," "Easter Parade," "God Bless America," and the holiday treasure "White Christmas." About the time "Maybe It's Because" was released, Paulie Cohen, another of Decca's A&R men, took me to Nashville to record a few country songs.

Paulie felt that I sounded a bit like Eddie Arnold, especially since I hailed from Texas. Several folks had heard that I had left for Nashville and was preparing to work with the great piano player and conductor Owen Bradley. People concluded that I decided to change direction and turn country. Actually, as it turned out, it wouldn't have been a bad idea.

Paulie informed me as we were boarding the plane that Hank Williams had a song he wanted us to see, and that he was going to meet us at the airport. When we stepped off the plane, there Hank stood, waiting with a crumbled brown piece of paper in his hand. Because of my lack of formal training, I couldn't read the few notes he had scribbled down, but the words were there in such emotional clarity.

Hank Williams started off as a songwriter but shortly after began singing and playing guitar. After great success locally, Williams joined the Louisiana Hayride, gaining more exposure for his aspiring career. Scoring big with "I'm a Long Gone Daddy" and "Lovesick Blues," he was on his way. Having him write a song for me to sing was a great honor for me.

Ernest Tubb, one of the first superstars of country music, welcomed us into the recording studios in Nashville. Tubb had a long association with Decca Records. Having hits such as "Blue Eyed Elaine" and "Walkin' the Floor Over You," Tubb crossed over from country audiences to mainstream audiences. He later hosted *Midnight Jamboree*, a show that followed *The Grand Old Opry*, showcasing stars and performers on the rise. The association he had with Decca lasted more than 35 years.

When I entered the doors of Decca's Nashville studios, I handed the scrawled piece of paper to Ernest. We began to grind out about two dozen songs in the next three days, including that handwritten song Hank Williams had given me, "I Can't Help It (If I'm Still in Love with You)."

When the decision-making people at Decca heard my new Nashville recordings of "I Can't Help It" and "Grievin' My Heart Out for You," they loved it. Their publicity department began a huge media campaign. Posters were printed up and placed in record stores across the nation. Every major magazine featured a headshot they took of me, calling it "A Decca Best Bet," and my grinning face appeared on the sheet music that was now in popular demand.

Williams had already recorded it himself, and by the time they spent all their efforts, his version went on to become a legendary piece of history. My timing had always been a bit off—just as my string of hits was accumulating, rock and roll was waiting around the corner, and the demand for popular singers began to wane.

Hank Williams and I had a very similar upbringing. After losing his father at an early age, he was raised by a strong-willed mother, too. The difference between us was that Hank drank excessively. He was on top of the world in 1951 but died of an apparent heart attack on New Year's Day in 1953. Many speculate that drinking and substance dependency were the real cause of his demise.

While in Nashville, Irving Berlin got wind that I was in town recording country music songs and personally called Morty Palitz back at Decca. Berlin told Morty that my big hit of "Maybe It's Because" was one of the most beautiful records he had ever heard, and expressed the desire to meet me after I finished.

Upon my arrival back to New York, Morty called me into his office and explained who had called him. In my mind, it was almost like God wanting to meet me! I had Morty set up a day and time, and when it arrived, I walked into Irving Berlin's huge office with a bounce in my step.

Berlin asked me to have a seat and made me feel very much at home. He raved on about my singing, adding that he had written a song especially for me. Walking over to the enormous but elegant piano he had in the corner, he proceeded to play the song for me. In his mind, he must have thought that he had *written* a beautiful country song. My immediate thoughts were that Roy Acuff or Hank Snow didn't have to worry—a country song writer he wasn't. While Berlin sang the lyrics, I thought to myself, even God can make a mistake! I grinned, murmured a short but quick compliment, and walked out of his office in a bit of a daze. What did I just experience? How was I suddenly this expert of country music?

Shortly after releasing "I Can't Help It," I wondered what had happened to all the other songs I had recorded. I never saw them released and thought that Decca must have not liked them well enough, so I decided to switch gears back to more mainstream material. More singles were released over the next few months when my recording of the standard composition "My Mother's Pearls" made its debut. It was released in time for Mother's Day, and got great airplay. To this day, it's gratifying to know that "My Mother's Pearls" is still being requested and played every Mother's Day since I first recorded it more than five decades ago. Like the old saying goes, if I only had a dime for every time they played it. Well, it's really more like a penny, and with 50 years of inflation, "My Mother's Pearls" might buy me a bowl of oyster soup on Mother's Day.

With the coming of the new decade, new opportunities also arrived. The title-spin of "country singer" was still following me around when I got booked into the State Theater in Hartford, Connecticut, opposite Teresa Brewer. I would open the show while Teresa performed the second half. They were also going to pay me more money than I had ever seen in my life—a thousand dollars for four days. Since I was going to be performing on stage with a big well-known star like Teresa Brewer, I decided to leave the graduation suit Mother had bought for me, and opted to take my Easter suit. Each night I performed wearing a yellow jacket, green shirt, bright green tie, green pants, and no hair. I still didn't move much on stage, but the folks didn't take their eyes off me. Well, at least off my clothes! They probably never saw a more colorful performer until the flamboyant hard rock era of the '60s took over. Brilliant clothes sort of became my trademark from that point on. I actually have a huge walk-in closet still filled with patterns of every color and style you can imagine.

HOLE
4

Swingin' with the Clubs

||||||||||||||||||||||||||||||||||||||||||||||||||||||||||||||||||||||||||||||||||||||||||||||||||||||||||||||||||||||||||||||||||||||||||||||

OKAY, I HAVE BEEN BABBLING ON so much about my singing career that many of you are probably wondering what happened to my love for golf. No, I didn't give up the game. I just didn't get around to squeezing in a word edgewise. Things were b-u-s-y as you can tell, but when I wasn't working in a nightclub or recording new songs at the studio, I could always be found somewhere on the greens, chasing around that little white ball with dimples.

Up until 1952, I hadn't had much time to enter into any real tournament play, but when all those songs of mine were being heard over the radio waves, I entered and I got beaten in the semifinals of the National Amateur in Seattle. I'm not sure if this helped or hurt to keep my place in the golf standings.

When March 1952 came around, my picture started appearing on the covers of some of the nations best-selling music magazines—*Popular Songs* and *New Sensations* are just two that come to mind. With the ink barely dry, I entered and placed in the semifinals of the USGA Western Amateur event, winning a medal with a score of 141. The event was held at the Exmoor Country Club in Highland Park, Illinois, and I came in third under my good friend E. Harvie Ward. Frank Stranahan won the event by a three in two margin. As much as 40 years later, a fellow by the name of Tiger Woods would take the same crown home with a two in one win in 1994.

Seeing my face plastered across newsstand magazines back then was a bit eerie to me, but having my name and picture appear in golf publications because of something I had competed in and actually won made the experience concrete. I also got a sense that I was being drawn in closer by the public, which made me focus more on seeing what I could achieve.

Back when I had first moved to New York, I met the legendary Perry Como and we became instant friends. I even appeared and sang on his 15-minute TV show a few times. Perry had given me a complimentary membership to the Garden City Golf Club, where he was also an active member. Not only did we have fun playing golf there, but I had managed to score the winning title in the Long Island Amateur Championship two times in a row—not bad for a free membership.

Another fellow I met while playing at Garden City was Frank Strafaci. At one time or another I must have told him of my prowess as a sprinter. Well, one early afternoon when Frank and I were out on the course, we were paired up with another well-known amateur golfer, Frank Stranahan. Stranahan was the son of the founder of the Champion Spark Plug Company. A big health-food nut, he also worked out as a bodybuilder. Wherever Frank traveled, he would take a set of free weights with him. Stranahan was a great golfer but had a mischievous way about him. Little jokes often amused him. Many times he liked to ask the bellboys at the hotel or the caddies at the clubs to carry his bags, which were often stuffed with his overly heavy weights. He got a kick by watching them struggle with the bags behind him.

During a golf game, the two Franks and I had been playing a $20 Nassau (bet), and coming up to the 18th, Stranahan had already lost nearly $80, and somehow the subject of running had come up earlier in the round. I explained to Stranahan that I jogged every morning, and that's why I was so quick on my feet. He asked exactly how fast I was, and not realizing what he had in mind, I said, "Fast enough!"

Stranahan shot back, "I'll just run you 100 yards for the $80." Thinking the worst I could do was lose the 80 bucks back to him, I accepted his offer. Frank Strafaci stepped off 100 yards ahead while we got on our marks. When Strafaci gave the word, we both took off. After about 40 yards, I realized that I was running alone, but finished the hundred yards and jogged back to where Stranahan was.

"Why did you quit?" I asked. He replied that his cleats got caught in the grass, and he slipped. Without any hesitation and full of confidence, I said, "Well, let's do it again and this time run for a thousand."

He replied (which I thought was very wise at the time), "I didn't slip that much."

I ran into Stranahan just weeks later when I decided to go to Washington and compete in the National Amateur at the Seattle Gold Club. In the process of getting to the semifinals, and with a bit of luck, I had beaten Frank and two other very good players—Gene Littler and Bob Rosburg—in the fourth round to play against Al Mengert in the semifinals. Al Mengert was the one who won the Mexican Amateur right above me that same year, defeating seven-time French amateur champion Henri De Lamaze, one-up.

At the '52 National Amateur I lost the first six holes of a 36-hole match but somehow came back and was one up going to the 32nd hole. I lost the next three holes and was beaten two down with one to play. This is how I got my first invitation to every golfer's dream: The Masters. More about that later . . .

Bob Rosburg, who competed in the 1959 Ryder Cup and won the PGA championship that same year, became an ABC Sports analyst and commentator in the '70s. Bob had a great sense of humor when it came to golf and life itself. Two funny stories come to mind, the first going back to 1953, when Bob and I were competing in the All-American Tournament in Akron, Ohio. As usual, I was working in a nightclub nearby and competing by day. We were both staying at the same hotel, and my room was very close to Rossi's. On the last day, I finished hours before Bob—if I'm not mistaken, he was one of the leaders—and I caught a plane to Seattle as soon as I finished. Once in Seattle, I discovered that I had left my hairpiece in the room of a very pretty lady whom I had spent the night with in Akron.

Immediately, I made a frantic call to Bob, who was due in Seattle the next day for our next golf competition. Knowing I was going to open that night at the Town and Country Club he said not to worry, he would bring the hairpiece. Bob then telephoned the young lady at 2:00 in the morning, and she met him at the airport by six the same morning with my hairpiece. Bob arrived just 30 minutes before I was due on stage. I related the story to the audience at the first show, and Rossi received a standing ovation. Phil Harris and Bing Crosby just happened to be in the audience, clapping along with a full house.

The following year, Rossi was having a bad day at the Arizona Country Club in Phoenix. On the 12th hole, he called for a ruling from Jack Tuthill, who was in charge of the tour at the time. Jack informed Rossi that if he came out there in his cart, and found the ruling to be obvious, he was going to give him a two-shot penalty anyway.

Rossi waited until Tuthill showed up, then he informed him that he didn't need a ruling . . . he just needed a ride back to the clubhouse.

Jimmy Demaret... By a Hair

Now I HAVE TO TELL YOU ABOUT MY HAIRPIECE, rug, toupée, whatever you want to call it. It just happens to be a very important part of my life. My manager, Howie Richmond, took me to see an important showbiz agent who he knew could be helpful. The one bit of advice I was given by the agent was that it would enhance my appeal on stage if I could hide my prematurely thinning hair. Taking his advice, I went out and shopped around for a good maker of hairpieces until I found the one that suited me best.

At first I was *very* self-conscious and shy about having it. My first recollection of anyone mentioning it was, who else?, Jimmy Demaret. (All you golfers out there know who Jimmy is.) Phil Harris and Bing Crosby both said that Jimmy Demaret had the greatest sense of humor of anyone they were ever exposed to. It sure didn't take me long to agree with them! I first met Jimmy in 1937, when I was a mere 13 years old. It was back home at the Wichita Falls Country Club, when I got a job caddying for Dave Marr Sr. in the Texas PGA. Jimmy Demaret was also there playing in the tournament. One day, he arrived late after his caddie already left, so my brother Paul asked if I would go out on the course and shag balls for Mr. Demaret. The word "shag" didn't mean a whole lot to me then. All I ever knew was when you played a sport like baseball or football, you would catch the ball while it was airborne. Well, I went out to shag for Mr. Demaret.

Jimmy was very accurate, so I was catching them in the air, on the fly, as I thought I was supposed to do. When Jimmy started hitting them with the longer clubs (especially the woods), I realized that as my palms turned burning red, I needed his leather shag bag to use like a catcher's mitt. Out of the 43 balls he hit, I missed five. Jimmy used to say that the ones I missed "scalped me, that being the reason for my hairpiece."

I never really wore my hairpiece on the golf course, only on stage when I was singing or on TV. Actually, it also turned out to be a great prop. I joked about it quite often, like the time someone in the audience requested the song "Little Green Apples." It was a huge song, and started with the line, "If I wake up in the morning, with my hair down in my eyes. . . ."

I'd stop the song after that point and say, "I can't sing that song because it just isn't true. My hair is usually under the bed or back in a box." Then, after the audience got a good laugh, I'd add, "We even found it hanging on a clothesline one morning, but then you are really taking a chance flitting through backyards at 4:30 in the morning!" The audience would roar, and my hair earned its keep.

Come to think of it, there was this one time I wore my hairpiece on the golf course. It was when I was asked to play in an exhibition tournament with Jack Nicklaus, Arnold Palmer, and another great, Dave Regan, on a golf course in Orlando called Bay Hill. Dave Regan was married to a lady named Joan, whose father had owned his own golf course called Dubs Dread, and he had booked me into his club that night to sing. Naturally, I brought along my hairpiece.

Frank Chirkinian (the very famous CBS Sports producer) suggested that I wear my hair on the golf course because he was filming and it would help "give it some class. Besides," he said, "Everyone here has hair, so it would look good if you would wear yours." I was a little leery because the wind is subject to blowing quite strong in Florida. I only use two small pieces of tape to hold the piece in place, so if the wind started to blow very hard, that hairpiece was apt to wind up in the next county.

Nevertheless, I agreed, thinking only positively. Everything went well for about six holes, then the wind started to kick up. As I tried to make a shot with a 6 iron, the wind decided to blow really hard. I tried hard to position my head as I swung to keep my hair from falling off, but when I did, I took a divot that you could bury a dog in.

Being a little upset, I did not go and retrieve the divot. Instead, I jerked the hair off my head and covered the hole with it. I took one look at my hair lying there and wondered how far a ball would go if you hit it from the hair. Here is a little tip you may use—it travels anywhere from six to nine yards farther off the hair than it does off the grass, but it can get expensive! Hairpieces cost about $850.

Arnie shot a 65 that day and about three months later he wound up buying the golf course.

Talk about a sense of humor, the great James Newton Demaret was probably best known among golfers not only for his colorful outfits but also for his keen sense of humor and the amount of liquor he could hold. Every player at one time or another has told a Jimmy Demaret joke or two without even knowing it. One of his most famous one-liners went, "Golf and sex are the only things you can enjoy without being good at them." Asked by a partner he was once teamed up with, "Is there anything I can do to improve my game?" Jimmy replied cold turkey, "Sure, play shorter courses."

Jimmy was truly golf's first show business star. "Demaret is the funniest amateur comedian in the world," Bob Hope once told a group of reporters. It was commonly known that Bob Hope's starring partner, Bing Crosby, invented the Pro-Am. Bing could sing, tell jokes, and greet the people, but it wasn't a party or a golf tournament until Demaret was on the premises. One time it snowed when Jimmy and I were playing the Pro-Am in California. Jimmy opened the clubhouse door, looked at me, and quipped, "I know I was drinking last night, but how did I get to Squaw Valley?"

Demaret was a member of the Golf World Hall of Fame. From 1934 to 1938, he won the Texas PGA five times in a row before joining the professional tour full-time. Jimmy was also the first golfer to win The Masters three times. The first time over Lloyd Mangrum by four strokes in 1940, then in 1947 over Byron Nelson and Frank Stranahan, winning by two shots, and finally in 1950 by beating Australian Jim Ferrier with a

283–285 win. He came in runner-up to the great Ben Hogan in the 1948 U.S. Open. After that, Jimmy was chosen to play in the famed Ryder Cup of 1951, and was winner of the 1952 Bing Crosby Tournament in Pebble Beach.

Jimmy also loved to serenade a song. Two of his favorite songs were "Mam'selle" and "Where or When." Actually, on top of being a wonderful golfer and comedian, he was a better than average singer. Every time he showed up where I was performing, I'd introduce him and ask if he would honor the audience with a song. Sometimes it would turn out to be *six* songs!

I recall this one particular night, he started with "Mam'selle," and after going back to the bridge, I grabbed him by the arm and said, "Hey, I'm—" but before I could finish the sentence, he said, "Shut up, kid, or I'll hit you in your hair!" I never heard laughter like that before. We were like a comedy team . . . Abbott and Costello or Martin and Lewis. For you historians, some of the golfers laughing along that evening were Cary Middlecoff, Bo Wininger, Sam Snead, Ed "Porky" Oliver, Lew Worsham, Craig Woods, Chick Harbert, Walter Burkemo, Lionel and Jay Hebert, and Tommy Bolt. The room was filled with the greatest golf champions in the world. (That night was also the first time I ever met Vic Damone. He was serving in the army, and Jim had talked him into showing up that night. Vic and I later became very good friends, even working together, as I'll tell you about soon.)

Jimmy Demaret and I were both from the great state of Texas and had a lot in common. Don Wade put it best when he wrote, "The difference was, Demaret got paid for his golf and Cherry got paid for his singing." Jimmy was already an established player, but just having the presence of his company and the friendship he bestowed upon me helped secure my relationship with many of those other sportsmen.

Harvey Penick, one of golf's greatest teachers, also wrote of Demaret and me in his book *The Game for a Lifetime*, "When I asked his opinion of Don Cherry as a player, Demaret said jokingly, 'The reason he won't get his swing back too far, is that he carries his money in his right trouser pocket.' Jimmy went onto say, 'Don Cherry doesn't know what out-of-bounds means, because he had only seen the fairways. Nobody hits the ball closer than this kid. I don't care if his swing is one inch long, just so he finishes it.'"

There was probably some truth to that. No, really, my swing was short but had a lot of power. On my downswing, I would snap my wrists toward the ground, a mannerism I had learned as a youth. It was simple and it worked. It also gave me a powerfully long drive.

Take another time when I was performing at the St. Anthony Hotel in San Antonio, and also playing golf in the Texas Open at Brackenridge Park, a municipal course there. It was one of my first engagements wearing a hairpiece, and Jimmy (who always came to see me perform) was there. Jim had persuaded most of the pros in the tour—a total of 56 people—to come see my act. He had all of them seated on each side of me and in front of the floor where I was to perform.

As I walked out, the band played the intro and the host announced, "Ladies and Gentlemen . . . Don Cherry." Back in those days, I usually opened with an upbeat song written by Peggy Lee called "It's a Good Day." Well, before the show and unbeknownst to me, Jimmy had supplied half a dozen golf balls to each of the golfers that came. As I walked out on stage and began to sing, they proceeded to bounce the golf balls across the floor in front of me. Stunned at first, I didn't know what was happening, but as I struggled to get through my first song, my laughter became barely containable. As you can imagine, it was quite a production.

A wannabe nightclub singer, Demaret once admitted having "a burning desire to entertain the gallery." Jimmy's flashy clothes stood out from across the field, commonly wearing bright blue and shocking pink shirts with bright yellow and green pants. Jimmy would even have his shoes made from the same color swatches as the flamboyant clothes he wore, just to make sure he matched correctly. Maybe it was a ploy to distract the other players or maybe it was the performer Jimmy had burning inside him. He entertained and was entertained himself by the game of golf. That's why he was so good.

Jimmy's way of needling me (from his subtle to most outrageous antics) over the years was his way of expressing affection. He was most like a father that I never really had. Take for instance the night I was booked to sing at a nightclub that Paul Berlin owned. Jimmy planned his grand entrance that evening by pulling up in a huge limousine. I knew it was going to be quite a memorable evening when the limo's door opened and Jimmy came out with this huge smile on his face.

I went backstage to prepare for my introduction while Jimmy found his seat. I always felt a little uncomfortable with performing, but this night I was a little more apprehensive than most. As the show began, and I started my first song, I heard some of the folks in the audience laugh during my ballad. Then, as I reached the fourth line in each verse, I heard the sound of a grown man weeping. I kept my composure and continued as the weeping became louder and the laughter followed at the same level. Before I could finish my song, a paper airplane shot past the edge of the lights and made its way to land on stage right in front of my feet. I kept the audience in suspense by pretending not to notice. When I finished my number, I walked right up to the little paper plane and, with a downbeat, squashed it with my right foot as the audience roared, watching to see if I was going to acknowledge Demaret. After the show he said to me, "You're almost as good as Crosby." I didn't know if he was keeping the pressure going or giving me a backhanded compliment.

A short while later I was truly honored to hear Jimmy respond to a question during a TV interview after playing the Bing Crosby Tournament. When asked who his favorite singer of all time was, the interviewer was setting him up to say "Bing Crosby." Instead, Jimmy turned and looked into the camera and said, "Don Cherry is my favorite. I think he's a bit better than Bing Crosby, himself." Not a finer man there could have been.

Jimmy left us in 1983, but not before bequeathing a huge legacy to the world of golf. You might have noticed on the first few pages that I dedicated my book in part to Jim. I will never forget him. He not only taught me many things from experience, and could make me laugh, Jimmy was the best friend I ever had.

Tommy Bolt

ANOTHER GOOD FRIEND I HAD AT THE TIME was the great Tommy Bolt. Many of you might remember him as Terrible Tempered Tommy Bolt. He also went under the pseudonyms of Tommy Thunder-Bolt and Tempestuous Natured Tommy (T-N-T). No matter what nickname Tommy Bolt had, he was surely one of the most colorful and interesting men I had ever known.

My first introduction to Tom went way back to Wichita Falls again. It was a year after caddying for Jimmy Demaret when Tommy came into the clubhouse, and I was able to do the same. Tom told me that he started playing golf at about the same age that I was. I turned 14 at the time, and Bolt was about eight years older than I. He hadn't quite perfected throwing objects yet, and was just working on perfecting his swing without letting go of anything.

Bolt recounted the time when he sold newspapers on the street corner as a kid. He'd rip open the stack when they were delivered and head straight for the comic pages. *Ben Webster: Bound to Win* was his favorite, as the inspiration of that comic strip would impact him for life.

Tom told me that growing up poor and not having much of anything was the drive he needed to overcome obstacles in life, much like little Ben Webster in those comics. If others could do it, so could he. If he failed at his attempt, Tommy would get pissed and throw things. He first noticed his anger grow as he entered his teens.

Tired of competing in spelling bees, pitching pennies, and seeing who could kick the farthest, Tommy took a job as a carpenter's assistant. He laughed once telling me, "In that line of work, you're occasionally going to whack your thumb with the hammer. One day I slammed my thumb good, and my boss made the mistake of laughing at me. He stopped laughing when the hammer I was holding missed his head by two inches."

Upon entering the army, as just about every eligible male in the country did during World War II, Bolt was assigned to a tour of duty in Rome. There, close to where he was stationed, Tommy played professional golf and also ran the gambling operations at the local golf course. Primarily consisting of craps tables and golf wagers, while competing in golf games himself, Tommy learned that he could make tons of money. He lost his accumulative fortune one night when professional gamblers suckered him into a game of high stakes. Nevertheless, upon his release from the service, Tommy came back and took up golf seriously, wanting to reclaim some of his lost fortune.

Bolt's reputation of breaking and throwing clubs was to become more popular than the games he played in. The higher the stakes, the farther the clubs would fly. People would often listen to the radio or stand in the gallery (sometimes ducking) just to see what he was going to do next.

During a minor tournament we were once playing in, Tommy was one stroke ahead as we were nearing the end. He had this new caddie and instructed him that morning to keep quiet and just answer by saying either, "Yes, Mr. Bolt," or "No, Mr. Bolt." Tommy then proceeded to hit the ball and watch it come down near the base of a big tree. Studying what shot he was going to have to make to clear the tree's branches, Tom looked at his caddie and asked him, "Should I hit a 5 iron?" Of course, the caddie answered as he was instructed, "No, Mr. Bolt."

Angered that the caddie did not agree with him, Tommy hit the ball with the 5 iron. Into the air it went and came to rest 3' from the pin. With a hint of anger, Tommy declared proudly to his caddie, "Okay, there, how do you like that. You may talk."

The caddie took a beat, looked at where the golf ball had landed and then back to the place under the tree where Tommy hit the ball from, and flatly replied, "Mr. Bolt, that wasn't your ball that you hit."

I moved away quickly as clubs were sailing over my head. That cost Tommy 2 strokes and the game. After calming down, Tommy came over to me and gave me a piece of good advice: "If you helicopter those dudes by throwing them sideways instead of overhand, the shafts wouldn't break as easy." I took his advice, since I, too, was known as a club-throwing golfer. Tommy had a sense of humor that only a mother and Don Cherry could love.

||||||||||||||||||||

Speaking of Mother, the royalty checks for my recordings were starting to come in a bit more often.

Singing would pay me as much as $1,000 to $1,500 for two or three nights' work. After spending $30 or so on a room, and a few dollars for food, I continued to send more money back home. Although Mother never asked for anything, I knew she could use money for upkeep on the house and to pay the bills. My brother Paul and I were the only two that might help, but I knew he was in need of help himself.

By now, my brother had been out of the service for a few years. Paul originally enlisted under the army's buddy system, where, if two friends signed together, they would put you through basic training and assignments together for their whole enlistment. I guess it didn't work out that way for him. During his four-year hitch, he and his friend were separated, and Paul was assigned as a combat engineer to a post in Burma. There, he contracted malaria, depending on cigarettes and alcohol to see him through his agony.

Upon Paul's treatment and release, Millie Walker, his wife, insisted that he return home to Clovis, New Mexico, and start a family of their own. Paul was a very funny fellow, but he chose an opposite path in his life from mine. He began to gamble and do everything in his nature that was wrong for him. I, on the other hand, never took a drink or had the desire to gamble in my life. To some, the nature of my strict upbringing was much too overbearing to understand.

I often thought, at times, it seemed strange that I became close with friends like Jimmy Demaret and Tommy Bolt. Both could hold their liquor, and both had dispositions that were so opposite of each other, yet so similar. Jimmy's sense of humor and Tom's impatient anger were wearing off on me. As much as I loved their friendships, their vices were never of an interest to me.

Tommy once whispered to me, "It's a wonder that I didn't become a full-fledged alcoholic. At one time I had a contract to endorse this famous brand of scotch. In return, they reimbursed me for all that I could drink. When my own dermatologist took one look at me, he suggested that I lay off for a while. My nose had grown red and swollen, and was a gauge that others could use to see how much I consumed."

Tom had won the Los Angeles Open in 1952. When he came back the following year to defend the title, he signed a new contract with Kroydon Golf instead of the scotch company. My observation at the time was that Tommy, who had a perfect swing, was the only man in the world who could play and win with their golf clubs. To me, they all looked like little shovels.

As he always did, Tommy marched over to the practice tee to hit balls before he started the first day's competition in the L.A. Open. As he was beginning to hit the balls, the president of Kroydon Golf walked up behind him. Shirley, Tom's wife at the time, was watching, so to be proper and polite, Tommy introduced them. It was cold and misting that morning when Shirley, wearing a raincoat, didn't remove her hands from her pockets when greeting them. As the president of Kroydon left, Tommy turned and shouted to Shirley, "Damn it, Shirley, when I introduce you to someone as important as—"

Shirley didn't wait for him to finish. Instead, she said in a very impatient voice, "Tommy, we are two different people. I am basically an *introvert* and you are an *extrovert*—"

He interrupted her, shouting back, "Call me another name and your ass is going back to Houston!" Yep, that's my Tom. The press was not always kind to him, either, and Tom was always the first to notice. In 1958 Tommy was leading in the third round at Southern Hills during the U.S. Open in Tulsa, Oklahoma. It was a common fact that, if you were leading or had a chance to win, the correspondents would expect an interview. That was the case as Tommy walked into the club. He was obviously not very happy. Someone asked him why the long face, so he pointed to one of the reporters and said, "I see where you put my age in the paper as 49. I want you all to know that I am 39!"

The reporter he pointed to replied that it must have been a typographical error. To that Tommy retorted, "Typographical error my ass! It was a perfect four and a perfect nine! I seen it!"

Bob Hope once related a classic Tommy Bolt story to me about the time they played Pebble Beach together. After easing his drive straight down the middle at the 16th, Tommy requested the yardage to the hole from his caddie.

"One-thirty-five," the caddie replied.

"Soft 7 iron?" Bolt asked.

"Gotta be a 3 wood or a 3 iron," the caddie answered. "Those are the only clubs you have left."

I think you can now see what I meant by Tommy Bolt being colorful, with the colors of black and blue included.

Mickey Mantle—Bobby Layne

WHETHER HE'S FROM COMMERCE OR PITCHER, OKLAHOMA, take your pick, everyone has heard of the great Mickey Mantle. I am positive that anyone who knows Mickey Mantle has already formed an opinion, but a lot of folks don't know the whole Mickey Mantle story. One thing is true: Mantle had a career awed by millions of fans across the world.

Mickey was actually struck with a terrifying bone disease in his high school years. After being kicked in the shin while playing football, doctors told him that they needed to amputate his leg because osteomyelitis had set in. Mickey's mother and father wouldn't allow the doctors to do what they wanted. They decided instead to drive young Mickey to the "crippled children's hospital" in Oklahoma City, 175 miles away. Every three hours for many days, Mickey received injections. Then a miracle healing took effect. His leg was saved. The new drug they used was penicillin.

After he was able to use his leg once again, Mantle began playing baseball, far surpassing everyone his age. Mickey signed on with the Yankees' "C" team in Missouri and reported for spring training at their camp in Arizona. Following a quick rise in the Yankees organization, Mickey became an overnight legend, known for his speed and hitting ability during the 1951 World Series. If he had been totally whole (I am referring to his injured legs and knees), all the baseball records would have been his. To say he loved life is a gross understatement. I can understand his attitude because I have one just like his.

I can assure you the man's sense of humor is second to none. Mickey Charles Mantle and I became very good friends, mostly due to another sport: golf. When I met Mickey, he was at the height of his popularity. His hometown of Commerce, Oklahoma, wasn't that far from my hometown of Wichita Falls, Texas. In those days, we would play a lot of golf when we went back home. Mickey was probably one of the longest hitters of a golf ball I can recall. I don't know how many stadiums Mickey hit a baseball out of, but I do know that he hit it out of Briggs Stadium in Detroit more than once. If you ever saw him hit a home run, you'll know why the golf ball could not resist. Paul Richards, manager of the Baltimore Orioles at the time, said, "Parks were made for Mickey Mantle to hit baseballs out of!" That also goes for Yellowstone!

Mickey and I were playing at a golf course in Dallas, Glen Lakes to be exact. There was a dogleg par-5 on the back nine. Mickey drove the ball through the fairway into the rough. When we made our way there, we found the ball lying in a tire track made by the mower, at which time he asked if he got a drop.

I informed him that there was no white line indicating ground under repair, and that he was a victim of a term in golf called, "the rub of the green" or, simply, tough shit. Being a little more than upset, Mickey took his stance and announced to me that if he did not get his ball out of the tire track, he was going to knock the crap out of me. I immediately discarded the term and gave him a free drop. I've always considered that one of my better decisions!

I was visiting Mickey at his home around Thanksgiving when there were a lot of football games being shown on television. We tuned in and were watching Texas play Oklahoma. I don't have to tell you which team each of us was rooting for. In between the announcer, I was popping off about the punter for Oklahoma. After a few minutes, Mickey started becoming a bit upset, shouting, "What the hell do you know about kicking a football?"

I told him that I was a pretty good punter in high school. Mickey immediately retorted that he could probably kick a football farther than I could. At that, I suggested that we get up and go out to the backyard and see. We bet each other $100, which he insisted that Mickey Junior hold.

Outside was this huge cottonwood tree at one end of the backyard that must have been 40' tall. Mickey decided that I was entitled to kick the ball first since I was the guest, so I did. I have to admit that I kicked left-footed and could really nail it. Wham! I kicked the ball straight up and air-mailed that tree. Mickey looked at me for a minute, paused, then turned to little Mick and said, "Give him the money, and let's get out of here." Once you really got to know Mickey, you couldn't help but love him.

||||||||||||||||||||

If you're keeping track, Mickey was also one of the five best friends I ever had. Another was Texas U's All-American quarterback, Bobby Layne.

I actually met Bobby right before I met Mickey. It was a time when I was invited to play in two golf tournaments at the same time in different states. Back home, in West Texas, if you played in a tournament, you always checked to see if they had a Calcutta pool. That is where the players are sold to the highest bidders. At the finish of the tournament, the person who had purchased the winning player would receive 40 percent of the pool. The buyer would then give the player part of his or her winnings—just another form of show business!

As it turned out, the biggest pool was in Hobbs, New Mexico. Packing quickly, I barely got there in enough time to qualify. As I signed my name in, I glanced over and noticed that one of my all-time heroes was waiting to play with me. That was my first meeting with Bobby Layne, and a long friendship to follow.

Not only was Layne an All-American football player, but he also was a pitcher on the Texas U baseball team. I was told by someone that knew him well that in three years he never lost a baseball game. He and the Detroit Lions won the world championship twice. Layne also played golf to a 6-handicap, but I discovered that Bobby Layne would rather have been a singer than do all of those things I just mentioned. I was very much in awe of him and, I must admit, a bit shaky when we first met, but after the second hole at Hobbs, there was a complete reversal.

The first hole was a par-5, and I made 3. The second hole was a par-4. I drove the ball on the green and made 2. I am not quite sure where the next par-5 was, but I also made three there. I had three eagles and a birdie and shot 28 on the front nine. When I played it the second time, I shot 32. My total score amounted to 60. Not bad for the first time around. I was a medalist, won the long-driving contest, and won the tournament.

For being a medalist, I won a Bulova watch, a trophy for the long-drive contest, and a set of Wilson gooseneck irons for the tournament. Oh, and $450 from the fellow who had bought me in the Calcutta pool.

I had heard about the craps game, probably from Tommy Bolt, at these tournaments but, of course, never participated in any—remember, my upbringing. Well, Bobby talked me into shooting craps. In less than an hour, my watch was gone, my gooseneck irons were gone, and my $450 was gone. I had sold my trophy for $50, and that was gone, too. That was my first experience with Mr. Layne!

In 1954 I was singing in a nightclub called (don't laugh now) "Mickey's Gay Haven" in Dearborn, Michigan, a suburb of Detroit. Bobby called me and invited me to Briggs Stadium to work out with the team. My life's ambition was to play football, so I eagerly said "yes" and went.

I was given my own football shoes and warm-up suit by Coach George Wilson. The team let me run pass patterns and punt the football (which I could always do). It was quite an experience, and I became friends with many of the Lions players. One of them in particular was Doak Walker.

I remember they had a play where Doak would delay for just a second. Bobby would then fake a pass, and hand the ball to Doak. That one-second delay got Doak in a trap, so he pitched the ball back to Bobby. You could hear Bobby yell all the way up into the stands, "Don't ever give that son of a bitch back to me!"

Bobby had another saying that you have to be familiar with football to understand. He loved to look at pretty women. Every time I would point one out to him (picking an unattractive girl on purpose), he would say, "She looks worse than third-and-1."

Bobby was traded to Pittsburgh, and his new coach was named Buddy Parker. Everyone, including Buddy, used to say that Bobby was one person who knew more about football and what to do with it than anyone they ever knew. I am reminded today about the kind of equipment that Bobby used to wear. He had very little protection. In those days, no quarterback ever heard of a face mask.

I went to Pittsburgh one time to visit and stayed with four gentlemen, Bobby, Ernie Stautner, Tom "the Bomb" Tracy, and Harley Sewell. Bobby's vice was betting on Saturday college football games. He never bet on Sundays, especially when his own team played. Saturdays, though, were a different story.

That weekend, Bobby placed bets on 14 different college teams. He lost 12, tied one, and won one. The last game finished about 4:30 in the afternoon when he picked up the phone and called his bookie. All we heard was, "Anything left on TV?" The bookie informed him that the Canada Grey Cup was on, but it had already been played. Bobby's reply was, "Don't tell me who won it!"

I remember one other time I got home before Bobby and Ernie Stautner, and I was pretending to be asleep. Bobby asked Ernie, who weighed 240 pounds and was one of the best and strongest defensive linemen of all time, "Who is this bald-headed son of a bitch laying there?"

Ernie replied, "Beats me!"

Bobby asked back, "What are the odds of you whipping his ass?"

Ernie got up, walked slowly over to my bed, looked right at me, and said, "Pick 'em!"

Both Bobby Layne and Mickey Mantle were the best friends I could ever have. If I were singing in a nightclub someplace, they would always be there—most of the time just to needle me. One New Year's Eve I was working at the Cabana nightclub in Dallas when they both showed up. The maître d' informed me that all the tables were reserved, and that he had no place to seat them. Perplexed, I found a solution.

There was a little card table by the entrance door where a young lady was checking coats. I suggested to the maître d' that he could take that little table and set it up on the right-hand side of the stage.

He asked if that would bother me, but I told him that I didn't move around much while I was singing (remember Betty Furness?). The card table was moved to the stage, where they placed a tablecloth and a few glasses on it to make it appear classier and not so bare. To even add a bit of ambience, they placed a basket of fruit in the center.

When Mickey and Bobby finally arrived by themselves, you could tell that they had been drinking. Since it was only minutes before I was to go on, the maître d' seated them at their new table. Bobby proceeded to sing "Ida Red," while Mickey, as he nearly always did, put his head down on the table and pretended to be sleeping.

When the spotlight came on, they announced to the audience, "The Cabana proudly presents the one and only Mister Don Cherry!" As the spotlight hit me, the band played my introduction number and I began to sing. All of a sudden, out of that basket of fruit on the table flew a bug zooming right through the spotlight. It probably would not happen again for a million years, but as it whizzed through the light, I caught it in midflight!

Bobby jumped up and shook Mickey, shouting, "You should have seen what Cherry did!" Mick asked out loud for the audience to hear, "What did he do?" Bobby said, "He caught a fly!" at which Mickey replied, "Big deal! I get $100,000 a year for doing that shit!"

The Mastins, The Masters, and The Walker Cup ... Big Time

KEEPING SCORE IN CHRONOLOGICAL ORDER is not an easy feat. I'm still in 1952, the year that the Sands Hotel in Las Vegas first opened its doors. Originally the Sands was just a gaming casino with a few hundred rooms, but over its 44-year history, it grew into one of the most historic places in Vegas. Before its demise in June of 1996, every United States president had one time or another stayed there, and just about every major Hollywood star or entertainer played there. The Sands is probably most famous for being home to the Rat Pack—Frank Sinatra, Dean Martin, Sammy Davis Jr., Peter Lawford, and Joey Bishop. I was the third act they had ever booked—an honor I am happy to claim.

Speaking of the Rat Pack, I eventually became good friends with ole blue eyes, Frank Sinatra, and ole red eyes, Dean Martin. As a matter of fact, Dean was included in my top circle of five best friends. We'll get to him in due course, but as for Rat Pack stories, I have a great one with the other Rat Pack member, Mister Sammy Davis Jr. I actually met Sammy in 1953 and still acknowledge the fact that he was probably the greatest all-around entertainer that ever lived.

Because of my hit record "Thinking of You," I was being booked into a lot of nightclubs and theaters. GAC, the agency that booked me, called my manager, Howie Richmond, and asked if I would be available for two weeks at the Chicago Theatre. It was a very prestigious job, so naturally we accepted the engagement. The next day, Howie received a call from Dinah Shore. Dinah and her husband, George Montgomery, were two of Howie's best friends. She had told him that she just finished working at the Capitol Theatre in New York with an act called The Will Mastin Trio, featuring Sammy Davis Jr., and how absolutely great they were.

Knowing that it was the very same act I would be working with at the Chicago Theatre, Dinah suggested the smart thing for me to do was go on first and let them close the show. The reasoning behind her thinking was that the headliner, or best act, always closes the show. This was one of the most valuable pieces of advice I ever received. I accepted her advice on demand.

When I got to the Chicago Theatre and watched them rehearse, my immediate thought was that no act in the world could follow these guys. The Will Mastin Trio consisted of Will, Big Sam, and little Sammy. Later on, little Sammy would go off and make history on his own, becoming an honorary member of the Rat Pack. The story I am about to tell is told only with love and out of respect.

Big Sam, Will, Big John (their road manager), Sammy, and their friends would play poker between the shows. One day they invited me to play. I loved poker and knew how the game was played, so I anxiously said yes. Of course, there are four suits in the deck of cards—clubs, hearts, diamonds, and spades. In every card game I had ever seen, there was a certain way of determining who dealt first. Now you have to remember that I was the only Caucasian in the group. I broke the seal, shuffled the cards, and the first words out of my mouth were, "The first spade deals."

Six hands hit the table and six voices in unison retorted, "What do you mean by that?" They finally laughed, and that line became standard among Sam, Big Sam, and Will for a long time. They never let me live it down. Rest well, my talented friend.

|||||||||||||||||||||

A few days after celebrating the new year, I appeared on the popular *Colgate Radio Show* along with Marilyn Maxwell, Bing Crosby, and host Bob Hope. Seventeen days later, I was also asked to sing another wonderful balled on Hope's own radio show, which featured his regular singer, Margaret Whiting, and actress Zsa Zsa Gabor. The public was heavily bombarded seeing and hearing me on the radio, TV, and in jukeboxes back then. Over the last year, Decca had released a total of eight of my singles, 16 songs if you count both sides. That amounted to having a new disc out about once every six weeks. In the meanwhile, keeping pace with the record company, I had accumulated about as many golf wins in just about every tournament I enrolled in. By placing in the semifinals of the famed National Amateur, the prestigious honor of being invited to the world-renowned Masters Tournament was bestowed upon me.

Before the thrill of the invitation had settled in, I padded my position further by nailing runner-up in the Metropolitan Amateur. Played in Ridgewood, New Jersey, the Metropolitan was the icing on the cake. A telegram arrived within a matter of days informing me: "Don Cherry: After careful consideration, selecting the top 10 best amateur players in the United States, the committee hereby invites you to participate in the 1953 Walker Cup."

During my playing time, I also took home first place at my old stomping ground in the West Texas Amateur. Ernie Vossler, who also hailed from Texas, was my opponent during the finals. As a full-fledged PGA tour member, Ernie would go on to win five times between 1955 and 1962, but this story shows another side of Ernie. We were playing the 18th hole in the afternoon, which was actually our 36th hole. The clubhouse was on the left of the 18th fairway, and there was an out-of-bounds there also. A little farther left was the swimming pool. I was first to tee off, and I hit the ball with a very bad hook. My caddie, who had a different sense of humor, shouted back in disgust, "In the swimming pool!" Then Ernie approached his ball and swung at his tee shot, only to hook it even worse than I had.

My caddie, with a much louder and more jubilant sound to his voice, shouted back, "In the deep end!" Finally, at the finish, I made 3 in the first extra hole and won it in 37 holes. I suppose caddies all sit around and tell golfer stories among each other, too.

One other time, when my self-discipline left something to be desired, Ernie and I played again in Denton, Texas. When things weren't going my way, I had a habit of dropping my putter and kicking the middle of the shaft between the grip and the head. Sometimes it would travel for 25 yards just like an arrow.

I came up missing two short putts in a row at 10 and 11 and did one of my famous drop kicks. It was actually one of my more sensational kicks, if I do say so myself. From the green, it flew over a tree and into a cow lot. I went to retrieve it and, much to my surprise, there was a bull in heat just waiting for me. Needless to say, I was mad, but I wasn't stupid. I wasn't about to go in to retrieve my putter, so I made two putts in a row on the next couple of holes with my 2 iron. We got to the middle of the game when Ernie abruptly excused himself. I shouted, "Where are you going?"

Calmly, but firmly stated, Ernie answered, "Bull or no bull, I am going to get your putter." Eventually I won the match, but my club is probably still in that cow lot.

That was a stunning year for golf. The year 1953 was my first time participating in both the Walker Cup and The Masters. Everything just seemed to click and I was on top of the world. I would go on to play in The Masters nine times and the Walker Cup three. It was astonishing.

The Augusta National Invitational, which started in 1934, was formed to give an ultimate tournament to all those who could qualify at the top of their league. A few years later it was simply renamed The Masters. As a yearly event, qualifying consisted of playing a four-day stroke period, covering 18 holes each day instead of the usual 36 holes on the third day that was customary in other major competitions. The Masters is always held during the first full week in April each year when the scenery is alive in its vibrant color. Top prize not only includes the monumental trophy but also the honor of receiving The Masters green jacket to proudly wear. It represents the green of the grass and the victory over all the other top-notch players. The winner is allowed to take his jacket home so he can value it for the rest of his life. To this day, The Masters is one of the top four events in the world of golf.

While preparing to arrive for my inaugural participation, it was reported in the press that I was the singer who had recorded the song "Thinking of You," which had placed on the *Hit Parade*. A fellow who owned a nearby nightclub called The Club Rio heard about this. He managed to contact me and asked if they could book me to sing at the club. He stated that it would be for four days, beginning Wednesday of that tournament week, and that the club was in the same city, Augusta. Did I mention the offer was for $2,000? I only had to do one show a night at 9:30, and not being one who indulged in alcohol or cigarettes, I saw no reason it would have an effect on my golf score. After all, one would have to finish in the top five in the tournament just to come close to making that kind of money. It was a no-brainer. I accepted quickly.

About a week before I arrived on a Monday, the club owner began to clear the strippers out his club and advertise that I was singing there. When I finally got to the country club and checked in, I was immediately handed a note at the front desk by Helen Harris, who eventually became a huge fan and wonderful friend, to see Mr. Cliff Roberts.

Bobby Jones and Cliff Roberts were the two men who originated The Masters, so I knew it had to be something of importance and I found my way to Roberts' office right away. Cliff was very cordial to me and asked if I would have a seat. Through the pleasantries, I knew right away that he had something on his mind. Then the chitchat stopped and his message came: "We never had anyone play in The Masters and sing at a local nightclub [which had the reputation of being a strip joint] at the same time."

I sensed he was implying that The Masters carried more prestige than any other golf tournament. My reply, without being disrespectful and with a little Texas naïveté was, "Mr. Roberts, I have looked at the people playing in this tournament and can't see anyone else who can sing."

I must admit my answer was given with a little tongue-in-cheek. Cliff told me that it was nice to meet me, and our conversation ended. I went back to check in and meet some of the other players. On Wednesday, a couple nights later, I attended the dinner that was always held for the amateurs. It was then I found out how good (or bad) my answer on Monday had been.

Bobby Jones always sat at the head of the table. It was actually the first time I had ever seen or met him. In his later years, Bobby had become disabled and was confined to a wheelchair. I was introduced to him and took my place at the huge table. As soon as I was seated, I looked up to see him motioning for me to come back to where he was. "Yes, Mr. Jones?" I asked, looking him right in the eyes.

"I heard about your conversation with Cliff Roberts. Your response to him was a very good one, but I don't think you should ever use that answer again," Bobby stated. More good advice I took.

Playing against the likes of Ben Hogan, Cary Middlecoff, Byron Nelson, and Sam Snead, our group (No. 45) consisted of Bill Campbell, Charlie Kocis, and Jimmy Demaret. Ben Hogan broke The Masters record that week by five strokes, totaling a 14-under-par 274. It was such a great thrill to compete among the best.

What an experience and joy it was just to be standing on that course in Augusta, Georgia. Gazing out over its fully layered lush green grass, breathing in the beauty of the terrain and how they utilized its natural slopes and mounds instead of building an overabundance of manmade bunkers, I took it all in as if it were the one and only time I would be passing through. Little did I know that I would be back again in the near future. With the exhilaration of golf still pumping through my veins after playing in The Masters, I couldn't sit still for a moment.

iiiiiiiiiiiiiiiiiiii

My old pal Frank Strafaci and I took home the Anderson Memorial Trophy when we played at the Winged Foot Golf Club in Mamaroneck, New York. That's the same place that the Amateur Championships (the oldest golf championship matches in the United States) are held. It is quite an interesting-looking trophy that still gets a lot of attention from friends who get a chance to see it in my modest display case at home.

A year earlier, in Highland Park, Illinois, I had taken medals in the Western Amateur Championships at the Exmoor Country Club with a score of 141. But in 1953, right after playing in The Masters, I went on to lose the Western competition that year at Blythefield Country Club in Grand Rapids. It didn't seem to have a big effect on my playing, though, when I made up for the loss by playing in the Canadian Amateur shortly thereafter.

The RCGA (Royal Canadian Golf Association) had been formed way back in the late 1890s to help develop, govern, and regulate the game in Canada. There are over 300,000 members who play in more than 1,600 associated clubs across the continent. With museums, training centers, and academic scholarships, it is recognized as the governing body of golf in Canada. It's considered one of the world's finest.

In 1953, the competition was held in Montreal at the Kanawaki Country Club, named after a tribe of Indians who lived on a reservation right outside of town. The entire upcoming British Walker Cup team (Tony Duncan, Roy C. MacGregor, Joseph Carr, John L. Morgan, Norman V. Drew, Ronald White, Arthur Perowne, Gerald Micklem, James Wilson, and John Langley) was entered in the tournament and had arrived a week early in order to get accustomed to the time change and to get some practice in. It was nice to be able to see whom I was going up against.

A caddie by the name of Lawrence was assigned to me for the length of play. His Indian name was Soft Wind. His name fit him perfectly to a tee. Soft Wind hardly spoke two words to me in five days. Each morning he would say, "Hello," and as he left he would say, "Good-bye." Whenever I would ask him a question, he would nod his head yes or no. I recall having one easy and four very tough matches on the way to the finals. That last day I was playing opposite an excellent Canadian golfer by the name of Don Doe.

Soft Wind hadn't given me much information about yardage or which club I should use, and especially the distance to the green. Now remember, I just had four very tough matches. Then the finals came, and we were playing the last hole of a 36-hole match. We were tied. Both of us drove our balls into the middle of the fairway, with Doe's being slightly away. He hit his shot, and it stopped 8' right of the hole, pin high.

I wasn't sure which club to use, so I picked a 5 iron, thought for a minute, put it back, and selected a 6 iron. Before I could take my stance, Soft Wind (in a voice I will never forget) said very emphatically, "That's the wrong club."

Geeze, he never had anything to say before, especially an opinion. After an awkward pause to register whose voice said that, I looked at Soft Wind and asked him which club I should use.

"A 4 iron," he replied.

I hadn't realized it, but it was late in the day and the wind had started to blow against us. I figured that anyone with a name such as Soft Wind probably had some inside information. I grabbed my 4 iron, took aim, and hit a perfect shot. The ball traveled its distance and stopped about a foot right behind the hole. Don Doe missed his 8' putt, and I became the Canadian Amateur Golf champion!

As we left the green, I asked Soft Wind why he had not helped me before. His answer came in four words, "You didn't need it." Now, that is one caddie after my own heart.

The famed Walker Cup panel had previously placed out a search for the 10 best amateur players in the U.S. I deemed that my winnings over Frank Stranahan, Bob Rosburg, and Gene Littler in the earlier Seattle National were the catalyst that secured my invitation.

Started in 1922 by George Herbert Walker (then president of the USGA), the Walker Cup began out of the ambition to have the best players culled from Ireland, Great Britain, and the U.S. compete for the USGA International Challenge Trophy, much like the Olympics of the golf world. (Injecting an interesting bit of information, George Herbert Walker was grandfather to George Herbert Walker Bush, the 41st president of the United States, and great-grandfather to George W. Bush.)

Our team was made up of the finest names—Captain Charlie Yates, James Jackson, Bill Campbell, Jack Westland, Sam Urzetta, E. Harvie Ward, Gene Littler, Charlie Coe, Dick Chapman, Ken Venturi, and myself. We headed out with the competing team for a peninsula near the island of Martha's Vineyard, to a golf course named the Kittansett. It was the first week of September, and the weather was extremely hot. It was so hot, in fact, that many members of the British team, not prepared for the weather, used scissors to cut the legs off their trousers to make themselves customized golfing shorts.

The course itself was a bit of a challenge. A coastline followed much of its path as it stretched out into an area known as Buzzards Bay. Therefore,

Kittansett, meaning "the sea," created some surprising winds that came in from the southwest on this nearly 6,500-yard course. Nevertheless, the Kittansett Country Club was in an excellent, first-class, beautifully admired setting, included a vast array of rare roses that lined the path toward the left of the clubhouse. I consider this to be one of the 10 best golf courses in the United States.

The camaraderie among all golfers, whether new players or on opposing teams, was something very unique and special. This is why many of us players from the old school have a very special bond and love for each other. There wasn't a lot of money involved as there is today. Managers and agents did not abound in the golf world until the business of show business started slipping in. To give you an example, one such story came out of that first day on September 4: Gene Littler and Jimmy G. Jackson were teamed up to play in the first foursomes against Jim C. Wilson and Roy MacGregor of the British team. As the quartet approached the 3rd tee, Jimmy noticed that he had mistakenly packed 16 clubs in his bag instead of the limit of 14. As soon as it was discovered, and without hesitation, Jackson informed the members and rules committee. With full knowledge of being disqualified from play, both team members were saddened and distraught giving the opposition the win by default.

Before Jackson and Littler could make it back to the clubhouse to sulk in what had transpired, Tony Duncan, the captain of the British team, rushed over and stopped them, exclaiming, "Not so fast! There's no way all of us came over three thousand miles to win a 36-hole match by default . . . on the second hole mind you! This is ridiculous! We have sent out a couple players to find the USGA president and see what can be done about this."

It took about an hour, but a decision was granted in writing: "The committee has no power to waive a rule of golf. A penalty of disqualification, however, may in exceptional individual cases be waived or modified or be imposed if the committee considers such action warranted." The game was back on, thanks to the absolute kindness and sportsmanship provided by the British team. This is such an example of what I meant by the camaraderie among golfers. The U.S. team was penalized two holes.

Even with the 2-hole loss, we played well. Scoring was very close during first-day foursome play, with three for the Americans and one for Great Britain and Ireland. I did not get to play the first day in the doubles, but I did play on the second against a young Irishman named Norman Drew.

Starting into the singles matches on the second day, Ronnie White of the British team held a 1-hole lead, which allowed him to retain his record of 100 percent singles wins in the Cup. Continuing through the day, the scores mounted for us. All matches were 36 holes. Our match lasted 29 out of the 36 holes. I beat Drew 9 up with 7 to play. Fortunately for me, he obviously didn't play very well. When Norman conceded the match, and before shaking my hand, he turned to the gallery and in his Irish brogue, shouted very loudly, "Sometimes I play worse than this!" E. Harvie Ward beat Joe Carr 4–3, while Gene Littler grabbed 5–3 against Gerald Micklem. Sam Urzetta beat John Langley 3–2, while Charlie Coe lost to John Morgan 3–2. Ken Venturi scored a 9–8 against James Wilson, and fellow teammate Jack Westland took 7–5 against opposing Roy MacGregor. With my 9–7 playing against Norman Drew, that gave us a total of 6–2, resulting in a grand total of America 9, Great Britain and Ireland 3, to win the Walker Cup.

President Eisenhower sent a congratulatory telegram, as did the senator from Texas, Prescott Bush (father of George H. W. Bush), who spoke before our 29th Walker Cup dinner. The speeches included how generous and especially gracious all the players were. As far as I was concerned, we were all winners.

Snakes and Sinatra

||||||||||||||||||||||||||||||||||||||||||||||||||||||||||||||||||||||||||||||||||||||||||||||||||||||||||||||||||||||||||||||||

YOU MUST REALIZE that the purse for winning any of the major events wasn't like it is today. We're talking a few thousand dollars, and that's if you can make it to the top to win. Of course, playing as an amateur meant that I could not accept any money even if I did win. Unless you happen to come from a wealthy family to begin with, most amateurs had to nestle their play within the limitations of their regular jobs. Performing in nightclubs netted me a nice income, and I figured out a way to sing in the towns where I could golf.

While playing in the U.S. Open at Oakmont in Pittsburgh, I took a job, as usual, singing in the evenings. The place was The Copa Club, owned and run by a man named Linnie Littman. I had worked at the club many times in the past and knew that Linnie hired what was referred to in the business as "record acts." Whenever you were hired as the record act or the featured star, another lesser-known singer or comedian would usually open for you. To this day, I can't figure out why Linnie booked a novelty act on the bill with me.

I have to say, at first she appeared very pretty and charming (I think Linnie had something going on with her), then I learned that she also charmed snakes, and not the kind who came in to see the shows late at night—*real* reptiles. She called herself the "Snake Lady." During her act, she would have five or six snakes out of their cages at the same time, on stage with her, while she danced and pranced about.

The first night I asked her how she could manage all those snakes at one time. She told me that about two hours before she went on stage, she would give them liquor that would keep them calm and about half asleep.

That Friday night a lot of my golfing pals decided to come to the early show. There were Sam Snead, Cary Middlecoff, Lew Worsham with his brother Buck, Walter Burkemo, and some others. One fact I must interject: golfers do *not* like snakes! You see, in our lifetime as golfers, we are exposed to more of those slithery creatures than the average person probably sees. I hadn't thought about that fact, so I didn't even mention to the group that Snake Lady opened the show.

On both sides of the stage, where the audience sat, were long drinking bars. The golfers were seated along the bar, stage left. Then the announcement came, "Ladies and gentlemen, presenting Snake Lady!"

Snake Lady made her way out, dressed in a very skimpy costume. I stood backstage and peeked through the curtains, wanting to see the reaction of Lew and his buddies. There were lots of oohs and aahs. Snake Lady took a few bows, and then her assistant brought out the huge cage full of snakes. Right away the oohs and aahs came to a screeching halt. Every one of the golfers in the audience moved their stools back about 3'.

The actual star attraction of her show was this big black snake that was about 15' long. He was introduced to the audience first, then put back in his cage for the finale. Snake Lady would then perform with two or three smaller snakes, put them back, and exchange them for the others. I guess her act lasted about 25 minutes on stage, as she had them crawl around her arms and legs while charming them and the men in the audience. When it came time for her finale, she looked around, but the big black snake had disappeared! Then someone spotted it slithering around on the floor under the curtains. You never heard such a commotion as soon as the audience became aware of this.

The Copa Club was located downstairs from the street level, so naturally, you had to go up some steps to get out. Everyone in the place moved to the stairs at the same time. Lew Worsham and his buddies were leading the way. Knowing that black snakes have no poison, I stood singing "Don't Worry About Me," a current Sinatra hit that I later recorded with Artie Shaw, to them as they plowed out of the joint. Good thing for the others that the golfers didn't have clubs in their hands at the time. The snake was found later in the ladies' dressing room, right behind the stage. He was under a cot, sound asleep.

|||||||||||||||||||||

Speaking of Sinatra, not long afterwards I was booked to sing on one of Frank's radio programs. When my turn in the show came, I sang that Hank Williams song I had a hit with a couple years earlier, "I Can't Help It (If I'm Still in Love with You)." Frank and I became friends in the time we spent together. I told him all about golf, including the famous snake story, and we'd talk about musicians and arrangers while he related some of the problems he was having in his own personal life. We really got along great. Shortly thereafter, as a gift of friendship, Frank gave me a beautiful watch that he had engraved, "To Don from Frank Sinatra." I still wear it occasionally to this day.

Not too long after that radio program aired, Frank invited me to the premiere of his new motion picture release, *Meet Danny Wilson.* I asked Mel Torme, a friend of mine whom I was working with at the time, if he wanted to come along. We had a good time, and thought it was a great movie. The movie's storyline seemed to parallel Frank's own life. Unfortunately, the critics didn't see it that way and gave it poor reviews. They said it was never to be one of Sinatra's better films. It was a miserable blow, and a miserable time for Frank. Little did he realize at the time that his next role, in *From Here to Eternity,* would earn him an Academy Award for best supporting actor and turn his life back around.

Many years later, not long after Frank had married actress Mia Farrow, he wanted me to meet her. I was playing in the Palm Springs Desert Classic (before it became known as the Bob Hope Classic), when ole blue eyes brought her to the game. They were standing behind one of the greens of the golf course, and Frank called me over, saying, "I want to introduce you to someone."

Looking at his new wife, then back at me, Frank said, "This is Mia. Mia, I want you to meet '*I Can't Help It*.'"

"I Can't Help It" became Frank's new nickname for me all because of that one song I had sung on his radio show. In our conversation at the time, I asked him, "Do you or Mia ever play golf?" Frank's answer was, "Sorry to say, I don't have a set of golf clubs."

A week later I called the MacGregor Golf Company on the telephone. Within five days, MacGregor made up a special set of clubs with Frank's name emblazoned upon them. Back then, many of the golf companies would give their sporting goods to some of the featured players free of charge. Not only was it a way to get the players accustomed to their products, but it also served as a way to promote their brands. At the same time it made for great advertising when it came to the public's perception of what products were being used. A practice not recommended by the Golf Association, no one saw a need to strictly enforce their policy since everyone seemed to benefit from it.

Founded in 1897 and the second-oldest golf company in the United States, the MacGregor Golf Company was gracious to me. I would reciprocate their gesture by helping to promote many of their golf clubs and bags, which I found to be of the very best standards back then. Needless to say, Frank loved the clubs they made for him and the keener interest in the sport the gift gave to him.

I found this out later, when a letter arrived back home on 26th Street addressed to "Mr. Don Cherry, Pro." Inside it read:

> *I don't know where the time goes—but I am finally getting around to thanking one of my favorite golfers for making me the chic-est shod golfer-singer on Delfern. It's nice to have such a thoughtful friend. My thanks again.*
> *—As Always, Frank Sinatra*

Sinatra hired a personal valet by the name of George Jacobs in 1953. As an African American, Jacobs amazingly became part of Frank's inner circle. His duties included everything from massaging President John F. Kennedy's neck to dancing with Marilyn Monroe. Jacobs even golfed with reputed mobster Sam Giancana.

One evening I was invited to have dinner with Frank at his house in Palm Springs. Arriving early, we spent a little time catching up on current news. George joined us for a few moments in our discussion about the great Jazz influences we had, and about the close friendships I had with Dizzy Gillespie and the legendary Billy Eckstine.

The time soon came, and George announced that dinner was ready. Naturally, it was an Italian meal, and it included cooked Italian sausage. When Jacobs removed the lid, all I saw through the smoke were these very dark and quite large rolled sausages. Jacobs put one of them on my plate, waiting to see if I wanted another.

Now you have to remember, I was born and raised in Wichita Falls, Texas. Up until then, I had never been exposed to Italian food of any sort. I also never experienced much when it came to the concept of a color-barrier. Italian, Jewish, black, brown, or white, I considered everyone equal. So did Frank. His friendship with Sammy Davis Jr. alone (whom I consider the greatest entertainer ever) is a testimony to the fact.

With tongue-in-cheek, I took one look at those sausages and blurted out a one-word question . . . *"Relatives?"*

As what I had just remarked sank in, Frank coughed up . . . "Hell, I wish I had thought of that!"

George couldn't contain himself as he retreated back to the kitchen, closing the door. His baritone laughter still came through loud and clear.

Peggy Lee and '53

ONE OF THE CLASSIEST, MOST TALENTED and deserving persons I have ever known was Miss Peggy Lee, both as a human being and a person with tremendous talent. I will be one of her most ardent admirers for as long as I draw breath. As far as I am concerned, she interprets songs better than anyone I have ever known, both lyrically and melodically.

The first time we met was in Washington, D.C., when we were booked to do four shows a day at the Capitol Theatre. Another glib comedian, Gary Morton, was also added to the bill to sandwich in between Peggy and myself. Gary was a very likeable fellow and, by 1960, had won over the heart of Lucille Ball.

I had just finished a two-week engagement at the Sands and had arrived in time for my scheduled rehearsal. Waiting and waiting, I was told that Miss Lee had taken more than her allotted schedule and that there would be no time left for me to rehearse. Angrily, I walked away, having to do my best when the first show began.

Actually, after trying to figure out my cues and marks, the first show turned out just fine. In my lineup of about six or seven songs, I included "I'm Just a Country Boy," a song I had just finished recording with the famous conductor/arranger Gordon Jenkins. I'd often add little stories in between to make the audience feel comfortable, even if I was somewhat insecure on stage myself.

I guess it was during the second show that day that Miss Lee happened to be walking through the theater midway through my set, when she heard me singing "I'm Just a Country Boy." Peggy marched over to her conductor, Jimmy Rowles, and in a slightly raised voice, asked, "Why would they book a country singer to sing with me?" Jimmy followed after her saying that Don Cherry wasn't necessarily a country singer and that she should give me a listen.

Later, after the show ended, Jimmy came up to me and said, "A number of disc jockeys are going to have a party for Miss Lee after the show tonight, and she wanted you to join us."

Still reeling in the fact that she hogged all my rehearsal time and didn't seem to have much concern for me at all, my reply came from an old Texas saying. I responded, "Tell Miss Lee to go shit in her hat!"

With me not thinking he would really repeat it to her, Jimmy stuttered, "Ah . . . Ah. Yes, I will relay your message . . . ah," as he found a quick exit. The following morning, when I wandered back to my dressing room, there waiting for me on my table was a small vase with a single red rose in it. A note was attached that read "The Hat Is Full."

From that time on, we became very close, dining out almost every evening after the last show. We'd usually go to a restaurant or a nightclub, where oftentimes the musicians or our friends would join us. Our sense of humor worked well together, and we paralleled each other's point of view.

Sometimes before dinner, Peggy would order a pernod—a cocktail with a blend of herbs and a mild licorice flavor that helped to stimulate a person's appetite. It also seemed to settle her a bit, and since she wasn't much of a drinker, made her a bit more talkative.

Peggy loved to dance. I was convinced that I was a very poor dancer myself, and whenever she would ask, I'd politely say, "No, thank you." Ignoring the opportunity to swing and sway with Miss Peggy Lee shows you just how insecure I still was then. I knew she understood my shyness without becoming irritated.

To make up for not dancing, Peggy and I used to play and talk about gin rummy quite a bit. One night on our way back to the hotel, we passed a White Castle hamburger joint. As we started walking past it, Peggy stopped, looked at me, and commanded, "Go get eight hamburgers!" When I told her that we'd never eat that many, she ordered, "Go git 'em!" Following her command, I did just that. Then, with a big bag tucked under my right arm, I inquired, "What are we going to do with this many hamburgers, Peggy?"

"Follow me!" were her words. I followed her to her suite, where she instructed me, "Take them to the bed and shake them out." I was stunned, not possibly knowing what she had in mind. She proceeded to tell me, "We are going to do something with hamburgers that has never been done before."

Swallowing hard, I shook the burgers out as quickly as I could. Seven made it onto the bed, while the eighth hit the floor as I picked it up before she changed her mind.

"Shuffle 'em!" she commanded.

I was game to whatever we were going to play, so I tried to shuffle them. I don't know if you have ever tried to shuffle eight hamburgers, but it ain't easy! Then came her next order: "Deal!" I did as requested. Then Peggy began to pick up the hamburgers I had dealt her. After giving them a once-over glance, she exclaimed, "I am going down with one pickle!"

I don't know where it came from, but I shot back, "You're undercut, I've got half a piece of lettuce!"

People who say that gambling can eat up your savings never played with food. Soon after, Peggy and I worked together again at the Sands in Las Vegas. Her part of the show always brought people to their feet. Dressed on stage usually in a sparkling white or pink show-through dress lined with glimmering silver, Peggy looked radiant every night. She always pleased the crowds with a melody of her hits, "I've Got You Under My Skin," "Why Don't You Do Right," "Lover, It's a Good Day," and "Mañana," to mention a few.

During our engagement at the Sands, Peggy would sometimes accompany her manager and a few of the musicians to Lake Mead after the performance. Peggy would go along for the boat ride on the lake while the others would fish. The vessel was owned by the Sands Hotel, and could easily accommodate quite a few passengers with its large forward cabin.

One night I was invited to go along. While driving to the lake in the car, we stopped by a boat repair and tackle shop. The guys wanted to pick up waterdogs, bait that looked like tadpoles or little lizards. I am sure that Peggy had no idea that these waterdogs were purchased for fishing bait. Once on the water, Peggy saw Kelly, her manager, start to bait his hook with one of these waterdogs, and with much alarm asked, "What are you doing?"

"We are going to fish with it," Kelly answered back, not realizing something had upset her. As he reached again for the bait bucket, Peggy grabbed the bucket up and said, "Not tonight!" Then she proceeded to walk over to the side of the boat and pour the entire contents into Lake Mead. That one gesture made me realize what a heart and soul this person possessed.

I'll also never forget the night I was discovered red-handed. I didn't have the heart to tell Peggy that I caught the eye of a cute line girl who wanted to go out with me. Knowing that Peggy and I would always go out together after the show, I waited until I thought the gang was going to be out on the lake fishing. I gave her some excuse that I wasn't feeling all that well and that she should just go ahead without me.

As the curtain came down for the evening, I met Linda around the corner and decided to stroll across the street to The Castaways, far away from the Sands, so that nobody would spot us. It wasn't as though Peggy and I had any understanding, I just felt a bit uncomfortable coming up with some explanation why I wanted to have dinner with someone else.

Linda and I walked in and were given a table down in the front where we could see the show. After ordering and getting a chance to talk for a bit, I looked across the room to see some of Peggy's musicians seated. It occurred to me that they should be out on the fishing boat when, lo and behold, Peggy sashayed up behind me, murmuring as she passed, "Crazy lookin' bait!" I pondered what I was going to say to Peggy the next day, but she never brought it up. Things were back to normal. Peggy married actor Brad Dexter later that same year.

I have to let you in on how wonderful a songwriter Peggy was. She could paint pictures with words that were unbelievable. During that year in 1953, Peggy had written a collection of verses titled *Softly, with Feeling*. To me, it explained her whole life and attitude, and impressed me more than anything to date. Over 50 years later, I still have this precious little book tucked away in the top drawer of my clothes dresser. I often open the pages and read from it. Inside the cover are these words, "Privately Printed—Beverly Hills 1953."

> *I give my will to life and let it live me*
> *All my mistakes to love*
> *Love will forgive me . . .*
> *And then I turn my face up to the sun*
> *And know that I am one*
> *With all the sunlight that I see.*
> *So let my spirit soar*
> *All unforbidden*
> *And let the light shine*
> *That none is hidden . . .*
> *And tell my soul to know that it is free*
> *And I am one with all the beauty*
> *That I see.*
>
> *—Peggy Lee*

Later that year, Peggy performed one of her eloquently written poems from that book before an audience at the Hollywood Bowl. She was accompanied by Victor Young, the gentleman with whom I made my first recording. It was titled "New York City Ghost" and brought a standing ovation from the audience.

〰〰〰〰〰〰〰〰

Before 1953 comes to an end, I have a strange but funny story that happened to me in Springfield, Illinois. I was hired to sing in a famous place at the time called the Lake Club. Many famous entertainers like Bob Hope, Ella Fitzgerald, Pearl Bailey, and Mickey Rooney played there. Why they booked me was both a surprise and an honor.

I was scheduled to perform for 10 days, including two weekends. After the first weekend, the owners, Harold Henderson and Hugo Vagnoli, received a call from a gentleman who told them about another singer who was getting a lot of publicity. The actual reason for all the attention was that the singer, Christine Jorgensen, just returned from having a sex-change operation in Denmark and *he* was now a *she*. Well, back in 1953, this was something quite unheard of. The owners of the club asked if I would mind if she came in and did a little part of her act before mine.

I thought about it and informed them that I thought it would be a great move—since she was getting so much attention, it couldn't hurt. By now, she was on the cover of every major newspaper, and the whole world knew who she was.

When Christine arrived, I took a seat in the back of the club to watch her rehearse. Much to my surprise, she was better than I thought she would be. Christine opened the show that night and was very well received by the audience. After a short intermission, I took to the stage with my part of the show. After singing a few well-known hits, I began singing a popular ballad called "Stranger on the Shore" when I noticed Christine standing in the wings gazing at me.

The next night she was gazing from the wings again. After the third night, Hugo, the owner, came up to make me an offer: "Don, we've been noticing Christine's fascination with your singing and infatuation with your every move. We think she's falling in love with you. We'll offer you $500 to find out if the operation was a success."

I never knew if their offer was real or not. Trust me, I did *not* take their offer!

Another offer of a different sort was made that night. The comedian we worked with on the same bill at the Lake Club was a huge Chicago Bears fan. He was leaving to see the Bears play Detroit the next morning, and asked if I wanted to tag along with him after the show. I didn't feel like going, so I told him to have a good time and that it was great working with him. That turned out to be one of the best decisions I have ever made.

He had just bought himself a brand-new convertible, and was so proud of it that he couldn't wait to drive it. In a hurry, he quickly took off out of the parking lot. About 50 miles up the road, he must have fallen asleep at the wheel. The car ploughed under a 16-wheeler, killing the driver.

I had my share of sex and violence for one night.

‖‖‖‖‖‖‖‖‖‖‖‖‖‖

One last note about the Lake Club in Springfield: around 1974 odd sounds were being heard inside. The piano would start to play by itself and, with no one else around, footsteps were heard walking across the wooden floors. The story continues that a couple years later, in 1976, things began to intensify. Empty glasses on tables would suddenly be filled with chocolate. More patrons began hearing and seeing strange things. Glasses from the bar would suddenly rise into the air, then fall to the ground and shatter into pieces. Lights would flicker and mysterious screams and moans were becoming more and more common.

It was discovered that back in the heyday of the 1950s, a fellow by the name of Albert "Rudy" Cranor had worked there. He was usually found in the backroom, where illegal gambling was held, taking care of custodial work. As Rudy experienced some personal difficulties of his own, he began drinking heavily on the job and eventually committed suicide on June 27, 1968, with a high-powered rifle in one of the club's back rooms. Others say the comedian whom I declined a ride with might have some sort of connection to the mysterious happenings. No one will ever know. The Lake Club burned to the ground in August 1992, but rumors of strange lights and noises emanating from where the Lake Club once stood on Fox Bridge Road still abound to this day.

‖‖‖‖‖‖‖‖‖‖‖‖‖‖

As they say, bad stories always seem to happen in threes. As 1954 began I received a call from Mother. She was distraught by what she was about to tell me, so I told her to calm down. She informed me that my brother Paul's wife, Millie, had lost her life in a terrible automobile accident.

We all knew that Paul's wife had been seeing a fortune-teller for years. Actually it was the same fortune-teller who once told Mother and me that I was going to become a famous singer. When Paul's daughter Anna

Lee needed to have her tonsils out, the fortune-teller had given Millie the name of someone in Oklahoma who would remove her tonsils without surgery. Believing that was true, Millie talked my brother and their two children, Anna Lee and Donna Dale, into driving there. Along the way, someone failed to make their stop and struck Paul's car from the side. The blow was so hard, Anna Lee blacked out in the backseat. Paul looked to see if her sister was all right, but when he glanced over to check his wife, the force had been too powerful. Millie was thrown from her seat into the windshield. Grief-stricken, Paul was never right after that. Knowing he was a mess emotionally, Mother offered to take care of the two girls while he sorted out his life in New Mexico.

Paul put both of his daughters, Anna Lee and Donna, on a bus to Wichita Falls, fighting back tears as he waved good-bye, not knowing what was to become of his life once they were out of his sight. Those poor girls suffered tremendously with the horrors of what they must have gone through.

Mother transformed my old bedroom at our house on 26th Street into a room for the two girls. She made sure that they had plenty to eat and enrolled them right away in the nearby school. She gave them a secure home with plenty of love and her own brand of strict upbringing. Shortly thereafter, Paul became very ill and lost his job. Down on his luck, Paul sold the house he built for his family. He settled his business in Clovis and then headed back to Wichita Falls to move in with Mom and the girls.

Taking a job in a local Kmart-type department store, Paul had compounded his life of gambling, smoking, and drinking by hitting rock bottom emotionally and financially—something he would struggle with forever.

I visited them often, bringing money or useful items whenever they needed them. So many years later, Anna Lee remembered, of all things, the car I used to drive when I visited them. Specifically, she remembered that Mother used to have me park it around the corner. It was a brand-new black Cadillac El Dorado. I purchased it from a dealership in Michigan. They asked me if I wanted to order it equipped with air-conditioning. When I asked how much extra that would be, they informed me that it would add an additional $450 to the price. I told them no thanks. When it arrived from the factory, I drove it straight down from the dealership to Texas, where I sweated even with the windows down.

The smell of the my leather golf bag lying on the contrasting leather seats gave me the cognition of some success while I drove in solitude. Arriving back home and showing my mother what I had just purchased, she asked me how much I paid for it. I told her, "An even $5,000." She thought for a moment and said, "That's $4,000 more than the house cost!" Around the corner it went.

My mother never really got to travel to many places in her lifetime. When I made it back to New York, I sent her money for a plane ticket to come out and visit me on the East Coast. Although I heard that she would visit the beauty parlor once in a while, I never in my entire life saw my mom with much makeup on. Usually, whenever I got a check for working, I took out what I needed to live on and had my manager, Howie Richmond, mail the remainder to her. I always figured she sacrificed everything she had to raise me, and it was the very least I could do to help out.

I drove out to the airport to meet Mother when she arrived and was somewhat taken back by her appearance. After hearing that she had spent a lot of money on remodeling portions of the old house, I guess she opted to pay a visit to the beauty parlor and buy a mink stole for her plane trip. Never seeing my own mother in makeup, I played a little joke on her. As she stepped off the plane and rounded the terminal, I walked right past her, pretending to not recognize her. She screamed, "Donald!" To my amusement, we shared the laughs back to where I was staying at 400 East 57th Street.

Ross Alma had the time of her life, spending about a week in New York. I not only took her to all the finest nightclubs and restaurants, but she also got to meet a friend of mine, Perry Como. Returning back to Wichita Falls, Mom raved on and on about having so much fun. On one of my return trips home, I took along my old '53 Buick Century and gave it to her as a much-needed present. I was so happy that I was able to give her a little sparkle in the daily grind of everyday life.

In 1954 I wasn't spending as much time in the studio making records. As a matter of fact, Decca had only released three singles the whole year. I concentrated more of my time on golfing and performing in nightclubs. I traveled to the town of London, Ontario, to play in the Americas Cup and to defend my title in the Canadian Amateur.

Started in 1952, the Americas Cup had been formed as an outgrowth between competitors from Canada, Mexico, and the United States in an attempt to stimulate golf in all three nations. Each Americas Cup event rotated between the three countries and was played ever other year in between the years of the famed Walker Cup. The USGA selected its team of players with the same criteria that was used for the Walker Cup series—playing ability as reflected by records in important tournaments, unquestioned amateur status, and qualifications to represent our country internationally. Each team's seven-member squad was solely comprised of amateurs from their respective countries. Their first tournament was held in Seattle, and in 1954, I was invited to play in the second one along with Bill Campbell, Charlie Coe, Joe Conrad, Dale Morey, Bill Patton, and E. Harvie Ward. Originally designed for fox hunting, the London Hunt and Country Club was comprised of hound kennels surrounded by tennis and archery courts. With the encroachment of residential buildings and the growing interest in the game of golf, property at the west end was purchased, and the kennels moved out. Our U.S. team played to a win on Thursday and Friday, August 12 and 13, and we were never so proud.

Three days later, on August 16, the Canadian Amateur began play at the same place. I tried to carry over the excitement from the Americas Cup win, but during the first match of the game, I got beaten by a guy named Joe LeBlanc. I must admit, I wasn't very gracious about losing, which resulted in some bad press from the newspapers and radio. You know, it was that same old breaking of clubs and pouting like only I could. What's so bad about saying, "On a good day, I could beat LeBlanc with one club, a five iron!"? E. Harvie Ward, an excellent golfer and very good friend, made *Time* magazine's August 30 edition, stating he had taken top place. Oh well. Win one, lose one.

The tournament was over, but I still had to stay and finish my job at Campbells. It was a very beautiful nightclub, and as usual, I took the booking while playing golf in town. In London, Ontario, where Campbells was located, the town held a yearly Shakespeare festival. On Thursday, the owner of Campbells told me that a very famous actor by the name of James Mason and his party were going to be attending the show. Mason was in town appearing in one of Shakespeare's more famous plays. Needless to say, it made me a little nervous. After all, I hailed from Wichita Falls, and all of these famous people I had only seen or heard of were in the movies. It also happened that James Mason was one of my favorite actors.

I went on stage feeling a little apprehensive and hoping to please the audience, especially Mason and his party. Remember the song that Peggy Lee first heard me sing, "I'm Just a Country Boy"? Well, one of the three records that Decca had just released was that same number. It was a great song written by Freddie Hellerman, who was with a famous group himself, called The Weavers. I recorded the song with Gordon Jenkins, one of the greatest songwriters, conductors, piano players, and arrangers of all time. I remember at first Jenkins didn't want to record it with me, but Peggy Lee convinced him that I was a good singer, so he consented to doing it.

That night at Campbells I sang that song and received so much applause that it scared me. The one person leading the ovation was James Mason. He was standing and insisting that everyone do the same.

Over the next three days, we became good friends. James wanted a couple dozen copies of my new record, "I'm Just a Country Boy," and said that he would give them out while he was being interviewed, promoting his new movie. Wow! James Mason was promoting my record. What could one say to that other than profusely thanking him? He asked when I was going to be out in California next. I replied that I was going to Los Angeles to play in the L.A. Open. Mason then insisted that I stay with him at his place when I got there.

When I arrived in Los Angeles, I didn't trouble him with his invitation, but did accept when he invited me to have dinner at his house. What a dinner that was! Let me tell you who was there: Tyrone Power with Linda Christian, Joseph Cotten with Patrica Medina, and of course James and his wife, Pamela, with their very young daughter, Portland. A few others were there also, but after all these years, my memory fails me a bit. The main footnote is that I never had attended a dinner or party like that back home.

James walked over to his record player in the dining room and began to play the record of "I'm Just a Country Boy" I had given him in Canada. He walked back and announced, "*That,* my friends, is our honored guest, Don Cherry."

I was seated next to Linda Christian, and I'll never forget her reaction. She looked directly at me, and asked, "You?" My very intelligent answer was, "Yes, ma'am." She later asked me why I called her "ma'am," and I responded, "It's because you're older than me." That didn't sound right, so I quickly added, "My mother always told me to address ladies and gentlemen as 'ma'am' and 'sir.'" I think it impressed her. A little respect goes a long way. To this day, I still address people with that lost art.

Another gentleman whom I had the utmost respect and admiration for was my very good friend, Buddy Hackett. I have known Buddy for more than 50 years. We met in 1954 at the Concord Resort Hotel in Kiamesha Lake, New York. My close friend Jimmy Demaret was the pro at the club, and I went to visit him.

Jimmy told me that he had met the funniest man he had ever seen there. That was something coming from the mouth of Demaret, who was inherently funny himself. As it turned out, he was dead right! Buddy would do a routine about a Chinese waiter in his act. It has become a classic bit ever since, and Buddy instantly became world-famous. I really found out about Buddy's incredible humor the next day when Jimmy, Buddy, golf pro George Fazio, and I started out to play a round of golf. The foliage and trees at the Concord were simply awesome, and the game started out very well. All of a sudden, on our 6th hole, Buddy came up missing. We started to wonder where he could be and began looking around. Suddenly we heard this crash come out of the bushes. It was Buddy. He jumped out nearly stark naked, yelling, "The locusts are coming! The locusts are coming!"

Another time Buddy and I were playing golf. He was a better than average player, and this time he had just finished making a motion picture called *The Love Bug*. It was a movie about a little Volkswagen named Herbie. After filming, the producers gave Buddy the car, which he proudly drove around. We had been playing a round with a friend of Buddy's named John Pransky. All of us crammed into Buddy's little car to travel to the course. After the game, John proceeded to bend over to take off his shoes. When he tried to bend back, he couldn't straighten up. "Buddy," I asked, "how are we going to get him back to the clubhouse? There is no way we are going to get him into that car."

With a look and a voice that only Buddy could come up with, he replied with authority, "We'll tie him over the fender!"

My first thought came out as a question: "What if a cop stops us?"

Out of the side of his mouth (as Buddy always talked) he replied matter of factly, "We'll tell him a deer shot him." He always had the answers, that was Buddy.

||||||||||||||||||||||

I also had my share of playing in some wonderful events during 1954. Making it to the quarterfinals of the USGA Amateur Championship, I lost to a golfer named Arnold Palmer.

In his book *A Golfer's Life*, Arnold writes, "I had something more immediate to worry about—an afternoon quarterfinal match against Don Cherry, the reining Canadian Amateur champ. I didn't know much about Cherry's game, but I found myself 2 down to him at the turn and had to battle back to square the match by 16. At the long 17th, both of us missed the green, but I pitched close enough to make 4. Cherry bogeyed and we halved 18, meaning I moved onto the semifinal round."

Moving on, my trip to The Masters was my third. I was paired with Walter Burkemo, who had just won the PGA Championship the year before. During the first 10 holes, I had hit some very strange putts, made a couple, but had already 3-putted four times. If you have watched The Masters on television or in person, you'll know that Amen Corner is where you find a large part of the gallery. The people who watch golf from there are looking for a little excitement. Well, I provided a little this day.

Eleven is a very good par-4 hole that measures a little over 440 yards. A lake borders the left side of the green, so that's where you try to stay away from. Playing it to the right side, I hit my second shot and pushed it a little more than I wanted. It left the ball about 65' right and short of the pin.

As they often did, they had placed the pin in the back left corner of the green. Being just a foot or so off the edge of the green, I decided to use my putter. Bad decision! Walter was standing just to the right of me with his arms folded and his putter under his left arm. I putted the ball, knowing the minute I hit it that it had stroked a bit hard. I also saw Walter turn his back to the hole and drop his putter. I realized soon what that meant.

The ball had gone past the hole, down the left side of the green, and into the water so hard that it splashed. There was a lot of mixed reaction from the gallery, who had never seen anything quite like that. The rule in golf is that you must play the ball from the same spot. I was now shooting 5. Putting the putter in the bag, I took out my 6 iron and chipped the ball. It proceeded to go straight into the hole for a hard 5! In all my years, I have never heard a cheer from the gallery like that one.

Up until this time, the nationwide amateur format of playing was called match play. Match play consists of pitting one golfer or one team against another golfer or team on a hole-by-hole basis. The USGA had defined a set of 34 rules with their explanations. A hole is won by the side that holes its ball in the fewest number of strokes. Whoever wins the hole gets one point toward their total. In July of 1954, the Sunnehanna Amateur was inaugurated with a new idea of qualifying to play called medal play or stroke play. That meant each golfer would play four rounds of golf, and their total number of strokes were counted to win. The lowest score won the tournament.

As stated in a column by Rick Granger of *Golf Playing* Magazine:

Originally the Sunnehanna Country Club had sponsored
match-play games from 1936 through 1951 when the
board of Governors decided to terminate the yearly event
because of problems with waging and gambling associated

with Calcutta pools (betting on players). Two years later, the board decided to sponsor the Sunnehanna Amateur, but they need a golfer that can add legitimacy to their new event. Their goal is to attract a player from the U.S. Walker Cup team. Since Don Cherry has also recently been a member of the winning Americas Cup team, along with playing in The Masters, he is considered the prime candidate to approach.

I guess it also didn't hurt that I presented coverage in the entertainment field as well, with my appearances on TV, radio, and nightclubs, including my current six-week engagement at the Sands in Las Vegas. An agreement was made that I would sing each night and also play in the event itself. On my way back east, I was able to stop in Indianapolis to play and win the Western Four-Ball Championship with another former Sunnehanna competitor and Walker Cup player, Dale Morey.

It was in July when I made it to the hills of Western Pennsylvania, known in history as the site of the Johnstown flood of 1889. Only a golf swing away, the Sunnehanna Golf Course has one of the most spectacular views on earth, flowing out in a 360-degree full circle to nestle the clubhouse, which sets up on a veranda.

I guess I amazed them all back then. Not only did I help to host their event, I shot a 287 to win the title that inaugural year, and helped Sunnehanna gain a foothold toward notoriety. Unfortunately, I returned the following year to play again, and lost by 1 stroke to fellow Walker member Hillman Robbins Jr.

Phil Harris: The Bear Necessities

NOW FOR THE FOURTH PERSON in my claim of five best friends. By the way, there isn't any exact order to the five. All I know is that all five were known worldwide as having big drinking reputations. How I fell into and remained in their company was a mystery to them and me. Nevertheless, I have to tell you about Mr. Phil Harris.

Phil was known as a longtime film actor. In the 1930s, he played the drums with Francis Craig and led his own groups. Between 1936 and 1946, Phil was a regular on the *Jack Benny Radio Show*. His voice became recognizable to millions of Americans when he married movie actress Alice Faye and continued in radio with his own show from 1947 until 1954. A laid-back, good-natured, overindulging playboy image was based on a self-parody of his earlier film and radio roles. Many kids today have grown up hearing Phil's voice in many Disney animated classics, such as *The Aristocats* and *The Jungle Book*. You might remember Phil singing the endearing song "The Bear Necessities" as Baloo.

I feel like Phil and I had known each other since the beginning of time. We actually met somewhere on a golf course after being introduced to one another by Jimmy Demaret. Both Jimmy and Phil could hold their own when it came to the ladies, but if I met a gal first, they'd usually wind up asking me if she had a sister.

On one occasion, Phil had spent a productive night drinking. The next morning we both arrived on the golf course while the sun was coming up. On our second hole, while Phil was making a 3' putt. As he stood over the ball, a huge black dog came leaping over the fence and almost ran him over. Phil didn't move a muscle. He made the putt, looked at me and Joe Dyer, and said, "Please tell me that was a friggin' dog!"

Phil is the star of one of the classic stories of all time.

The Palm Springs Desert Classic, which was founded in 1960, changed its name five years later when Bob Hope took it over, and it became known as the Bob Hope Desert Classic. Phil Harris loved golf so much that he actually lived right on the Thunderbird Country Club in Palm Springs where the original tournament was played from.

A week or so before the first Classic teed off, Phil had invited Forrest Tucker, another good friend, and myself to stay in his guest house during the event. Most folks remember Forrest Tucker as the actor who appeared in more than 50 films, such as *The Yearling*, *The Sands of Iwo Jima*, and *Hellfire*. Others remember him for his comedic flair when he played opposite Rosalind Russell in *Auntie Mame*. But to most, Forrest was probably best known to television audiences as Sgt. Morgan O'Rourke in the classic series *F Troop*. Most people didn't know that Forrest played semipro football in Arlington, Virginia, before turning to acting. At 6'5", he was a natural for many sports and loved the game of golf in between all his film and stage roles.

Forrest, I must say, had the reputation of having the largest sexual organ of all time. I'm not making this up. It was something that was only whispered about back in those times. Well, here we were, staying at Phil's guest house, and guess who was sharing a room with Tuck? We each had our own small single bed. How a 6'5" man could sleep in a single bed was already a picture to behold.

That first night there, Phil came over to ask me a favor. I knew he already had a couple of drinks as he said, "If you wake up in the morning before Tuck does, and he has an erection, you make sure to come and get me. That is something I have to see!" Well, as awkward as it sounds telling this story, we were both giggling like small boys at summer camp.

I awoke at 6:45 the next morning and couldn't help but take a glance over at the other bed. It looked like Tucker was sleeping in a pup tent. In a flash, I pulled on my shirt and pants and ran to get Phil. Throwing on his clothes, too, we both ran quickly to the guest house. As Phil opened the door to the guest house, I'll never forget the look on his face. He tip-toed inside, walked up to the bed, and yanked the sheet off of Tuck before beginning to shake him awake.

In a startle, Tuck awoke confused and asked what the hell was going on. Phil then took a step back and pointed his finger at Tuck's famous organ and said, "You better leave a saucer of milk under the bed for that son of a bitch, 'cause it's liable to turn on you in the middle of the night!" Phil took two steps back so Forrest couldn't reach him as we all howled with laughter.

I was invited to Forrest Tucker's 52nd birthday party in 1971. I was told that his birthday cake was made to resemble his sexual organ, which was referred to as "the Chief," and I agreed that it had every right to be called that from my one-time assessment.

When Tuck blew out all the candles and cut the cake, I was also told that you could tell how much he cared for you by the part of the cake he offered you. When I glanced down at my piece of cake on the plate, Tuck had given me the part of the head. I was informed that it was the supreme compliment.

Mom heard, all the way back in Wichita Falls, about my hobnobbing (no connection with that piece of cake above) with the stars. Before I knew it, my picture would be in some magazine or newspaper caught out on the town. The current issue of *TV Fan Magazine* ran a photograph of me having dinner with Mary Healy, Sheila and husband Gordon MacRae, and Peter Lind Hayes.

Peter Lind Hayes was a popular actor, entertainer, songwriter, and author. Admired by reining radio and TV host Arthur Godfrey, he would often be asked by Godfrey to sub for him four or five times a year. Peter and I had developed a good friendship by playing a lot of golf together, and as a result, he would take me on the morning show with him when he could.

Godfrey discovered many talented people along the way, including Pat Boone, Anita Bryant, and Italian singer Julius LaRosa. LaRosa became the permanent singer on Godfrey's television show until a famous incident took place. Toward the end of 1954, after performing his usual number on the show, Godfrey fired Julius outright on the air over a small quarrel. After that, Mr. Godfrey used me many times on the show on a semiregular basis.

A favorite friend of both Phil Harris and Bing Crosby was a comedian by the name of Joe Frisco. His memory has since faded with the public, but back in the days of vaudeville, Joe Frisco was a legend. Joe really made his mark in entertainment as a dancer. Later, after he established himself with his series of shuffles, camel walks, and turns across the stage, Joe began to speak in his act. In real life, Joe stuttered, which only worked as an asset to his comedic delivery. Credited as the first jazz dancer of the 1920s, Joe even appeared in over a dozen movies, including his last, *The Sweet Smell of Success*, in the later 1950s.

Bing Crosby owned a house right across from the Thunderbird Country Club in Palm Springs. Nestled up against the base of the majestic foothills, many of Bing's golfing buddies and friends would drop by to visit.

One afternoon, to show off his new swimming pool, Bing had invited a few people over. Joe Frisco was among the guests, along with his buddies Phil Harris, Jimmy Van Heusen, Johnny Mercer, and myself, just to mention a few. Everyone was inside gazing through the huge window in the back when a hermit whom everyone had seen at different times flitted across the foot of the mountains and disappeared into a small cavity in the rocks.

Phil finally asked out loud, "I wonder what a guy like that does for a living?"

Without missing a beat, Joe answered, "He . . . he . . . he pro . . . probbbbabbbly s . . . s . . . sells c . . . c . . . caves!"

Frisco was a horse bettor, second to none. One time Joe's friends had invited him to Florida for the racing season. They explained to Joe that for business reasons they needed to go to New York for about a week, but he could stay and look after the house for them, wishing him luck with the horses.

Two days after they left, Joe ran out of money. He remembered that he knew another friend there who ran a pawn shop. Looking around the house for something to hock, Joe decided on a painting of the Last

Supper that hung on the wall. He tore the sheet off the bed, covered the painting, and proceeded to take it to the pawn shop.

When asked by his friend what he brought in to hock, Joe removed the sheet and displayed the painting of Jesus and his disciples. The man looked at the painting and said, "Joe, this is the most famous painting in the world! I have no idea what to offer you for it!"

Joe looked back at the painting, then back at his friend, and answered, "H . . . H . . . How a . . . a . . . a . . . bout tw . . . tw . . . twenty dollars a plate?"

I also can't forget the time that Joe went to the track and began to place bets on his favorite horse. As his lucky number would be leading in the final stretch, the horse would all of a sudden jump the fence to the left and throw the jockey off toward the right. This happened two or three times in a row during a race. Joe finally took it upon himself to find the horse's trainer.

"M . . . m . . . may I off . . . offer a suggestion?" Joe asked the distraught trainer.

"Sure" he replied, thinking that any kind of advice would be helpful.

Stuttering out his suggestion, Joe said, "W . . . wh . . . why don't y . . . yo . . . you p . . . p . . . put some le . . . lea . . . lead in his right ear?"

The trainer thought for a minute. "How do you do that?" he asked Joe.

"You p . . . p . . . pu . . . put a g . . . g . . . gu . . . gun in his left ear!"

Band of Gold, St. Andrews, and Rock and Roll Takes Over

As 1954 DREW TO A CLOSE, so did my recordings for Decca. The company didn't seem to promote their artists as they had done in the past, and now Columbia Records was courting me to come over to their label. Columbia was known for having a huge roster of popular vocalists, including Doris Day, Tony Bennett, Guy Mitchell, Buddy Clark, Rosemary Clooney, Percy Faith, The Four Freshmen, Jerry Vale, Frankie Laine, Ray Conniff, Marty Robbins, Gene Autry, Sarah Vaughan, Duke Ellington, Jo Stafford, and a zillion others. Besides me, Columbia was also courting the likes of Miles Davis and Johnny Mathis.

Howie Richmond, my manager, signed me to a nice deal, and I immediately began recording a few songs for them to release. The first was with legendary arranger and conductor Percy Faith and his orchestra called "Clean Break." Another couple records were slowly released, but nothing much happened except for a little interest in a song called "Fifty Million Salty Kisses" they put out toward end of summer.

Then, it happened like an earthquake. Probably the single most important event in my entire singing career. Howard had just published a new song, recorded by a lady named Kit Carson for Capitol Records. Her real name was Liza Morrow, and the version she released was done with a very slow tempo. It managed to make it onto the charts, but didn't go anyplace once it got there. Howie called and asked Mitch Miller, their A&R man at Columbia then, if we could record the song, saying that he knew it had a lot of potential. Mitch agreed with one condition.

*Still singin' and
swingin' through life.*

*I haven't changed
all that much.*

Mom and I. This is my favorite picture.

My sister, Anna Lee, brother, Paul, and I posing with a pony.

Left: Practicing on Shepard Field.
Top: Personal Management:
Howard S. Richmond.

Perry Como and I.

Jimmy Demaret wearing my hairpiece.

Bobby Layne (left), me, and Mickey Mantle.

Our 1953 Walker Cup Team.

The biggest influence in my life.

Left: Singing rock and roll.
Above: Having a laugh with Arnold Palmer.

Dean Martin, Phil Harris, and I.

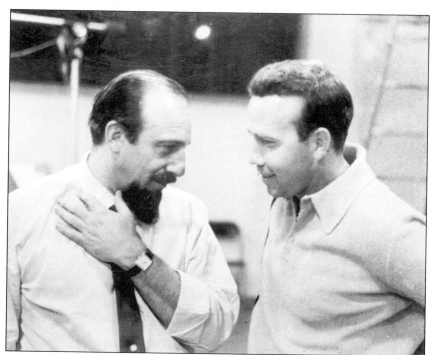

In the studio with Mitch Miller at Columbia.

The 1955 Walker Cup Team at St. Andrews.

A TV moment: Sammy Cahn on piano and Mike Wallace standing.

Singing with Arnold Palmer.

It seems that Miller had taken a bass trombone player by the name of Ray Conniff out of Tommy Dorsey's band. If we would use Conniff, we could record it. Ray came up with an idea, and he was the first arranger to combine voices with brass. Hot off the presses, before the vinyl could cool down, Columbia sent promotional copies to four cities in America: Philadelphia, Boston, Cleveland, and Chicago. You would be able to find out in five days if your record was a hit. The radio stations embraced it immediately and were playing the song every other hour. Three days later, it shot up to the top of the charts! The rest, they say, is history. That little song was called "Band of Gold," and brought me all the gold I could ever imagine.

I am a firm believer that Ray's arrangement had as much to do with that song being a hit as I did singing it. After all, if you know anything about music, you know how successful Ray Conniff became himself.

If you are a child of the disco years, you'll probably remember another song with the same title by a singer named Freda Payne. But my "Band of Gold" is a true "singer's song" as described by Mel Carter, another great singer who is best remembered for his own hit, "Hold Me, Thrill Me, Kiss Me." Eleven years after my hit version of "Band of Gold," Mel honored me with recording his own version.

I crossed paths with Mel a couple of times over the years, but in 2004 we finally got a chance to really get to know each other during a TV show we were appearing on together. He not only gave me so many wonderful compliments but also told me of his love for my music and what "Band of Gold" meant to him. I received a note from him in the mail stating what a wonderful time he had with our encounter.

> *Dear Don,*
>
> *It was a pleasure seeing and meeting you. I must say it was great sharing the same stage with you. Thank you so much for the magazine—the only thing missing is that you didn't autograph it.*
>
> *God Bless, Mel Carter*

Needless to say, that song has followed me around for the last 50-plus years. "Band of Gold" has become synonymous with nearly everything

I do. Fans from all over the world still send thousands of letters and emails every year, describing what memories that song brings to them. My American Express and Visa cards can be cut up and thrown in the trash because I am truly blessed to have a universal calling card that has become a part of me as much as my own signature. That's truly my Band of Gold.

As strange as it seems, I also became a part of rock and roll history, too. When "Band of Gold" was riding high on the charts, a disc jockey named Alan Freed booked me in a rock and roll show he was producing at the 17th Street Theatre in Manhattan. Alan Freed is credited with coining the phrase "rock and roll." If you have ever seen the movie *American Hot Wax*, you'll know how influential Freed was. He did much to promote the careers of so many—Buddy Holly, Little Richard, Chuck Berry, etc.—and change the face of music in America. Strange as it might seem, Freed was born in Johnstown, Pennsylvania, the same town that hosted the Sunnehanna Amateur I played in. I never felt like I had anything to actually do with rock and roll becoming a success, but I was glad for the job, especially because Count Basie was the accompaniment for each artist and group.

Listen to people who were on the bill with me: LaVerne Baker ("Tweedle-Dee"), The Chuckles ("Runaround" and appeared in the movies *Rock, Rock, Rock* and *The Girl Can't Help It*), The Cadillacs ("Speedo" and "Gloria"), and a few other well-known groups. I did "Band of Gold" and one other tune that was popular at the time. Then, I was informed that because of the crowds we were playing to, we would have to perform an R&B song also. I had no arrangements that would fit Basie's band, especially for a rhythm song, so I didn't know exactly what to do.

Basie had a hit called "Smack Dab in the Middle" that Joe Williams sang. Joe is one of the greatest blues and ballad singers of all time, and he and Count Basie suggested that I do that song. Well, I did, and it sounded just fine. I can't express what a great feeling I had, singing "Smack Dab" and appearing with the famous Count Basie! I felt like I had come a long way from that little house on 26th Street in Wichita Falls.

To add further claim to my presence in the rock and roll sphere, a record was released without my knowledge that not only made it to number three on the charts, but also sold over a million copies at the time. The titles were "The Flying Saucer," and on the flip side of the 45 was "Flying Saucer the 2nd." Two comics, Bill Buchanan and Dickie Goodman, came up with a way to pose as radio news reporters, having their spoken questions answered by snippets from current rock and roll hits. Clips from records out by Frankie Lymon and the Teenagers, Little Richard, Fats Domino, Carl Perkins, Bill Haley, Chuck Berry, and even Elvis were used on both sides, including snippets from my own release of "Band of Gold." Wow, I hadn't any idea that "Band of Gold" had fit in with rock and roll.

Once the record companies heard what Buchanan and Goodman had done, they went after them with a lawsuit to close down their distribution and their company, Luniverse Records. The charges were dropped within a matter of two weeks. The "borrowing" of selections from all these artists didn't hurt anyone involved. In fact, sales of these artists went through the roof as the public raced out to find the full-length records they heard just bits and pieces of. The artists couldn't have asked for better advertising!

Decca finally decided to release my final recordings, "The Thrill Is Gone" and "Wanted, Someone to Love Me," after witnessing the success of "Band of Gold" on their competitor's label. I could have gotten mad, but was actually happy to learn that the people at Decca must have been kicking themselves.

In April of 1955, I was invited to play in The Masters for the third year in a row. Cary Middlecoff, known as the greatest golfing dentist in the world, won the title that year. With a 7-stroke victory over Ben Hogan, learning to fill teeth must have helped him fill those 72 cavities at Augusta. It was a great time to be there and see history in the making— even if it wasn't my history. An interesting note was that a 25-year-old relative newcomer also played with us that year. He managed to tie for 10th place with a 297 to take home a whopping $695. That fellow's name was Arnold Palmer. It was his first Masters.

While I may have enjoyed watching history, I didn't always show it. I am reminded of the time Sam Snead put things into perspective during one of my Dr. Jekyll/Mr. Hyde occurrences. Jackie Burke, Sam, and I were paired up at the Milwaukee Open, one of the largest golfing tournaments in the country. I always got a good pairing even though I was an amateur, because the PGA field staff knew I could play. They were especially good to me, especially Ray O'Brien and Jack Tuthill, two lead staff members.

I shot a 67–67 the first two rounds, and even though I wasn't paired with Sam on the third round, I shot a 68 anyway. My three-round total was 202. As a result, I received two telegrams. The first was from (who else?) Jimmy Demaret: "You'd better check the paper. Someone is playing under an assumed name." The second telegram came from E. Harvie Ward, which read, "Hang in there and beat those pros."

After 54 holes, I was tied for second place with Ted Kroll and Sam Snead, and my pairing for the last round was with both of them. As late as the 15th hole, I was tied with Cary Middlecoff for the lead. I made a bogey on number 16. Cary Middlecoff made a birdie on the same hole. When I lost the tournament with those two shots, I also lost my cool. At that point, I forgot all about the large gallery that had been watching us. Now they were watching me as I had reacted so many times before, cursing and kicking, throwing clubs and kicking the dirt or grass, whichever one was available.

Sam, very composed and somewhat embarrassed at the show I was putting on for the crowd, walked over. He leaned over to me and said, "Don, why are you so pissed off? Stop acting like a child." His words were actually a little stronger than that. He finished by saying, "Hell, if you win the tournament, all you're gonna get is a f*ckin' wooden bowl anyway!"

To play with the likes of Sam Snead was playing with "class." His words proved to be the humbling experience I needed to realize how I looked. I would have been one of the very few amateurs to win a professional golf tournament, but, being an amateur, I would only be able to take home the wooden trophy, not any prize money. His words that day have come back to me on many, many occasions.

I may have moaned and groaned with anger then but could not have been more jubilant when a telegram from the USGA arrived. I remember tearing it open with a bit of caution, only to find that I was invited to represent the United States in the prestigious Walker Cup for the second time in a row.

As the first week of May 1955 began, I was boarding the *S.S. America* in New York for a six-day journey to St. Andrews in Scotland. Here, I met the other members of our team, most of whom I already knew. The enthusiasm was high, and we were all excited to be traveling to the country from where golf originated. Even though the journey would take six days, there was a method to the madness of traveling by ship versus flying. It was determined that by spending a few days together, we would get to know each other like a family or team before we arrived. They were right.

A large net was erected on the exterior of the ship's deck so that we could all practice. It was a bit odd not having grass under my feet, moving along at 25 knots trying to find an imaginary flag in the ocean to hit, but it gave us something to socialize about around the liner's huge red, white, and blue funnel smoke stacks.

Checking the room assignments, I was happy to see that my great friend E. Harvie Ward and I were sharing a compartment. Actually, team captain Bill Campbell came to the conclusion we were the only two who could put up with each other. On the second day, while making our way to dinner, one of the ship's stewards approached Harvey and myself. He mentioned that there were some German girls aboard ship who had married G.I.s and were on their way back home to visit their homeland. He added that there were some very pretty ones, and made us a deal—for $25 he would get us a key to the third-class deck, two floors below us, where they had a dance each night and all the girls attended. We figured that for $12.50 each, what could we lose? We forked over the money and he handed us the key he had burning in his uniform pocket.

I'm not much of a dancer, so as we set foot on the third-class deck, I decided I would sing a song with the band. As soon as I finished, a very pretty girl approached me. Apparently, my version of "Unchained

Melody" made a huge impression on her. We conversed on and on throughout the evening. I can even remember her name. Before the evening came to a close, and we started to leave, I gave Heidi a hug and said goodnight. The next thing I knew, she asked if she could come and visit me at my stateroom the next day. A definite "yes" sprang from my lips.

That night I told Harvey all about the girl I had met. I also asked him a favor. Since he and I had both been hitting golf balls into the ocean in the mornings and jogging around the deck to stay in shape, I wondered if he would run a little longer around the deck until Heidi left the room. "When you get back, just knock before you come in," I told Harvey.

The next day, before she arrived, Harvey left to go jogging. I knew he would stay away for a while. About 45 minutes later, he came back and knocked on the door. I called out, "Not yet!" and in another 10 minutes, the same thing happened. This went on for quite some time. Well, by the time we got to Scotland, Harvey was in the best shape of anybody at the awards ceremony. He gave my sex life full credit for that when he announced, "I am the only human being who ever walked and ran from New York to Southampton!"

E. Harvie Ward and I had met and played in the previous 1953 Walker Cup together. I guess you could say we gave Bill Campbell, our current 1955 captain, the feeling that we were better than the rest of the players. On the American side, no one had made it to the finals of the U.S. Amateur, with the exception of Dale Morey, who took second in 1953. (Unfortunately, Arnold Palmer, who was the reining U.S. Amateur champ, had just turned pro months earlier. Palmer needed to serve out his apprenticeship, touring for six months, all to earn enough money to marry his girlfriend, Winnie. Thus, Arnold missed the opportunity of joining our Walker team that year).

We landed in Southampton with a whole day to ourselves before reporting to the train station. Most of us spent the morning at the famed Sunningdale Golf Course to play on real grass. The early evening was spent taking in what we could in London's main city. All of us turned in early and awoke to travel north by railroad and arrive at the grounds of St. Andrews.

As we stood before the old iron entrance gates, our excitement turned into silence. It was raining, but no one seemed to notice. We were caught in the euphoria of a place that was legend to many of us. The quietness was like being in church on a Sunday morning. I remember one word that kept rolling over and over in my head as I stood there in the rain— *awesome!* I had heard about this place my whole life, and just the respect we all had for it was something I can't even put into words.

With about a week to practice before the game began, we checked into the hotel that was reserved for us. The historical and elegant Rusacks Hotel, which overlooked the 18th hole of the "Old Course," as it was called, provided a transforming panoramic view from sunrise to sunset.

The first thing we noticed upon making our way onto the course was a sign posted on the first tee. It specified who had the right of way while on the fairway. There was a road or path that crossed going to the North Sea. First right of way was granted for mothers pushing baby carriages. The second was for shepherds and their sheep (hoping it was a small flock), and third was for golfers teeing from the first tee. According to the weather, they also posted par for the day. Sometimes it was in the middle 80s.

The weather remained cold and rainy for the first three or four days, but we still played, some of us with pajamas under our clothes to keep warm. In the midst of the second day, a 12-year-old boy came up to me and asked if I was the singer Don Cherry. "Band of Gold" was on *Hit Parade* and a huge success at the time, even in Scotland. I said yes, and asked him his name and how he knew about me being a singer.

He answered that his name was Johnny and that his father had told him I was the singer. It started to hail, with the wind getting speeds up to 25 miles an hour. In spite of the bad weather, I noticed that Johnny was wearing a short-sleeved shirt and short pants, and asked him if he was cold. His answer made me think he was the wisest person I had ever known. In a Scottish accent he simply said, "I am not allowed to get cold." The next day I saw him again, still without a sweater or coat.

It wasn't until we started actually playing in the matches that I saw little Johnny again.

E. Harvie Ward and I were picked by Bill Campbell, our nonplaying captain, to play as the number one team going against Joe Carr and Ronnie White, both returning Walker players who had led off for Britain in the past, four times in a row. They had never been beaten in a Walker Cup match.

Back in those days, it was the norm to play 36-hole matches. We hit alternate shots during the team matches, with Harvey playing first. As we approached the 16th hole the first afternoon, we were 1 down. The 16th hole at St. Andrews has the most famous bunker in any golf course in the world. All of the bunkers there have their own names, and this one was known as "the Principal's Nose." Most fairway bunkers there are called "pot bunkers." The Principal's Nose is about 6' deep, not very big, and located right in the middle of the fairway. That's where I drove the ball, right into the sand trap. I had to use a sand wedge to make sure that I got it out. At the time, we were still about 145 yards from the green in 3.

In the meantime, Ronnie White had hit their second shot on the green about 20' from the hole. Then Harvey hit our fourth shot. Again, not a very good one, and it stopped about 50' short of the hole itself. The putt had a huge break, and the first 20' were uphill. Harvey looked at me. I looked at him. And he shouted to me, "Hit it!" It was like a sergeant's command. I hit the putt and it went right in back of the cup. Joe Carr had no confidence in his putter and was using a 3 iron to putt with. He left the ball about 4' short. Ronnie White missed, and we tied the hole.

Harvey drove on the 17th hole. I hit a 4 iron about 4' from the pin. Harvey made the putt. We won the hole with a birdie. On the 18th, they left their second shot at the bottom of the green in what is called "the Valley of Sin." They 3-putted, we 2-putted and won, 1-up. A miracle had just taken place!

The next day I played Joe Carr, the only Irishman to be named Captain of the Royal and Ancient Gold Association, and a two-time winner of the British Amateur. As the announcement was being made, "Playing next, Mr. Joe Carr for the British and Mr. Don Cherry for the United States," I heard a small boy's voice. It was little Johnny.

"Mr. Cherry," he called in his accent. I found where the voice was coming from and made my way over. "I should pull for Mr. Carr, but I am not," he said emphatically, still without a coat.

It hadn't affected me earlier, since I shot a 67 in the morning, had Joe 6 down, and didn't play as well in the afternoon (even though I beat him 5-up and 3 to play). With the look in little Johnny's eyes, and his words to me, the American flag flying proudly above the crowd, and the ceremony with all its pomp and flair, tears started to roll down my cheeks. Right now I could try and tell you about the feelings that I had inside, but wait, my story isn't over . . .

After the matches concluded, the final ceremony was held. Lord Brabazon, who was the reigning Captain of the Royal and Ancient Golf Association, walked up to the microphone and said the following words: "A couple years ago we had two fellows [Bob Hope and Bing Crosby] come over here to play the British Amateur. Because they did not qualify, that did not happen. We now have a fellow who can sing and play golf! . . . Mr. Cherry, would you honor us with a song?"

It was a request I did not know about ahead of time. In my excited stage I thought quickly, and remembered a song that Howie Richmond had just published. Actually, it was recorded by another friend of mine at the time, Frankie Laine, and became an overnight hit. I thought what an appropriate song it would be, and with no accompaniment I began singing the song "I Believe."

A hush fell over the crowd of 10,000 spectators on the green at the fairway of the 18th. It was so quiet that you could hear a pin drop as I sang a cappella without choking up with emotion. The ovation I received when I finished was the loudest and longest I ever got in my whole life. No one knew how, inside, I felt a deep sensation and emotion I had never experienced before, and haven't yet again to this day. Despite many other wins, that single moment singing from the steps of St. Andrews was truly the highest point in all of my golfing career.

The following day, all of the sports pages reported that the meaning of that song was the reason the Americans dominate golf.

More Than Golf Is Needed to Beat These Americans

They don't think much of crooners in St. Andrews. Even Bing's swing leaves them cold. But when cheery night club singer Don Cherry stood on the wet, grey steps of the Royal and Ancient clubhouse and cooed into the mike, only the bronze face of old Tom Morris frowned from its plaque.

Here is a man to respect. A man who could beat Joe Carr 5 and 4. A man who helped give Britain's best amateur golfers their biggest home defeat in the Walker Cup by ten matches to two. The secret? In this Hit Parade cheerful Cherry sang "I Believe." He couldn't have picked a better song, for in those two words is the secret of the American Cup supremacy.

Americans believe they are the best players in the world— and are shocked if they lose. We are pleasantly surprised if we don't get beaten, and say so. Americans believe they can play their best when the pressure is on, and do.

—Laurie Pignon, The Daily Sketch, *May 23, 1955*

During the entire game, Arthur Godfrey had been reporting my daily progress on his show every night. TV coverage was limited and new. It was in 1955 that Great Britain first used television to broadcast a golf tournament, and one of the events they covered was the Walker Cup. Since no previous television cameras were ever there before, the broadcast engineers had to install cables in the ground. While we practiced, they worked putting them behind the 18th green and down the 18th fairway. They were the ones against the fence. About 50' or so behind and to the left are the steps leading up to the clubhouse. Here, a small part of the cable was left exposed.

Joe Dey, the secretary of the USGA and a supreme stickler concerning the rules of golf, took notice. "I don't see a white line here!" (A white line would indicate ground under repair.) "What do we do if a player hits a ball here?" he questioned loudly.

In typical British humor, Lord Brabazon replied, "I dare say we should raise his handicap!"

The British press attacked their own Walker Cup members and were especially hard on Joe Carr and Ronnie White, the two that E. Harvie Ward and I defeated. White's record in the singles had been untouched until that defeat, and many called our match the "Walk-over Cup." On the last night, at our Walker Cup dinner, Bill Campbell got a chance to say a few words. He praised the challenging team and told of the real meaning of the Cup—it's the meaning we all learned as kids. The match is not about who wins, the match was "about a unique sporting encounter that mattered to the participants."

A little fact that I didn't realize at the time was told to me by Bob Drum, one of Arnold Palmer's best friends and a noted sportswriter who specialized in the field of golf. Up until this time, the cut in The Masters was placed at the low 40 players, and in the U.S. Open it was any of the tying scores after 36 holes. I am not quite sure about the PGA and British Open, but it seems this rule changed because of me. Here's what Drum had printed many years later to explain: "The 10-stroke rule was adopted at The Masters after an undistinguished amateur, Don Cherry, who was a nightclub singer by trade, holed a lengthy putt on the 18th hole to eliminate Ben Hogan and Cary Middlecoff even though they were trailing by fewer than 10 strokes with two rounds to play." It was a hard job, but somebody had to do it!

Our team members kept the party going by competing in the British Amateur Championship held in Lancaster at the Royal Lytham and St. Anne's on May 30. E. Harvie Ward could not attend because of prior job commitments back in the States (his regular job was as a salesman). Nevertheless, Harvie blasted back, winning the U.S. Amateur title in September. Harvie would also make the record books by becoming one of only nine amateurs to win consecutively again in 1956.

For the British Amateur, Harvie was replaced by Ken Venturi, whom I also met during the '53 Walker Cup game, after receiving a release from his duties in Germany. All I can say is, what comes around goes around. Lieutenant Joe Conrad, a former U.S. Air Force member, wound up taking top place, defeating Alan Slater of England by 3 and 2. As for myself, I blew it early on in the eliminations.

By the end of 1955, a first-class postage stamp cost three cents. The Warsaw Peace Pact was signed and Disneyland had opened its doors. Albert Einstein and Charlie Parker had died. The Dodgers had beaten the Yankees in the World Series, and a girl who was soon to become a well-known actress, Lee Meriwether, was chosen as Miss America. Little did I know that the next Miss America was in my future.

Over the last six years, I had recorded nearly 100 different songs. Each was released on one side of a two-sided 78 rpm or 45 rpm disc. The executives at Columbia decided it was about time that a full-length album was put out. *Swingin' for Two* made its debut with a collection of a dozen songs. The title "Swingin' for Two" was a play on words to associate the golfer Don Cherry with the singer Don Cherry. The cover employed a picture of me in the studio holding the lyrics, singing into a microphone. But some art director decided to place a drawing of a young man and young woman on both sides. The young man was drawn in casual clothes and the lady in a dress made for dancing. I guess, being it was my first full-length record, they were trying to tell the public something about my singing style.

The selections on the album ran the gamut from original standards, like "I Don't Care if the Sun Don't Shine" and "So Rare," to some newer bouncy numbers, "For You" and "My Future Just Passed." We recorded all the songs over a period of four days, and the best part that sets this album aside from the rest is the backing by Ray Conniff and his orchestra.

Columbia also decided to release a couple of my other songs as singles. They didn't want to include them on the album, I guess to sell more product. Both singles, "Ghost Town"/"I'll Be Around" and "If I Had My Druthers"/"Namely You" turned out to be successful sellers. They were released simultaneously with the sheet music so fans could sing or play along if they wanted.

Howie Richmond and I found ourselves in the Philadelphia area to help promote my new Columbia recordings. Philadelphia was becoming a hub of the current music explosion. One of them was a radio show hosted by a young disc jockey named Dick Clark. The trend of an announcer playing records and having the audience commenting on them was a new format.

WFIL also found another fellow by the name of Bob Horn to attempt the same format on their sister television station. Teenagers were invited to come and dance while Horn played records on the air. The show was very successful, especially with the high school students in the area. When Bob Horn took vacations, Dick Clark filled in for him on the TV broadcast.

While in Philly, I was invited to be interviewed by Dick on his radio show. He and I were both about the same age and hit it off very well. Afterwards, news broke about the trouble Bob Horn had gotten himself into. It was a touchy situation for the station because not only did it involve drunk driving, but there were two additional charges, which involved underaged girls. Howie Richmond overheard the managers of the station talking about a possible replacement for Horn, when he chimed in, "Don had just been interviewed on your radio station, and that Dick Clark fellow was very good. He could really talk! Why not let Clark take over the *Bandstand* show?"

I'll never know if Howard's comments made the difference, but on July 9, it came to light. Less than a year later, the show went national with its new title, *American Bandstand*. I returned a couple times to sing from coast-to-coast with its new host, Dick Clark.

Back in New York, home base had changed from 400 East 57th to 400 West 57th, and I was still rooming with friend Marty Mills. A call came through inviting me to sing on yet another popular TV show. Patti Page, famous for so many hit records, "Mockin' Bird Hill," "I Went to Your Wedding," and "Tennessee Waltz," the biggest selling single ever recorded by a female artist, invited me to sing on her weekly TV program. Patti's show was only 15 minutes in length, but that was normal for a lot of musical variety programs at the time. I obliged by choosing a selection from my current new releases. A few days later, I learned about the enormous amount of fan mail that arrived because of my appearance. Even way back in Wichita Falls, I was told that Mother would turn on the television set, close all the doors, and demand it be quiet until my part of the show was over. The power of television! Show business had its high point at times.

|||||||||||||||||||||

Two of my golfing buddies, Bo Wininger and Bobby French, decided to come to New York and pay me a visit. Bo and I had played a lot of amateur golf together before he turned pro and made quite a success of it. Not only was he a wonderful golfer but also quite a character.

When they arrived, I decided that they should see some of the finer sites in New York, deciding on the Radio City Music Hall. That night the symphony orchestra was performing Ravel's *Bolero* with the famous Rockettes dance group. Being from Texas myself, I had never seen anything like it before, and was lost in all its splendor and elegance. I could not wait for them to see it, and from such great seats in the third balcony where you could see everything. About 15 minutes into the production, I looked over to see their reaction. They had both fallen asleep! Needless to say, we did not go there again. I opted the next night to take them out for a classy dinner at a very chic restaurant called the Four Seasons.

Now, you have to remember that Bo was from Guthrie, Oklahoma. Bobby was from Brownwood, Texas, and I hailed from Wichita Falls. None of us were dummies, but we had not seen many restaurants with the caliber of the Four Seasons.

We were seated, and the waiter brought us menus. Looking them over for a while, we then summoned the waiter to come back. Bo and I had ordered steak, but there was one on the menu we had never heard of before called "steak tartare." Bobby commented that he never had that, so he decided to order that one.

Shaking his head to confirm he heard our food orders, the waiter inquired of Bo and me how we wanted out steaks cooked. Bo and I answered "medium" as the waiter plucked up our menus and began to leave. Looking left out, and with a little hurt in his voice, Bobby asked, "Don't you want to know how I want mine cooked?"

Now might be a good time for those of you who didn't get that funny story, to go and look up "steak tartare."

The Plunge... And Everything That Went with It

||||||||||||||||||||||||||||||||||||||||||||||||||||||||||||||||||||||||||||||||||||||||||||||||||||||||||||||||||||||||||||||||

My FIRST TRIP INTO THE UNKNOWN happened in late September of 1956. After "Band of Gold" came out, I had been turning down quite a lot of singing engagements because there were so many requests. One call that came at the right time was from the people who ran the local Miss America Pageant in my hometown of Wichita Falls, Texas. I was asked if I would be interested in hosting their pageant as master of ceremonies. All that was required was to learn a new song—"There She Goes, Miss America"—introduce some very pretty girls to the audience, and be my usual witty self. On top of that, they were going to pay me $1,500. Money? Pretty girls? How could I turn down my hometown?

About a week before the pageant, I received another phone call from the folks in charge. They were thrilled to inform me that the reigning Miss America had consented to appear at their event, too. Her name was Sharon Kay Richie, and she had won the title as Miss Colorado at the age of 18 for the national crown.

On the day of the actual televised pageant, we all reported for rehearsal at 10:00 in the morning at the Wichita Falls Municipal Auditorium. It wasn't until just about showtime when I was introduced to Sharon Kay Richie. As we started to talk, my first thought was, "Wow, what a beautiful girl she is!" Later, another thought came to mind—no, not what you think! I thought to myself, "What a good human being she seems to be, too." It turned out that I was right in both my judgments.

Sharon grew up in Grand Island, Nebraska, and in a way it was a lot like Wichita Falls, so we had no trouble communicating. Her beauty and infectious personality grabbed my attention so that I wanted to spend more time with her. As luck would have it, they were holding a dance at the country club that night. It was a big event, and they had hired well-known trumpeter Sonny Durham and his band to play for it. I asked Sharon if she would like to accompany me. At first she couldn't give me a solid answer because she first had to check with her chaperone, a watchful conservator assigned by the Miss America Organization. I guess her chaperone thought I was a very nice guy because she said yes.

Now, before I go any further with the story, I have to remind you of my hairpiece. You remember that I always wore it when I performed on stage, and the minute the performance was over or after my last show, I would always take it off. It became such a custom that I never gave it much thought. When I got back home, I removed it, showered, and dressed for my date that evening.

When I arrived to pick her up, I knocked, and the door opened a couple moments later. Sharon and her chaperone took one look at me and then looked at each other. I could see the shock in their faces. I'll admit, I did look a little different. Then the awkward moment of silence was broken by laughter as we left for the dance. Sharon confessed later that even she wore something on stage—huge, hard glass contacts because she was so nearsighted and didn't want to fall off the stage. We both laughed a lot and had a wonderful time.

I kept in touch with Sharon by telephone and even made it a point to visit her at a couple of the local pageants. We even made a date to spend three days in New York together—with separate rooms, of course—before I asked her to marry me as simply and quick as that. The answer was just as quick—"Yes."

Arthur Godfrey invited me back on his show again, only this time he wanted not only me but my new fiancée to appear as well. He wanted us to tell all of America about how we met, fell in love, and that we were officially engaged to be married. Two weeks after giving up her crown, Sharon and I were married on September 22, 1956, in Denver, Colorado. The October 1 issue of *Time* magazine reported the news:

"Married, Sharon Kay Ritchie, 19, prim, proper (no cheesecake) Miss America of 1956; and chubby-cheeked Don Ross Cherry, 32, amateur golfer (U.S. Walker Cup Team, 1953, 1955; Canadian Amateur champion, 1953) and nightclub crooner; in Denver."

As Sharon recalled, "The ceremony was performed by Val Wilson, president of the Colorado Women's College [Sharon's alma mater] and an ordained minister. My sister, Donna, was the matron of honor, and Bobby French, a close friend of Don's from Texas, was best man. The reception was held at Bauer's of Cherry Creek. We went to Estes Park, Colorado, for our honeymoon. Our short honeymoon was followed by a trip to Fort Worth, Texas, for an exhibition game with Ben Hogan at the Colonial Country Club. I went on to New York City, while Don remained in Texas."

To everyone around, including me, we were on top of the world with all the attention. But in real life, like in Hollywood, you usually know what happens to high-profile couples. From the start, Sharon and I both had possession of our own lives. Sharon had a career ahead of her, and I worked in nightclubs most of the time. We were always apart from each other, but during our five years together, we did manage to have two wonderful boys born to us: Sean Ross Cherry and Stephan Patrick Cherry. Stephan is the father of my first two grandsons, Jeremy and Peter. Jeremy, as a baby, is pictured with me on the jacket of my album *Something Old, Something New*. If you are familiar with that album, you know neither one of us is wearing a hairpiece!

Golf Illustrated's October 25, 1956, issue had this huge photo of "Four Happy Americans" emblazened on its front cover. The caption read: "Mrs. E. Harvie Ward, E. Harvie Ward, the U.S. Amateur; Mrs. Don Cherry and her husband, Walker Cup golfer and singer, Don Cherry." All four of us were smiling in the photo, but I knew that not calling Sharon by her name, must have beleaguered her a bit. Inside the magazine, I appeared in a photo titled "Don Cherry—Shut Face." Of course, the fine print explained that "shut face" is a term describing my golf-swing. The caption read, "U.S. Walker Cup player Cherry has very strong hands. The club-face points skywards at the top of the swing and the left wrist is not cupped or bent."

||||||||||||||||||||

People have been confusing two other men by the name of Don Cherry and me for years. Don Cherry the great jazz musician who plays trumpet has been given the *Downbeat Magazine* award countless times for being the best, and NHL hockey coach and broadcaster Don Cherry lives in Canada. The confusion started back in about 1956 or '57. I would travel to Edmonton and Calgary in Canada to appear in various telethons for different charities. We would usually show up a couple days in advance to appear at different functions and different places for publicity purposes. This particular time, I had also taken a job singing in Edmonton.

A week before I arrived, a comment was made by the "other" Don Cherry, who lives in Canada. Most people in Canada compared him to our commentator Howard Cosell when it came to his opinions. You either despised him or loved him—Don once implied that Wayne Gretzky was a pretty good player, but not the superstar that everyone made him out to be.

This Friday night, the Edmonton Oilers were playing the Boston Bruins. As in every sporting event, the national anthem was played. If they were playing a team from the United States, then both anthems were played. Since I was in town for the telethon, the team owners had invited me to sing the U.S. national anthem. I was dressed in western attire, with matching leather pants, jacket, cowboy hat, and cowboy boots. They instructed me to walk to the middle of the ice, where the microphone was located, to sing before the entire crowd attending the game. Cowboy boots are not meant for walking on ice! I must have slipped three or four times, catching myself before I totally slipped and fell. Finally reaching my spot, they announced, "Now, ladies and gentlemen, singing the United States national anthem . . . Don Cherry!"

You have never heard booing so loud in your life. Pillow seats and wadded up paper cups were being thrown on the ice at me. The announcer had to turn up the volume on the sound system to be heard over the roar of the crowd to announce, "This is not that Don Cherry. This one sings and plays golf."

Funny how one little announcement could affect 50,000 people. I finished singing, not wanting to look up from fear of an object hitting me, when I heard a thunderous roar of applause begin. I then received one of the biggest standing ovations I have ever experienced.

I also received a nice ovation from the folks at Columbia Records. Seems "Ghost Town" had made it to 22nd place in the all-time sellers of 1956. Another of my recordings, "Wild Cherry," hit 29th. Both beat out Little Richard's "Slippin' and Slidin'" at 33rd, and Chuck Berry's "Roll Over Beethoven," which landed at 29th on the vocal pop charts. Top place in every field went to—who else?—Elvis Presley for "Heartbreak Hotel." No one could top Elvis.

Even though I was thrilled that my records had been so successful, most of the other top selling songs were actually by rock and roll artists. The younger buying public was changing the face of music more than ever. Record companies were now in a frenzy to get the most they could out of their pop vocalists before the demand for them would disappear.

As a newlywed, I was the target of several new ideas from the Columbia Records executives. They had already had me record a song back in July called "The Story of Sherry" with David Terry and his orchestra. Originally, that song had been titled "The Story of Jenny," but they managed to get permission from the songwriters to change the name. It seemed to me like a nice romantic tribute to Sharon.

Session time was booked for me again at Columbia's busy sound studios. This time the executives had an idea to put out "The Last Dance" and "14 Karat Gold" on separate records. I soon discovered that the biggest buyers turned out to be wedding consultants and matrimony planners. Those two songs (along with "Band of Gold," of course), were, and still are, added to countless wedding reception playlists. It makes one wonder how many couples listened to my voice just hours before consummating their vows!

One person's voice many Americans *actually* heard before turning out the lights was that of Walter Winchell. As a newspaper columnist for both the *New York Daily News* and the *Washington Post*, Winchell was best known for his daily radio broadcasts. Each story he presented was fast-paced and delivered in a rapid-fire, staccato-style manner. Winchell often took on politicians or the rich and famous in a furious attempt to shake up the system. His trademark sound of telegraph key tapping signaled that more was on the way. People either loved him or hated him, but one thing was for sure . . . everyone knew who he was!

Walter Winchell was so popular that a television show was conceived for him to host. It was created to be a milder version of his controversial radio program, but the transition didn't work well with television audiences. Then, at the end of 1956, NBC offered Winchell a job hosting a variety show where he would introduce acts and interview guests who were in the headlines. *The Walter Winchell Show* had only been on the air for a couple of weeks when Howie got a call that Winchell wanted Sharon and me on his program to talk about our new marriage. Not only were we assured that he was going to keep it fun and positive, but he also made an offer of $5,000, thinking that our appearance would boost his ratings.

We hadn't even responded back with an answer when Arthur Godfrey got wind of his offer. Godfrey's producer called and told me in a few words, "Don, I know that the money is good, but Mister Godfrey has decided to end your appearances on his show." I was stunned—Arthur had been so good to me, I simply didn't understand the reasons.

Six months later, to the date, Godfrey sent me a telegram. A nice card and gift followed, congratulating Sharon and me on our new marriage. I realized then that it must have been something personal between Godfrey and Winchell, and I just happened to get caught in the middle.

ıııııııııııııııııı

Bobby French never communicated the word "friendship" to me in all the years we have known each other, but actions speak louder than words. Bobby had been blessed with a personality and attitude that one would not expect coming from a child in a wealthy family. His parents had made their fortune in the oil business, but Bobby's idea of a good time wasn't spending weekends on a yacht. Instead, Bobby was more intrigued with the game of golf and made it a habit of visiting the various courses all over the area. That's where we got to know each other.

Many times it was a love-hate relationship. When I was away from home and could use a place to stay, Bobby took me in while I played in the local events in his area. Once I remember him kicking me out of his house simply because I had a bad day at the golf course, but later things smoothed out, and we were back to being friends again.

With a keen interest in golf himself, Bobby would often come along and play. Three hundred and eleven miles southwest of Wichita Falls, we both found ourselves on the greens in Brownville, Texas. Bobby was a scratch golfer, to say the least. I always thought that I was 10 under his score. Well, he proved me wrong this one time, and whooped my ass, beating me by winning the West Texas Invitational. But before Bobby knew it, I struck back, taking the Mineral Wells Invitational shortly thereafter. Playing and competing were both fun.

As a wedding present, Bobby was not only my best man, but had given Sharon and me a gift that went beyond belief—a truckload of bedroom furniture to fill our New York home. Actions do speak louder than words.

ıııııııııııııııııı

I guess I was always quite quick on my feet. Take the time a different Bobby came to play golf at the Odessa Pro-Am. Quarterback for the world champion Detroit Lions and later the Pittsburgh Steelers, Bobby Layne showed he could run with a football, mostly out of desperation. Somehow the subject of running came up, and Bo Wininger had mentioned to him that I outran Frank Stranahan and a few others.

"Hell, I can outrun him!" snapped back Bobby Layne.

That got Bo and Bobby to wagering $500, and the race was on. It turned out to be a different kind of race than any I had ever run. Starting from the first tee at the country club, we were to race over to a cottonwood tree, circle it, and come back to the first tee. Back then, in West Texas, there was some grass, but most of it consisted of what they called goat heads. It was best described as a sticker patch.

We started running, when Bobby slipped and fell about twenty yards from the start. I kept running, circled the tree, and started back. About half way back, Bobby had taken a stance like a defensive back and was waiting to tackle me. He dove my way, but missed me completely and wound up face first in the sticker patch. His face and neck were covered with scratches and stickers all the way down to his arms. About a week later I received a phone call from Buddy Parker, the coach of the Steelers. He explained to me, tongue-in-cheek of course, that I didn't have to get Bobby into shape that early.

ıllılllılılllılılıllı

The Masters came around again in April, and I was invited for the fifth straight year. Faring much better than the previous year (when I think I played my worst), I managed to make the cut above a number of others (Bolt, Hogan, Littler, Middlecoff, Rosburg, Souchak, and more than 50 others). Strange, I always seemed to have done well in the odd years—1955, 1957, etc.

My luck followed through in 1957, when I journeyed to Chicago, Illinois, to compete in the All-American Men's Amateur, and also the World Championship game. Both events were sponsored by a fellow named George S. May, the preeminent promoter of golf in the world at the time. Even though George S. May was a golfer himself, he was more interested in the business behind the game and would stage a number of annual tournaments at his country club, the Tam O'Shanter. May's top prize money was the largest in the world, as he often supplemented his income with unheard-of concession stands, score cards, and bleachers set up for the gallery of folks who came. Many viewed it as a carnival atmosphere rather than a solemn game of golf, but his innovations helped bolster attendance and bring the game into the living rooms of many Americans who would have never had the chance to experience golf themselves.

Top prize on May's PGA stop was $50,000 at the end, and another $1,000 for each of 50 exhibitions during the following year. Back in 1957, that would be like $2 million today! There were three classifications: PGA Pros, LPGA Pros Women, and 15 Men Amateurs. All competition was medal play. The women played for $10,000, and the men's amateur winner would receive a beautiful trophy.

During the two weeks of tournament play, "the boys," as they were referred to, had a bookie taking bets on who would win in each division of the tournament. In my case, two professionals whom I had been

122

playing with in practice rounds knew how well I had been doing. They approached the bookie and asked what the odds were on me winning my division. He asked how many players were in my division, and they told him 15. The bookie then replied "15-to-1," which made the two gentlemen decided to bet quite a lot of money on me to win.

I was leading after 3 rounds by 6 shots. The next morning, while putting on my shoes, a good friend of mine, Mr. Neil Rosonova (better known as "the Tailor"), approached me and told me to be very careful. By just his manner, I knew exactly what he meant. I went and informed my two friends what had transpired.

They went back to the bookie and asked him if they could cancel their bet. Good luck seemed to happen when, amazingly, their request was granted. I've often wondered what might have happened if that bet had not been called off.

Good luck continued as lightning struck twice when I won both the All-American Tournament and the World Championship Tournament. Playing the Tam O'Shanter was pleasant. It was a warm and relaxed course—very open and flat, and only 15 miles from the Windy City.

You would not expect a kid from Wichita Falls to be the biggest fan of the second largest city in the United States, but it's true. Chicago, Illinois, where just a few years earlier, parents kept their children from attending movies and closed the public beaches. The number of victims contracting polio had swelled to over 1,200 in just Chicago alone. In 1957 Chicago was first to use a widespread polio vaccine developed by Jonas Salk to eradicate the deadly disease once and for all. I loved Chicago, and that year I talked Sharon into moving there for a bit of a change in my showbiz career.

On the way, I made a quick stop to appear on *The Ed Sullivan Show*, which was the highest-rated television program in the nation. Ed Sullivan was the man responsible for introducing Elvis Presley and the Beatles to American audiences. A well-noted newspaper columnist before becoming the host of his own variety show, Sullivan once wrote, "Elvis Presley considers Dean Martin, Jerry Vale, and Don Cherry his favorite singers." I must admit that I received a lot of attention from the appearance on his show.

A couple months later an invitation came to play golf at a beautiful club called Shawnee-on-the-Delaware in Pennsylvania. Shawnee is a beautifully constructed course with 24 of the 27 holes located on an island in the scenic Delaware River. Fred Waring owned the Country Club and Inn, and invited stars and celebrities from all over the world to compete in a yearly match play for prize money and charity.

Fred Waring was a huge celebrity himself, mostly known for his huge band of musicians and singers known as The Pennsylvanians. Many people don't remember that Fred Waring was also the inventor of the Waring kitchen blender. It was once noted that Salk used the Waring blender to help develop his vaccine for polio the same year I was to meet Fred. I remembered his weekly TV show that featured the patriotic songs he made famous during the years I was in the service.

Many huge stars and players were there to compete: Jackie Gleason, Art Carney, Perry Como, Bo Wininger, and E. Harvie Ward to mention just a few. Even Arnold Palmer met his future wife, Winnie, on the course while playing there.

Well, as fate would have it, during the second day of match play at the Shawnee, my partner and I were teamed up against none other than Ed Sullivan himself. Ed was a good player, and most of us were there having fun, not taking things too seriously. It was a common gesture among golfers to give their opponent the putt when the ball is very close to the hole.

We got to the 10th hole, when Ed got to within a couple feet, so I gave it to him as we marched onto the 11th. Same thing—a couple of feet, so I let him have it. Well, by the time we made it to the 18th, we were tied, so we needed to play one more. On the first hole, again, Sullivan overshot by about 3', but I considered it close enough, and we marched onto the second hole. Now it was my turn. I did the same by coming about 18 inches short. Sullivan didn't say a thing. I waited. Still nothing. I looked at his partner. Nothing. So I bent over, picked up my ball, and left there in a huff. Not even taking time to clean up, I jumped into my car and took off for Chicago for a singing job I had at the famed Playboy Club.

I wonder why I never did Sullivan's show again . . .

The attention I received from my appearance at the Playboy Club led to a week at a wonderful upscale club called The Tradewinds at my new locale in Chicago. A couple of guys who had a wonderful comedy act opened for me. Their names were Dan Rowan and Dick Martin. I wonder whatever happened to them? In less than 10 years, Rowan and Martin would change popular culture with phrases like, "Sock it to me" and "You bet your bippy" on a little TV series called *Laugh-In*. Speaking of having a TV series, I had a chance with one of my own, too.

Sharon and I settled into an apartment in a beautiful 20-story building at 400 North Lakeshore Drive, when our first son, Sean Ross Cherry, was born at Passavant Hospital. I was appearing regularly on a 15-minute TV variety talk show called *In Town Tonight* from the studios at WBBM, a CBS affiliate station. Guests like Sam Cooke, Mahalia Jackson, and Buddy Holly were some of the talented guests that appeared on the show.

Frank Atlas, the station's owner, had been informed that a sponsor was looking to put big money into a new morning show. Atlas liked what he saw in me on the 15-minute program, and he approached me with ideas for the show he wanted me to host. He suggested that a pilot episode be made for the sponsor, and a couple of big-name guests would help sell it.

Right away, we got to work and a set was built. We used the house band and singers that were under contract to the station at the time, and it all came together in about two weeks. My first guest of the show was famous cowboy singer and movie star Rex Allen. You can see, with my Texas underscoring, and guests like Rex Allen, that they were looking for a morning show with a bit of down-home "country" appeal.

In the meantime, people at the parent CBS network had gotten wind of what we were doing and quickly produced and submitted a show of their own. They had found their own host, another fellow Texan from Plainview named Jimmy Dean. Jimmy didn't have any television exposure up until then, but he had a natural ability to make folks feel comfortable. He was a very good storyteller and an equally good singer. Later, Jimmy would stray away from show business and make a little money selling sausage on the side.

The sponsors decided to go with his show instead, and for the rest of the year, *The Jimmy Dean Show* was seen every day, broadcasted from Washington, D.C.

Right about now, WBBM had a dilemma on their hands. What were they going to do with me? After all, I had signed a contract with them, so they needed to come up with something else. I wound up with a 15-minute show that aired at 10:15 in the evenings, right after *In Town Tonight*. Even though it aired at an unfortunate time, quite a number of celebrities and famous people, like Sidney Poitier, stopped by when they were in the Chicago area. It made for an interesting time, that is, until the ratings slipped down a notch or two.

Someone in charge decided I should get some help, so they hired this monkey. No, not an inept person, I mean a real monkey. His trainer had brought him in for an audition, and I guess Frank and a few others decided his antics would liven up the show. We rehearsed with the monkey for a week before the producer decided he was ready. His biggest trick was to run to the drums and begin to play. He was really a talented animal, but like most monkeys, he had a mind of his own. Actually, his trainer didn't want to tell us about the temper Chatter had.

That first afternoon of rehearsal, Chatter performed well and everything came off great. At about 8:30 that night, Chatter's attitude began to change. His trainer brought him in and immediately opened his cage door. Chatter proceeded to jump out and run up the curtains to the rows of klieg lights above. He made it above the band, and without hesitation, proceeded to pee on them. Chatter's trainer somehow convinced him to come down, and we finished the show, a bit pissed off, or should I say, a bit pissed on.

The second night I was convinced that Chatter was just nervous being in a strange place and would be more settled this time. During the day, he was taught to jump up in my arms, hug me, and begin to talk, in monkey language, of course.

When the live show began, I held his leash in my left hand while he sat beside me. We rehearsed so that when I said certain things, he would react on cue. The first thing I said to him, he grabbed my hand and bit me hard on my right thumb!

I was sure he wasn't going to turn my thumb loose, so out of sheer impulse, I slapped him with my free hand. The monkey immediately turned my thumb loose and his trainer put him back into confinement. Live TV wasn't Chatter's forte. Needless to say, it was also Chatter's last performance. Within a matter of hours, letters and phone calls began to arrive at the station. Most read the same: "How could you hit that poor little monkey like that?"

I really felt bad when I found out later that the day after Chatter's last performance on our show, his trainer went to see a movie at the Chicago Theatre and left Chatter in the car. It was one of the hottest days of the year when he parked his car on the street and locked the doors with the windows up, and Chatter suffocated. Sadly, it was truly his last performance.

We replaced Chatter with a girl singer by the name of Dori Cruz. She was a good singer, but because of the circumstances, WBBM's phones lit up with people shouting, "Bring the monkey back!" *The Don Cherry Show* didn't last much longer and by the time 1958 rolled around, we left Chicago and rolled back to New York.

In 1958 I cleaned up. I really mean *cleaned up!* I had no sooner returned back to New York when my manager Howie Richmond received a phone call from a fellow in Chicago by the name of Tom Cadden. He called to ask if I would consider doing a singing commercial for Procter & Gamble. Of course, Howie asked the usual: where and what did it involve, when was this to happen, how much time would be involved, and, most importantly, how much money would we receive?

Mr. Cadden replied that it was for a brand-new product that they were developing, and that nothing was for sure, but that they were paying only scale. Howie asked, "You want Don Cherry to record a commercial for scale?" Tom Cadden informed him that if the song was used in their TV and radio commercials, we could make a lot more in residuals. Howie didn't even have to think and told them that we would not be interested.

Two weeks passed and Howie received a call from Tom Cadden again, saying, "Procter & Gamble really liked the sound of Don's voice. How much would it cost to have Mr. Cherry record the commercial?"

Howie informed Mr. Cadden that it would cost $5,000 up front. Before we knew it, the deal was accepted. Soon came the day when I drove to Chicago and walked into the recording studio to meet everyone. There were five or six musicians going over the notes, as was the songwriter, Tom Cadden. They also introduced me to Betty Bryan, the singer who was to accompany me on some of the different takes that required a duet. Everyone was very pleasant, and it was a lot of fun. After completing the session that evening, I was informed by someone there that whatever money we would take out of the $5,000 advance we got, would be subtracted from the residuals that we agreed to. That wasn't a pleasant thing to hear.

While driving back home, I had thought about what they said, but those catchy lyrics that I had sung all day kept creeping back into my thoughts . . .

Mr. Clean gets rid of dirt and grime
and grease in just a minute,

Mr. Clean will clean your whole
house and everything that's in it.

Mr. Clean. Mr. Clean. Mr. Clean.

Thirteen weeks passed, and an envelope came with a check inside. Howie opened it and saw that it was in the amount of $176. Our response was the same—not a whole lot of money. Then we soon discovered that they had already taken out the original $5,000 and were sending it separately. That $176 check was only the first of many more to come.

Mr. Clean became a household product and household name, outshining every other liquid cleaner on the market. Most of the credit was due to the wonderful jingle that Tom Cadden penned, along with a clever series of television commercials depicting a powerful genie that I've been told resembled what I looked like in real life—minus the earring and muscles.

Debuting August 11, 1958, and for nine straight years, Mr. Clean was heard or seen in virtually every home in America via the radio, TV, magazines, and newspapers. The most successful commercial in advertising history, it played over and over and over, and the checks kept coming. I made quite a lot of money being the voice behind this superhero of dirt and scum, and consider it probably the single most important event in my career.

A few years ago, Procter & Gamble pulled out that old recording of Mr. Clean, dusted it off, and used it again for a whole new generation to hear. I smiled when I got a check in the mail that I didn't expect for $36,000. That brings the total amount I earned over the years from that one simple recording to close to $500,000. Thank you most sincerely, Mr. Clean.

The success was so powerful that I was asked again a year later to record a jingle for their new food product called Pringles. If only Procter & Gamble had decided to use it I would have really been counting potatoes.

Let the chips fall as they may, I returned back to golfing. The next tournament on the PGA schedule was the Buick Open at Warwick Hills Country Club in Grand Blanc, Michigan. I was still an amateur, and was given an exemption to play by the tournament committee. The exemption was given because I was an amateur player in a PGA game consisting mainly of pros who had to qualify themselves to be eligible. In my case the commission almost always granted me an exemption because of my extenuating record. Every time I considered it an honor to be able to play among the rest.

While playing in the Buick Open, I was also booked into a nightclub in Grand Blanc. I have forgotten the name of the place, but I do remember the special person that I appeared with there. It was Page Cavanaugh and his trio. They accompanied me during every performance. That was exceptionally exciting, knowing that Cavanaugh was a highly respected jazz pianist and vocalist. I had not only been a fan of the trio's music, but also remember the many motion pictures they appeared in. They gave each of my songs a special sound that made it wonderful to work with.

After checking the paper for the tournament information, I found that I was paired with my good friend Tommy Bolt and Gary Player, a fellow I hadn't the pleasure of meeting up until now. I decided that the Tuesday before the game, I would go to the practice tee and introduce myself to Gary and also invite him to my performance that night. Not only did he enjoy the show, but from then on over the years Gary would make it a point to drop in on my shows quite often.

The following Thursday morning, Ray O'Brien called us to the tee, and we all arrived at the same time. Now remember, Tommy Bolt had just won the Open, one of the most prestigious golf tournaments in the world. Tommy proceeded to greet Gary and me with a little concern in the tone of his voice. He was loud enough for the whole gallery to hear, when he turned to Ray O'Brien and asked, "Which tournaments do you have to win so you don't have to play with these amateurs?" It got a big laugh, but I could see that with Gary's South African sense of humor, he didn't quite understand.

We proceeded to tee off. I birdied 1 and 2, parred 3, then birdied 4, 5, and 6. As we walked to the 7th tee, Gary said in a voice so everyone could hear, "Tom, I understand now why you don't want to play with these amateurs!" That was one for Gary Player.

We didn't win, although it would have been nice. The Buick Open's winning purse was $52,000, the largest of any PGA tournament. At least we got to ride around in courtesy cars that Buick provided.

Tommy Bolt and I played in the Bing Crosby Invitational 13 times. We came close to winning a couple of times, but never did. One time while playing the 11th hole at Cypress Point, we were on the heels of Dr. Cary Middlecoff, who was leading the tournament. Doc was always known for his slow play, so you can imagine, playing in back of Cary had Tom a little uptight.

To give you a picture of Cypress Point course that day, there were no ropes and very few marshals to control the gallery. Also, it had rained so much that you could clean and place your ball completely through the green, which, except for the hazards, made the play even slower. With half a degree of patience, Tom drove his ball down the fairway and stood, waiting for Doc to putt his ball.

By the time Doc decided to take his putt, Tom was steaming. He had about 200 yards to the middle of the green and had selected a 1 iron for his 2nd shot. Finally Doc holed his ball and left the green. Tom stepped up and addressed his ball when about that time a deer wandered across the fairway right in front of him. About 30 yards down the fairway, Tommy turned around and said, "Very good! We are out here playing for all this money in a game sanctuary!" He waited until the deer got out of his way, then took his stance. Before he could take a breath, three little fawns peeked their heads out of the woods and started across the fairway after their mother.

Tommy backed away from the ball, pitched his iron into the air, and, in a very loud and angry voice that folks in Pebble Beach could hear, exclaimed, "Where in the hell are the marshals?" I have often wondered what he would have had them do to those little deer.

I remember once when we were paired up with James Garner and Bob "Rossi" Rosberg at the Bing Crosby Invitational a few years later. Bing found out about our pairing and had us split up. You see, Garner, Rosberg, Bolt, and Cherry were the four biggest hotheads in golf. Bing said that he was only thinking of the gallery. I remember Rossi telling Jim to always throw the clubs in front of him. They are much easier to retrieve that way.

Bing's movie partner, Bob Hope, also got a tournament of his own: the Bob Hope Desert Classic. Originally Hope's Desert Classic was known as the Thunderbird Invitational. That's what it was called when I first played it in 1958. What a wonderful course it was, and filled with great history. Did you know that the electric golf cart used today was invented for the members of the Thunderbird Country Club? Another interesting fact is the Ford Motor Company liked the Thunderbird's logo so much, they adopted the name and logo for their line of luxury Thunderbird automobiles.

Hollywood celebrities would flock to Palm Springs to become part of the Thunderbird's rich golf community. I remember the day I arrived for the Invitational and greeted all my celebrity and golfing pals. My old Walker Cup buddy, Ken Venturi, showed up, too, but had reservations about his playing. Venturi had served in the U.S. Army until a couple of years earlier, and because of this, didn't feel he was up to the level he once achieved. A friend of his, Eddie Lowery, gave a call to Byron Nelson and asked if he would come to Thunderbird and help Venturi get back in shape. Nelson arrived and stayed for over a week, working with Venturi every day on the course.

A day before the Invitational was to conclude, I received a call from a good friend of mine, Dan Wade, who lived in nearby Riverside, California. He discovered that Don Cherry *Senior* lived right down the street from him, and he had seen my father walking around the neighborhood. Dan described him as a handsome, well-dressed man, and said that he bore a resemblance to the drawing on the front of the Prince Albert can. He asked if I wanted to meet him since I was so close by in Palm Springs. After a moment of thought, I agreed to drive out to Riverside when the tournament ended.

I awoke the next day to the ringing of my telephone again. This time it was from the Golden Nugget in Reno, where I was scheduled to sing a couple days after the Invitational. They wanted to know if I could come up and start a couple days earlier because good singer and pal Don Cornell had suddenly taken ill. Since it was only about six or seven hours away, I agreed. I thought that the opportunity to meet my father would arise again, now knowing where he was located. So right after the final match, I left for Reno to make it on time. Ken Venturi won the Thunderbird Invitational that year.

Little did I know that before 1958 came to an end, so did the certainty of ever seeing my father again. A member on his side of the family, whom I hadn't seen for many years, called to tell me that my father had passed away on October 18, just a few days after his 75th birthday. It made me pause, if only for a moment. I remember the sadness that filled me at the time. The woman on the other end of the phone also informed me that it would cost $1,500 to have him buried and that no one there had enough money. I let her know that it would be taken care of and, as I walked to the mailbox to mail the check, I took it all in stride. Once again, he said good-bye without being there. A mixed sadness engulfed me.

They say that with everyone who passes, someone new enters your life. The birth of my second son, Stephen Patrick Cherry, was the highlight of 1959 for me. I often say he was born on the road, but he actually entered this world near the U.N. building in New York. He, along with his older brother Sean, made their debut in public just months later in some Hollywood-type magazines and newspapers. The media reported on our perfect little family to their readers. Little did they know that we weren't as perfect as they assumed. Being on the road a lot, Sharon and I were seeing less and less of each other. My thoughts began to stray a bit, and so did my actions.

With the distraction of singing in clubs and playing golf, I simply enjoyed what I was doing. Unfortunately, I now look back in despair about my ineptness to manage my recording career and marriage.

"Band of Gold" had been a huge hit just three years earlier, but my record company squeezed out only three Don Cherry records in '58. "Another Time, Another Place" received great reviews from the critics, but without proper advertising, the public didn't know that any new songs were released.

Actually, Columbia wasn't paying us correctly from the royalties of my recordings, and they wanted to concentrate more on their newer artists. After all, this was the late 1950s, and the competing record labels were hurting Columbia Records, who missed the boat during the rock and roll transformation. One more record, "Hasty Heart" was released in 1959.

Howie Richmond and I weren't too hasty in accepting a deal from Strand Records to record for them. For $10,000 I would go to Chicago and record four songs for them, one being a cover of my big hit from 1951, "Vanity." Two of the songs made it as a single release, but strangely enough, all four wound up on a long-playing album. The rest of the songs intermixed with mine were instrumentals. I should have realized how important it was to sell an album with my name attached to it, even if the consumer wasn't getting his full money's worth of Don Cherry. They say ignorance is bliss, and I let my recording career die. I was too busy running in a different direction.

Marriage Ills and Cherry Hills— Letting Go and Turning Pro

THE SUBJECT OF FOOT-RACING CAME UP AGAIN. This time in Greensboro, North Carolina, the stop of the PGA Tour in April of that year. Sitting in the men's grill with a lot of the other players, I began talking to Gay Brewer about the time I outran both Frank Stranahan and Bobby Layne. The other golfers, who had just finished their practice rounds, were having some beers and were listening in. John Brodie, who was a very fine golfer and one of the greatest quarterbacks ever to play in the NFL, commented, "I don't know about Stranahan, but Bobby Layne was never known for his foot speed."

Gay hesitated for a moment (the beer took over), then said to Brodie, "I'll bet you $100 that Cherry can outrun you in a 100-yard dash." Brodie had another beer, and after about 15 minutes, he looked over and asked my age.

"Thirty-six," I replied. (I later learned that John was 23.)

Without hesitating any longer, he commanded me, "Get up!"

What Gay didn't know, and neither did I, was that the only man on the 49ers who could outrun John Brodie was Joe Perry, one of the fastest running backs in the NFL. In a short time, we left the grill, headed out to the first tee, and stepped off 100 yards. Brodie started taking off his shoes and slacks; I was right beside him standing straight up. The only thing I took off was my hat. Then he got himself down in a three-point stance. I never did run from a three-point stance because I figured if you got down there, you only had to get back up to run, so that was how I ran.

I looked ahead and saw that Sam Snead was coming down the 18th fairway at Sedgefield, which paralleled the 1st hole. He was being followed by a large gallery watching him play a practice round. I have wondered many times over the years what those people must have thought—seeing John Brodie crouching in his jockey shorts like that. (By the way—Sam won the Greater Greensboro Open that year.)

Brodie looked at me and asked if I was ready. Then Brewer began to count off, "On your mark... get set... *go!*" Now I'll let John Brodie tell the rest of the story:

> *One of my fondest memories was a foot race Don and I had at the Starmount Country Club in 1960. Friday afternoon Tony Lema and I were sitting in the lounge with Gay Brewer, Jerry Pittman, and Miller Barber when Cherry walked in (also had missed the cut). There were a lot of missed cuts. Somehow the discussion turned to athletic prowess, and somebody mentioned that not only was I over my head on the Tour, but Gay said there was one guy at the table who could run faster. Looking around the table, it didn't look like a track team assembled for an Olympic ceremony. It came out that Cherry had broken 10 flat over 100 yards while in college, so I asked how old this person was. "Thirty-six," was the reply. Mine was, "Ain't no 36-year-old can beat me running." The game was on and only one man believed what I said—John Gustin; both of us were broke, as we all were then.*
>
> *About 100 people assembled on the 1st tee at Starmount, and discussions of distance were agreed upon as there was a tree about 90 yards from the tee. Of the 100 people watching, all were betting on Don. Between Jon and I, we accumulated about $1,000 worth of bets (first prize in the tournament was only $1,500) and started wondering what*

*hidden ability this southern bumpkin might still have in
another area.*

*So I shed my clothes down to my shorts and bare feet.
Don just ambled down to the 1st tee in his golf shoes, cap
(always a cap). I think I inquired about his confidence, but
it scared the hell out of me because a thought lingered—
maybe this SOB really could run. Question was, "Who
starts?" Don said, "Start when you're ready." Now I was
scared. I'm at a three-point stance and he's standing there,
two hands on his knees, casually saying, "Go when ready."
Somehow, we both started at once. I never looked back the
first 50 yards, but I couldn't hear anything. Glancing back, I
saw Don about 10 yards back busting his ass with spikes.*

*My last memory was of Gay Brewer kicking him like a
dog, telling him to get up, with some mention of it costing a
lot of money.*

*We all went out to see Don perform that night, and for
the first time his friends observed a new quality had set in.
Humility! It's a great quality and we should all have some.
It made the whole week worthwhile. "Golden Voice" and I
have been good friends since. Still think he sings prettier
than anyone.*

—John Brodie

After the race, I thought I was going to pass out. He must have beaten
me by 15 yards. In a 100-yard dash, that would be considered a "skunk."
I came back to the steps leading up to the 1st tee and sat down to rest.
Gay marched over to John and handed him the $100, then walked back
to me. Coming up from behind, Gay hit the back of my head with the
leather head cover from his driver. "You choking son of a bitch—you
cost me $100!" he shouted. (I also cost all the others who had bet on
me.) He began throwing beer cans at me and accused me of defaulting,
saying "You run like you putt!" *Yeah, hit me while I'm down.* I must
admit, this was the most embarrassing defeat I ever had in my famous
sports endeavors. John, I'm ready for a rematch!

You must realize by now that I love golf as much as singing, and singing as much as golf. It has been said that I am the only person to ever have a top 10 record on the *Hit Parade* and finish in the top 10 in the U.S. Open. It's true, "Band of Gold" sold well—more than a million copies—and in 1960, Jack Nicklaus and I shot the two lowest 72-hole totals that an amateur ever shot in the U.S. Open.

USGA Journal reported in 1960 that there were approximately 6,000 golf courses in the United States. That was also the first time in seven years that I didn't play in The Masters. Of course, I didn't realize that one of the biggest events to happen to me and to occur ever in the history of the U.S. Open would take place that year.

"You should play well—they named the course after you!" Sam Snead said to me as we finished a practice round at a beautiful place called Cherry Hills. Sam always liked to needle me.

Cherry Hills is located in a village cloistered inside the limits of Englewood, near Denver, Colorado. Sam was right, I did play well, and almost won the golden ring. Playing with Sam always seemed to inspire me. In 1955 I almost won the Milwaukee Open playing with Sam. (I finished second to Dr. Cary Middlecoff, another good friend.) Now being paired with Sam again at the U.S. Open for the last 36 holes, I almost took home the coveted prize—my playing was phenomenal.

The Open began in the middle of June. Of course, all the greats of golf were in attendance. The chances that an amateur would make it to the Open were slim to very slim back then. That was partially because of the guidelines they had established within which to compete, coupled with the longer and rougher courses the USGA had selected. I was lucky, and skillful too. My record—semifinalist in the 1952 U.S. Amateur, winner of the 1953 Canadian Amateur, two undefeated Walker Cups, seven Masters events, and all of the titles I mentioned previously—worked in my favor. Out of 2,472 golfers registered to qualify for the Open, a little over $\frac{1}{16}$ made the cut—it was narrowed down to 150.

Practice rounds at the Cherry Hills Country Club concluded on Wednesday, June 15. When the sun came up on Thursday, everyone was pacing, waiting for their tee time. It was warm, well into the 90s, but coming from Texas where the summers were sweltering, that didn't hinder me. During the first round, I scored a 36 and 35. That was better than a lot of others who didn't fare so well, and I felt comfortable with it.

There were so many great players, no one knew who to give the odds to. The new kids on the block, like Gary Player (23 years old), Arnold Palmer (30), and amateur Jack Nicklaus (20), were posing fresh threats. Current names, like Billy Casper (29), Jack Fleck (37), and Mike Souchak (33), were spectacular. Past giants, like Sam Snead (48), Ben Hogan (47), and Cary Middlecoff (39), were still in contention.

The second day gave us all an even bigger rush. A fellow Texan, Ben Hogan, took charge this time as he surprised everyone (which he had done many times before). Out of the first seven holes, Hogan birdied four. He bogied at the 9th, placing him 3 under par—he had the crowd holding their breath. When finally reaching the last hole, the gallery swelled to 6,000. With one swoop of his 3 iron, the ball went sailing across the bright hot sky to land and finally stop two feet from the hole. Hogan earned a 67.

Arnold Palmer started his first day in the middle of the standings. He knew if he didn't score better than a 72 in the remaining rounds, all the work that got him there wouldn't make a bit of difference. After the second day, his attitude wasn't as calm. Managing par (71) on the second day, it required a lot more work to catch up to 13 others ahead of him—Souchak (135), Sanders (138), Barber (140), Finsterwald (140), Fleck (140), Casper (141), Cherry (141), Crampton (141), Kroll (141), Snead (141), Boros (142), Hogan (142), Nicklaus (142), and Player (142). Six others were even, tied with Gary Player at the halfway point.

Out of 150 players, 128 were pros. I was feeling good, being the highest-ranking amateur coming in tied for sixth place (Nicklaus was tied for 11th). But this was only the midway point, and anything could happen.

Mike Souchak had played a wonderful game to this point—with good play and good luck. At his 9th hole, Souchak chipped back harder than needed when he used his 7 iron to avoid the bunker guards in front of the green. As luck would have it, the flagstick stood in the way of his passing ball, and stopped it from going any farther. That day gave him a 67 added to his 68 the first day.

Doug Sanders, scoring a 70 as I did on the first day, slowly gained the second day by birdieing many of the holes. At the 18th, it was a large cast-iron pipe that stopped his ball from falling into the water, where he chipped out and next to the hole. He played a good game to that point.

Back in 1956 Sanders defeated Dow Finsterwald in a playoff match during the Canadian Open. Because he was an amateur at the time, the only thing Sanders could walk away with was the top trophy. As a pro, Finsterwald got to pocket the money. Guess who turned pro after realizing what had just happened?

Finsterwald, now tied with Jack Fleck at 140, had been known to play slow and easy. He approached the ball one hole at a time, not thinking too far ahead of himself. Billy Casper, who ended 1 stroke ahead of Finsterwald, held the same mental picture, concentrating hole by hole.

Jerry Barber was another player who surprised quite a few. After 36 holes in the Open, he showed the crowd that he still had spunk, going on to have a wonderful 1960 season. Jerry has left us now, but I can only tell you what a privilege and a pleasure it was to be his friend.

The final day seemed to arrive sooner than expected. Unlike the two days prior, Saturday was to be a test of skill and stamina. Two rounds on the same day—36 holes. Saturday, I was paired with Sam Snead for the entire 36. Our time to play was scheduled late in the morning, from 9:54 AM to 2:24 PM.

Barber (210), Finsterwald (210), and Boros (210) surprised everyone with the biggest gains during the third round of 18. All three surged a stroke closer to Souchak, who still led the pack (208). The pairing of Ben Hogan and the new kid on the block, Jack Nicklaus, caused a roar after the third round when they finished tied at 211.

Arnold Palmer also caused a stir as he battled to get his score down, ending the round 7 strokes back.

The scores at the end of the third match were: Souchak (208), Barber (210), Julius Boros (210), Finsterwald (210), Hogan (211), Nicklaus (211), Cherry (212), Fleck (212), Pott (212), Player (213), Casper (214), Harrison

(214), Shave (214), Snead (214), and Palmer (215). Eight others were tied with Palmer.

As I wiped the sweat from my brow, the last and final round began. This was it—make it or break it.

Even with a rough time of putting at the start, Jack Nicklaus worked his way up on the 5th hole, driving the ball to drop an eagle 3. That moved him up to just under Mike Souchak, who was coming up after Arnold Palmer played.

As Palmer marched out to the 1st hole, he needed to do something in order to pull out in front. His mind-set was on clobbering the ball to get it where he wanted. With one huge, swift swing, his ball arrived only 20 feet away from the hole. The next hole he birdied again—and the next! Playing wisely, he didn't go past par and managed six birdies before he bogied the 8th. In 3 shots, he dropped the ball into the hole at the 9th, tying the record established in 1947 for the lowest score on the front nine.

Dutch Harrison had continued luck, with three birdies scattered between par shots, and managed a 32. Ted Kroll scored a 32, as well, by chalking up five birdies in the first nine holes. Jack Nicklaus moved into a first-place tie after Souchak had a hard time scoring lower than par on eight of the first nine. Then Jack Fleck pushed his way through like a race car on the outside. Making a series of birdies, he caught up with Souchak. The great Ben Hogan stayed the course, only managing one birdie in all nine holes.

That's when Sam Snead and I went out. I often wondered if his skill, expertise, and manner had inspired my play. I don't know, but it seemed true as I struck pars and birdies to shoot a 34, putting me 3 strokes away from Nicklaus.

Now it was all down to the back nine. The mood was so tense you could hear the grass grow. Palmer shot 30 on the front nine and a 35 on the back, putting him at 280, so I needed to play the last 10 holes 1 under to win. This wasn't a time for my anger to explode. I concentrated on keeping calm and playing my best. I 3-putted number 9 from about 8', but I birdied number 12, a par-3, to go back 3 under.

The 14th hole at Cherry Hills has a huge green, sloping mostly toward the creek that runs along the left side of the fairway and green. I pushed my tee shot into the right rough where the grass was very high, so all I could do was hit a layup shot very short of the green. I hit a very bad third shot and left it about 40 feet short and to the right of the pin. The break in the green must have been a minimum of 10' going left. But I made the putt to remain 3 under. On 15 I hit a 4 iron about 3' right behind the hole.

At that point, Sam Snead whispered, "You're going to win this tournament!" I missed the putt.

On 17, as I said before, we were playing right behind Hogan and Nicklaus. Hogan hit his third shot on the front of the green and watched it get sucked back into the water. He made a 7 and blew himself out of the tournament. I chucked my third shot into the water, made a 7, bogied 18, and shot 284 to Nicklaus' 282. Close, but no golden ring.

Many times in my life I have given thought to that tournament. As an amateur player, I could not win any money, just a trophy. But if I had won the U.S. Open that day—considering that I was an amateur and also in show business—the repercussions would have been priceless!

The final scores for the 1960 U.S. Open were: Palmer (280) winning $14,400, followed by Nicklaus (282), Boros (283), Finsterwald (283), Fleck (283), Harrison (283), Kroll (283), Souchak (283), Barber (284), Cherry (284), Hogan (284), Gammon (284), Bayer (286), Casper (286), Harney (286), Harris (287), Pott (287), Marr (288), Whitt (288), Hammond (288), Bradley (289), Goalby (289), Player (289), Snead (289), Feminelli (290), Mangrum (290), Rosburg (290), Venturi (290), Harmon (291), Hebert (291), Shave (291), Dick Stranahan (291), Harbert (292), Kneece (292), Baxter (293), Boynton (293), Douglas (293), Ford (293), LaClair (293), Crampton (294), Dudas (294), Mengert (294), Ragan (294), Johnston (295), Middlecoff (296), Ransom (296), Wall (296), Sanders (297), Sifford (297), Turnesa (297), Burkemo (298), Johnson (298), Penecale (298), Frank Stranahan (298), Verwey (301), Watson (302), Goetz (306).

The fifth biennial Americas Cup began August 11. This was my second time playing in this event. By the middle of the day, the U.S. team had only 1 point to show for a morning of three-ball sixsome play. That caused the United States team to rally, and we pulled into second place behind the Canadians that evening. During the second day, we just couldn't manage the lead until the next-to-last singles. When my turn came up, I managed to defeat Bob Wylie, Canada, 2 and 1, and Hector Alvarez, Mexico, 3 and 1. We were finally in the lead and managed to hang onto it until the event ended that night. Even if by a narrow margin, the U.S. was victorious in that breathtaking game. It also meant that the United States had won all five Americas Cup matches played.

I remember playing one fellow in particular during this time. His name was Moe Norman, better known to some golfers as "Pipeline Moe" or "Autistic Murray Moe." He could add or multiply numbers faster in his head than on a calculator. At a glance, he could count hundreds of pennies. He had a photographic memory. He spoke in repeated phrases and moved parts of his body in repetitive manners. He was also extremely shy and eccentric. Many biographies report that Moe Norman's affliction was a result of a sledding accident as a child. Moe was like a Harlem Globetrotter of golf. He was a master. Let me go one step further: he was a genius. There were players who didn't understand why Moe lived out of his car and would sell every trophy he won (I guess he had no room to display them in his Cadillac).

I couldn't help but like the man. I understood Moe and got along fine with him. As we played our game, Moe had me 1 down with one hole to go at the 18th. I proceeded to hit my ball to the right and it fell into the stream. We walked over, and Moe spotted it. Picking it up, wiping it off, and handing it to me, Moe was asked by the official on the spot what he had just done. When Moe told him, the official explained that it was against the rules for anyone to touch a ball. For that they gave him a stroke and he lost the hole. I felt terrible because Moe was ahead. He was just being a nice fellow and handed me my ball.

The scolding upset Moe, but he used his skills to get even with the official. Getting down on his knees, Moe hit the ball with great accuracy. He did it just to irritate the officials even more—making a point that their rules were full of shit. This was the first time I can recall ever being happy about losing a match.

There were only four more Americas Cup tournaments in future years, until they dissolved the game. Another competition, the Ryder Cup, was also being touted as a tournament that pits the U.S. against European countries. Even though the Americas Cup was prestigious, the Ryder Cup seemed to draw good attention.

A few pages back, I had dropped in what they call a "tease"—some words about not managing my own marriage very well. Yes, it's true, and this wouldn't be the first time either. I have already admitted to never smoking, gambling, or drinking liquor in my life. Unfortunately, unlike the cleanser that made me famous, I wasn't as squeaky clean as everyone imagined. Remember my phrase, "I never played the game"? I guess I treated relationships like a game too. Over the course of writing this book, I agonized at the thought of having to tell a part of me that wasn't so glamorous—every Cherry has its pit.

Being on the road, always away from home, takes it toll. Marriage can be a lot like show business and show business can ruin a lot of marriages. Between singing and golfing, my life was almost entirely on the road. I still never felt comfortable with singing on stage, and I even felt more uneasy with women in general. One thing that seemed to work both in my favor and against me was my shyness.

The romance of a top player on the golf course or the lure of a romantic love song sung by a nice-looking man in a tuxedo swept many pretty young ladies off their feet. When approached, my bashful demeanor made me seem aloof and uncaring. In turn, that became an obsession with some to win my attention. Most of my male buddies couldn't understand why I attracted many of the opposite sex, so now I've revealed my secret. Like Mick Jagger of The Rolling Stones once said, "Become a singer, and the girls come out of the woodwork."

I was brought up pretty much like an only child under my mother's very strict control. As a matter of fact, I think back now about how her controlling nature must have been what drove my father away. Mother was a wonderful, hardworking woman, but the relationship of marriage and its sacred values were something she couldn't pass down. I never even knew until much later how my mother kept any mention of my father away from me.

Okay—I'm still having a hard time admitting it—I fooled around while I was married. It is not something I am proud of. It wasn't something that I did all the time. I discovered that being away from the one you love for more hours than you're home, you find that you are confronted with others who are there for you at your time of need—such as when I was performing at a nightclub in Birmingham, Alabama. The owner of the club was married to a woman who was rumored to be a niece of some governor. Needing more attention than what her husband must have been giving her, she and I had a little fling that lasted for the couple weeks I was in town performing. Before leaving, I informed her that I was traveling down under to Australia next, and would be singing at a club called The Embers.

The Embers was a very popular place in Melbourne, owned by a fellow named Jimmy Knowles. When I arrived, legendary jazz singer Billy Eckstine was just leaving, and we crossed paths for a few minutes. Those few minutes of conversation were one of the most important in my life. During our chat, Billy told me that the owner of the club had a wife who was one of the prettiest ladies he had ever seen. He also stated that the owner was insanely jealous over her. His warning was stern—stay clear of her. I was soon to discover that Jimmy Knowles, the owner, wasn't just a big fan of jazz music, but was also a big member of the underworld. Stories abound about different men who had shown an interest in his wife, and how they "disappeared" shortly afterward.

Sure enough, on opening night as the show began, in walked his wife. Billy was right—she was very beautiful. It was hard to keep your eyes off her. Still, I was smart enough to keep my distance. The next night, and every night, this girl would always be there at my show, flashing a big smile from her special seat in the club. A couple of times following the first few days, she managed to find the door of my hotel room, and came knocking. Trying to be as nice as possible, I made light conversation, but never allowed her to come in to take her up on her offers.

Word of her confrontations got back to a friend and fellow golfer, Peter Thomson. You might remember him as the gentleman who won the British Open five times. Peter knew that the scenario was far more serious than I had recognized, and warned me of the consequences that might occur just by talking to this girl. Peter arranged to have me protected and found two security men to guard and walk with me for the balance of the time I was there.

The day before I was to leave, the girl phoned me in my hotel room to tell me she was going to try and find a way to travel to another part of Australia. From there, she would take an airplane to visit with me in Seattle, where I was heading to play in the 1961 Walker Cup. I took a big gulp after hanging up. Not wanting to waste any time leaving, I boarded a plane and headed back home, not hearing anything more from her—*I thought.*

I knew my marriage was on the rocks when I returned home to Sharon. We were not seeing each other much at all by that time, and had pretty much drifted apart by then.

Reflecting back, I realize that I messed up as a father too. When I was home, I spent a lot of time with my two boys. They were such a joy to hold and play with. I thought the world of them both, and I felt like I was a good dad back then. In my self-centered nature, they got caught in the middle. I could juggle a singing career with being a golfer, but when you added being a husband and a father to that, I failed. I didn't tell many about my personal life. As a competitor, I didn't face failure well.

I found out later what really was the straw that broke the camel's back, as they say. It seems that the governor's niece, whom I had a fling with back in Birmingham, decided to write me a love letter. Knowing I was going to Melbourne, and not having any other address, she mailed it to me at The Embers nightclub, where I was headed. Jimmy Knowles, the club's owner and an underworld figure, received the letter addressed to me. Since he was jealous that his wife was so interested in me too, he decided to put the letter into another envelope and mail it straight to Sharon back in New York City. I was caught red-handed. She never confronted me with that letter, but I think from that point on that whatever we had in our marriage was lost for good.

I took refuge back on the golf course, where I felt safe and in control. If I failed here, I could just break clubs, not marriages. The first stop was at Bing Crosby's tournament, a game I played in for many years.

You could tell how well Crosby regarded your friendship by where you were assigned to stay at the lodge. There was a cottage by the 1st tee, affectionately referred to as "the Snake Pit." If you stayed there, you were high on the totem pole. Surrounded by tons of trees, it consisted of four bedrooms with a large living room for playing cards and watching TV. I was lucky to be assigned one of the rooms, right next to Desi Arnaz (Lucille Ball's first husband).

Also, not staying in the clubhouse but playing in the tournament was the five-time Olympic gold-medal winner in swimming, Johnny Weissmuller. Weissmuller had won 52 national championships in his lifetime. It was back in 1939 at the same Bing Crosby Invitational that Weissmuller met and married his third wife, Beryel.

Weissmuller had always been in the media, from saving a 12-year-old boy's life off the coast of California to appearing on the Wheaties box. Ironically, out of all his high-profile achievements, Johnny Weissmuller is best known as the muscular, scantily clad, vine-swinging hero Tarzan, king of the jungle, in over a decade's worth of movies and their sequels.

A fellow by the name of Maury Luxford would call players to the tee at 7:00 AM, and Johnny was scheduled to tee off at 7:08. We all knew that Johnny drank a little, and that there would be no way he would make it that early. After hearing Murray call him to the tee for about the seventh time, I got a little excited. I opened my window, which looked out on the 1st tee surrounded by the greenery, and shouted, "Look up in the f*ckin' trees!"

Desi laughed his ass off with my reference to Tarzan, in his distinctive Cuban "hee-hee-hee" you remember from the *I Love Lucy* show. Tommy Bolt and I played with Desi and his partner later that day. I think Desi still holds the record for hitting people. I remember he had a snap hook, and that day he nailed seven people before we finished the 5th hole.

A few weeks later, while on a golf course playing in the Odessa Pro-Am, a messenger dashed out to catch me as the game had started, informing me there was a very important phone call from my wife. I went back to the club house to see who it was. Sharon was calling from somewhere in Mexico to tell me that she was filing for divorce.

When she finished with what she wanted to say, I replied in a moment of anger. "You mean you called me off the golf course to tell me that?!" I pretty much knew it was coming. Playing in Texas, and not having a marriage to go back home to at that point, I decided to make Wichita Falls home again. It's funny, but I really always thought of it as home, even when I lived someplace else.

Right around the corner came Augusta, Georgia, home of The Masters, where I was invited to play for my ninth year. I had arrived early to play in a little game that Jimmy Demaret put together for us with Ben Hogan and Byron Nelson. I told Jimmy at the time, "I think we are a little overmatched," meaning I would get a few shots. Jimmy mentioned to Ben that they should at least give me a shot a side.

Ben didn't even bother to look up. "Let him learn to play something else," was his reply. So we teed it up even as they proceeded to win 5 holes on the front nine. With the presses, we turned 5 down, 3 down, and 1 down. Ben finally relented, and on the 10th tee he agreed to give me a shot on the back nine.

For you, the non-golfing reader, this next part is going to sound like a foreign language, so please bear with me. If you are a golfer and place an occasional bet on the outcome, you'll howl at this.

My shot came on the 13th hole, which is a par-5. I was the only one to par 10; Jimmy birdied 11, and we were 2 up. Then I birdied the par-3 12th. At the 13th, the par-5 where I was to get a shot, Hogan made an eagle 3. I made one right with him! Okay . . . golfers, are you with me?

Now we were 4 up and 2 up on the 14th hole. I half bladed a 6 iron and wound up about a foot from the hole. Now that put us 5–3 and 1 up. Jimmy made a 4 at the par-5 15th; I made 2 at the par-3 16th, and then hit a very low shot on the 17th (it skipped over the trap). I then made the putt from about 20'. Jimmy birdied 18. We won every hole on the back nine. I believe, counting presses, that comes to 7–5–3–1. As we walked off the 18th green, Jimmy, who had no equal with the needle, turned to Ben and Byron and asked them, "You guys play out here a lot?"

New York Times sportswriter Link Warden commented to Ben Hogan, "I understand Cherry shot 30 on the back nine."

Remembering the bladed second shot on 14 and the skull shot on 17, Hogan replied, "And he never hit one shot!"

Ben Hogan was one of the greatest golfers to ever play the game, especially having to overcome so many tremendous odds against him. As a child, Ben witnessed his father commit suicide. Discovering golf at age 15, where he lost a caddie championship playoff to Byron Nelson, Hogan pushed on to turn pro at age 17. At age 36, considered one of the best golfers in the world, tragedy struck when both of his legs were crushed and shattered as the result of a head-on collision with a Greyhound bus. Being told he would never walk again, nearing bankruptcy, and struggling to eat at times, Ben fought back to prove to everyone and himself that he could still do it.

At Augusta, 10 to 12 amateur players would stay on the second floor of the clubhouse. Nicknamed "the Crow's Nest," they would charge a dollar per day for room and a dollar per day for meals. The USGA did not allow amateurs to accept money, gifts, or endorsements. The charge was really to make it all legal. I should also mention that if you were in the lower "cut" as an amateur, you would most likely be assigned to stay in the maintenance barn. That's how life was for an amateur.

Play in the 1961 Masters started on April 6. The weather was rainy all four days. My first day was simply awful; the second was a little better, but not enough to make the cut at 41. I stayed to watch the rest of the game when Gary Player excited the crowd by getting the ball up and down from the bunker at 18. Winning with a total score of 280 (8 under par), Player was given the title of "The Masters' First International Champion."

While in Texas, I was scheduled to sing at the famed Texas Hotel and play in the Colonial Invitational in Fort Worth. The hotel, owned by Amon Carter Jr., had a beautiful showroom with one of the finest orchestras you will ever hear. I was really looking forward to working there, and if I live to be a thousand, I don't think I'll ever have an opening night like the one I had there.

Amon had booked another good friend of mine to open the show for me. His name, which you may or may not recognize, was Norman Alden, better known as Norm. He appeared in hundreds of television shows and nearly a hundred movies. He played everything from bullies in the Jerry Lewis movies to a senator on the TV show *Dynasty*. You might also remember him as the fellow who drowned in his soup on the series *Mary Hartman, Mary Hartman*. Most people today can remember Norm as "Lou," the mechanic in a series of commercials for AC Delco. Back in the early '60s, Norm was still struggling to make a name for himself.

Another competition, which I was not participating in, was coming up while I was performing and getting ready for the Colonial Invitational. It was a pro event called the Canada Cup. Four members from the U.S. would play the four most outstanding players from Canada. Members of both teams expressed that they wanted to come by on opening night and see my show. Stan Leonard, who was the captain of the Canadian team, bumped into me on the golf course the next morning and asked if I would dedicate a song that night to his team. I told him it would be my pleasure and asked him if he had a particular song that was his favorite.

"I saw you at a nightclub in Phoenix this year, and I loved the way you sang 'High Noon,'" Leonard told me.

"You got it," I replied.

"High Noon" was a huge hit by Frankie Laine at the time. If you remember, Gary Cooper won an Academy Award for his performance in the movie of the same name. When the song played in the theaters, it began with a single drum played to a staccato beat. After four bars, the singer would begin, "Do not forsake me, oh, my darlin'." The orchestra would then come in and accompany the rest of the song, but the beat was the most predominant sound you would hear.

As usual, I rehearsed with the orchestra that afternoon and explained how important it was that we do our best with "High Noon." They assured me that it would be perfect. Everyone took a break and gathered back again a bit before showtime.

In Texas, establishments were not allowed to serve whiskey. You would have to purchase your own liquor at a licensed liquor store and bring it with you. Many states, as well as countries like Australia, have this requirement. Many refer to it as "brown bagging." Of course, the nightclubs would then charge a setup fee for the glass and ice to make their share of the dough. I peeked through the curtain before the show began to make sure everything was going all right and if we pulled in a big crowd. To my surprise, I saw that Jimmy Demaret had arrived with his constant companions, Little Red and Vic Ghezzi.

Little Red was a very beautiful young lady, and Vic Ghezzi was a very famous and successful golfer. I noticed, too, that Jimmy was carrying a FootJoy shoe bag, which I assumed had his scotch in it. I looked up, and it was about time to start. At 8:00 PM on the nose, the band played about eight bars before the band leader announced, "Mr. Norm Alden!" The audiences in Texas, in those days, were a little rowdy, so his first objective was to quiet them down. He was doing a pretty good job when a very drunk lady at one of the first tables was making a lot of unnecessary noise. Norm tried to calm her down, but to no avail. He became a bit annoyed, opening his mouth to say, "Hey, lady, I'm trying to work. How would you like it if I came to your place of business while you were working and busted your red light?" His line had an obvious meaning, as he did about three more minutes before announcing me.

To get on or off the stage, you would have to go through the kitchen. As I started on stage, the husband of the lady that Norm insulted ran up and attacked him from behind. I immediately ran on stage to escape the altercation. I found out later that Norm won the battle.

The band now played me on with a very popular upbeat number, "It's a Good Day." I sang a ballad next and started to tell the audience that I had received a request from Stan Leonard, captain of the Canadian team, to sing "High Noon." The band started the intro, or should I say the drum started the intro—"Bum-bum, bum-bum, bum-bum, bum-bum." I sang seven words—"Do not forsake me, oh, my darlin'"—and at that point I discovered what Jimmy had in the FootJoy shoe bag. It was an air horn louder than the *Queen Mary*'s. When he sounded the horn, it threw off the band and stopped me cold. My first reaction was to make a joke of it, which I did. I told the audience that he was my best friend, and that he was just having a little fun. He replied from the audience, "That's right! Now sing the song!"

We started again: "Bum-bum, bum-bum, bum-bum, bum-bum." He sounded the horn again. Now I became very upset and angry, which

I could do the best of both. I proceeded to leave the stage and go to my dressing room. I had not been there two minutes when there was a knock at the door. Guess who? It was Jimmy. He explained that he was just having a little fun and wouldn't sound the horn anymore. He said the crowd loved me and that we were just like father and son. I thought about what he was saying, hesitated for a minute, and with his assurance that the horn would not be sounded anymore, I went back on stage.

We started the song one more time. "Bum-bum, bum-bum, bum-bum, bum-bum." I started to sing, "Do not forsake me, oh, my darlin'—" This time the horn was louder and longer than it had been before. I left the stage, went back to my room, and did not come down again.

At 4:00 in the morning the phone rang. It was Bo Wininger, very sympathetic and very drunk. He said he understood why I was so upset and there was someone else who understood and would like to comfort me, Dr. Cary Middlecoff. Doc got on the phone, said he had heard what happened, and just wanted to say one thing..."

I thanked him and asked what he wanted to say. Jimmy's horn never sounded so loud! About a week later I realized how funny the whole thing was after learning that he, Jimmy, and Sam Snead won the Canada Cup.

Another great product of playing so well in the Open at Cherry Hills was the invitation to join the U.S. team in the 1961 Walker Cup on September 1 and 2. This was my third invitation (I played in 1953 and 1955), a feat that not many can lay claim to. The members of the USGA board would choose the 10 best amateur players in the country every two years, so it was not only a very high honor, but also one of the most meaningful things in my life.

At the time, the Walker Cup consisted of two 36-hole matches, with 10 players on each side. Only five double matches were played on the first day, and 10 single matches on the second (this would be the last time matches played more than 36 holes). We always hit alternate shots in the team matches.

Each team's captain decided who would play, so two players would be excluded during day one, but everyone played at least one of the days. This year the Walker Cup was played at the Seattle Golf Club in Washington. Jack Westland, who was a member of the U.S. House of Representatives, was chosen as the captain of the American team.

Because of his terrific play in the U.S. Open, Jack Nicklaus was scrutinized the most. He, along with Dr. Frank Taylor, Gene Andrews, Robert Gardner, Charles Smith, Deane Beman, Robert Cochran, William Hyndman III, Charlie Coe, and myself, made up the U.S. team. As luck had it, I was chosen to play both days, and I was just as lucky to have Charlie Coe as my playing partner the first day during alternate shots. We managed to stay pretty even on the first seven holes. On the 8th hole, a par-3, I hit a 7 iron. It carried the ball into the cup for a hole in one. Charlie had a sneaky sense of humor. He walked up, looked down at it, and said, "How am I going to hit it from there?"

Charlie and I beat David Blair and Martin Christmas by 1 hole on the first day foursomes. During the second day singles, I beat out David Blair 5–4. At the end, it was almost a skunk for America. The U.S. scored 17 to Great Britain and Ireland's 1. I never lost a game in all three of the Walker Cups I played in. Before I left, I stopped to take in the feel and excitement more than ever. I knew in the back of my mind this was going to be my last Walker Cup.

Turning Pro

ıınınınınınınınınınınınınınınınınınınınınınınınınınınınınınınınınınınınınınınınınınınınınınınınınınınını

I'VE MENTIONED TWO OTHER FOUR-BALL TOURNAMENTS I played in (the Anderson Memorial at Winged Foot in Mamaroneck, New York, and the Western Four-Ball in Indianapolis), but the one I'm most proud of is the Champions Cup of 1962. Jimmy Demaret and Jackie Burke started the event at the Champions Golf Club.

The greenskeeper at Champions was named Robert Young (not to be confused with the well-known actor). You could not possibly keep from liking him. I remember Jimmy Demaret would ask him every morning, "How do you feel today, Robert?"

Robert would always answer in the third person, "Robert Young feels fine."

This went on for quite some time when one morning Jimmy received a different answer to his question.

"Mr. Jimmy," Robert said, "I was watering the green over there on 13 last night. I looked over by the green and saw two big eyes staring at me!"

Jimmy asked, "What did you do?"

Robert Young's answer was, "I threw the hose down on the green and I took off."

"I've got a .22 rifle in the back of my car. Why don't you take that with you each night?" asked Jimmy.

"Mr. Jimmy . . . when Robert Young runs, he don't want nothin' in his arms!"

My partner in the game itself was a young man by the name of Gene McBride. Gene was also from my hometown of Wichita Falls and owned more hamburger stands than any one person in the state of Texas. (Later his stands were renamed Pioneer Restaurants.) Gene's short game was his best asset. There were times I needed saving, and Gene was always there for me. At the Champions game, we shot 4 under par (280). It was so much fun and very exciting. Everyone playing had such a wonderful time. It was also great that we won the game by 1 shot.

Soon after, they had started building little cottages for sale there at the Champions. Jackie Burke and I had purchased the first two. Mine was directly across the street on Champions Drive facing the clubhouse. It was a show model with a perfect view and location. I paid $19,000 for it—$1,000 down and payments of $140 a month. Two years later, I sold it for $30,000 thinking I made quite a profit. Today, its value is in excess of $150,000 (and maybe more with the real estate boom). Selling it was just another of my great decisions. Oh well—I have to admit, winning the Champions Cup and having two friends like Burke and Demaret are priceless.

The Mike Douglas Show had started broadcasting in 1961, from WKYW in Cleveland, Ohio. It began as a local TV talk/variety show that focused mainly on musicians, singers, and comedians, although Richard Nixon made a stop once to talk politics. Most of Douglas' musical guests weren't as well known yet, so the reception I received during my appearances was absolutely wonderful. The show was embraced so quickly that it was picked up and began broadcasting in four of the major cities across the nation. Wanting to make a good impression with his new audience, Mike Douglas invited me to be his cohost, much like Ed McMahon was to Johnny Carson. I did a little singing and conversing with the guests that dropped by. One in particular was the legendary Johnny Cash before his traditional black cowboy-gear days. That Thursday evening, Cash came dressed in a tuxedo, but looked very disheveled. He even had trouble walking when Mike introduced him. During the interview, Douglas leaned forward and asked what song Johnny was going to sing. Johnny replied, "My Old Leg Suckin' Dog," which took Mike by surprise. Douglas leaned back in his chair to give me a look that said, "What did he say?!" The show continued on, as Mike bit his lip and gritted his teeth.

Westinghouse, who owned the show and the station, recorded over the tapes after they aired to produce editorials to broadcast during their news programs. Can you imagine those early appearances by Barbra Streisand, Aretha Franklin, and Judy Garland lost forever? Worse yet—my appearances? Within a very short amount of time, *The Mike Douglas Show* went into national syndication from coast to coast. His salary rose from $400 per week to $500,000 per year. Maybe I should have hung around.

Instead, I gave much time and thought to another way to earn big money. It involved turning professional. As a pro golfer, I could take home any prize money I was able to win. Looking around, I saw many of my friends turning pro too. They were all doing respectably well, and I felt like I did all I could do as an amateur. I played in almost every huge event that was possible. "What more could I achieve?" I asked myself over and over. Not only could you take home winning purses as a pro, but making money endorsing products was becoming a new way to earn big bucks.

Bill Connors, editor for *Sports of the World*, quoted my disposition at the time, "Golf is like a disease with me. It's in my blood and sometimes I wish I could get rid of it, but I can't. On a tour there are maybe 200 amateurs who on a given day might shoot a 65. I decided I would really concentrate and try to make it [as a pro], although I am still very serious about show business too."

I played my first round as a professional at the Oakbourne Country Club in Lafayette, Louisiana. It was the fifth annual Cajun Classic that had 116 pros and 10 amateurs competing for part of the $17,500 prize money. Wednesday, the first day of play, I shot a 66 on the par-72 course and tied John Barnum for first. Right away I made $217. I thought to myself, "What have I been missing all along?" The next day I found out. On the first round of the second day I shot 74. I still remember Jimmy Demaret telling me, "There are two games going on out there. One is golf and hitting a ball. The other game is called putting." How often I have realized how true it is!

A letter arrived in the mail from the Office of Civil Defense. No, I didn't do anything wrong, they just wanted me to serve my country again. Not in uniform, but by guest-hosting an episode of their syndicated radio series, *Stars for Defense* with Jay Jackson. I felt it a public service and my civil duty to accommodate. The show consisted of my singing three songs, "You Made Me Love You," "In the Morning Sun," and "Too Close for Comfort" to the orchestra of Ray Bloch, while the interviewer kept America up-to-date about our civil defense. Even though I didn't have a record company putting songs out, my singing still managed to be heard.

Thanksgiving was spent in Columbus, Ohio, at a club called The Maramor. I must admit that I don't really remember the showroom, but someone found and sent me a terrific review from the *Citizen-Journal News* on Tuesday, November 20, 1962.

> *For the first time during my 14-month tenure here, the Maramor Trio, beyond any question a threesome of fine musicians, seemed inadequate, a statement in no way meant to reflect negatively on either the trio or Cherry. Actually, it is a tribute to the pleasing vocalist. His arrangements (and this includes his phrasing and choice of ad-lib movements) are geared to a big band sound. Not only would strings complement his voice—his voice would complement strings. In the low range, in the high range, lapsing into a sort of falsetto—he has a quality voice. I strongly suspect that the only reason he is not one of the biggest names in country is that no one has ever bothered to listen. I don't think I've ever enjoyed a nightclub performance any more than this. All this and a golf pro too.*
> —RON PATAKY

Some of the most receptive crowds that came to see my show didn't necessarily come to see me—take for instance the week I played Lake Tahoe. I was the opening act for comedian Shecky Greene. Shecky, along with Buddy Hackett, had the most natural talent for comedy of anyone I know. Shecky and I instantly hit it off and became good friends. I think it's because he shares with me a similar view about everything in general.

Every night Shecky would pull his car into the parking lot before the show. Ahead of time, he would tip the parking attendant a dollar to finish parking and to keep an eye on his precious vehicle. One night, after the last show, he came out and found that someone had stolen his car. Shecky began ranting and raving, a quality he was a master at. The attendant, not knowing how to calm him down, approached him and said, "Mr. Sheck . . . you want your dollar back?"

HOLE
16

Damone, Crosby, and Mother, God Rest Her Soul

E ARLY IN 1963 I PLAYED IN THE NEW ORLEANS OPEN at the Lakewood Country Club. Booked into Al Hirt's Nightclub at the same time, I would work until 1:30 in the morning. After a few hours of sleep, I would awake the same morning to compete in the golf tournament. Let me tell you about the nightclub first.

As admired, talented, and respected as Al Hirt was with the trumpet, he was that good and respected as a human being. His nightclub had a very unique look with the stage being elevated and surrounded by a bar where the patrons would sit. Out beyond the bar, there were tables and booths where the balance of the people could assemble. As the performer sang on stage, it would rotate in a circle so everyone would have a good vantage point to see.

There was a man who operated the lights and determined how fast the stage would turn. During the rehearsal that first afternoon, the stage was stationary, so I had no idea what would happen during the show. When showtime came, they announced me, and I started my opening number. When the stage started to turn, I instantly became nauseated. I thought if they slowed it down, everything might be all right. It wasn't. I barely finished the show and came off stage. One of the fellows in the band made a suggestion and handed me a Dramamine pill for motion sickness.

For six days, I took Dramamine, sang, and played golf. On Thursday I shot a 70 and on Friday I shot a 69. My total for the first two days came to 139, so I easily made the cut. I haven't figured out to this day whether I was lucky or unlucky. My pairing for Saturday turned out to be two of the great players on the PGA tour, Mike Souchak and Arnold Palmer.

In 1963 Arnie's Army consisted of almost everyone at the tournament. Needless to say, I didn't get much sleep on Friday night. Getting up very early on Saturday, I went to the club to practice, which is something I really didn't do in those days. I guess I didn't want to embarrass myself in front of Arnie's followers. People reacted to Arnie like they do to Tiger Woods today.

My driver wasn't working the way I thought it should, so I decided to use my 3 wood off the tee. Perfect strategy—just make sure I get the ball airborne. As we arrived at the 1st tee, there must have been 2,000 people on both sides of the fairway. Now, remember, I hadn't had much sleep and was nervous on top of that.

Souchak teed off first and hit a beautiful shot right in the middle of the fairway. Arnie teed off second and ripped one dead straight about 270 yards down the fairway. I teed up my ball next and offered up a silent prayer, "Lord, please, just let me get the ball airborne." My prayer was answered. I got my ball airborne, all of 12 feet in the air. It was the worst snap hook, and almost wiped out half of Arnie's Army. I guess they are right—be careful what you wish for.

At the Lakewood Country Club, the Spanish moss grows and hangs from the trees. Of course, this is exactly where my ball wound up—in the hanging moss. You might say I had an unplayable hang! I got the ball down, dropped it over my shoulder, took a penalty, and used a 6 iron just to get back to the fairway. I then buried my 4th shot in the front bunker, sculled the ball about 30' past the hole on the 5th shot, 3-putted, and made a fast-running 8. You see, the strategy worked!

In the meantime, while all this was going on, Arnold hit his 2nd shot from about 10' behind the hole. Souchak 2-putted from about 20' for a par. Arnold made his 10' putt for a birdie. And, as always, he sort of hitched up his pants. Then he did something I guess Souchak never heard him do. Arnold started to hum. As we were walking off the green,

Mike walked over to Palmer and said, "Man, don't start singing—you don't see Cherry out there trying to play golf!"

I did recover a little bit. I shot a 74 for the round.

In an earlier chapter, I told you I was given credit for changing the way golfers qualify for the last 36 holes or make the cut in all major golf tournaments. I had one other thing happen to me that had to do with a rule change.

I was scheduled to play in the 1963 U.S. Open at the Country Club in Brookline, Massachusetts. About a month before the Open, I had sung in a nightclub called The Red Barn in nearby Springfield. It was spacious, maintained well, and very beautiful. No one would have guessed that it was owned and operated by people with connections to the syndicate (I'm trying not to use the *M* word). Like *The Sopranos*, these guys had nicknames—"Big Nose" Sam Cafari, "Ski Ball," and "Tinneyann the Hitman." All I know is that they paid well and were very nice to me. I actually became friends with them, not giving a thought to their occupation.

I teed off on Thursday morning, and off to the side in the gallery were both Ski Ball and Tinneyann. I double-bogied the 1st hole, played the next three holes in 3 under, so at 9 I was 1 under. Ski Ball and Tinneyann were still following right behind me from hole to hole. When I got to 10, I hit a perfect shot. When my caddie and I got to the ball, we found it lying on top of a sprinkler head covered with water. I stuck a tee in the ground to mark the ball, picked it up, cleaned it, and dropped it.

An official, John English, came running from a hundred yards away. He asked if I had cleaned the ball before I dropped it. I told him yes. He then informed me that it was a 2-shot penalty for doing so. I went into one of my tirades and, as a result, shot 44 on the back nine.

All this time, "the boys" had been following me with the gallery. As I walked off the 18th green, a couple of the boys came over and asked me what happened on number 10. I related to them what had taken place. They replied in the form of a question: "What do you want us to do to him?"

My answer: "Nothing." I never told John English that I might have saved his life. It was later explained to me that casual water on a sprinkler head was the only place you could not clean and drop. That rule was changed the next year. Makes you think.

One of the most advantageous rewards that came about by turning professional was the endorsements that came my way. Everyone gave me clothes to wear—from shirts and caps to $400 alligator boots and custom-made leather gloves. When a big company gave a gift, they were only hoping that you would wear their products during the games. That way, the fans who came or watched on TV could see what was in fashion—kind of like being a male fashion model with a golf club.

The MacGregor Golf Company decided that I would make a good choice for advertising their brand of equipment. They made an offer to me to pose for pictures in their print ads, and wanted to put my name behind many of their products. Being one of the most respected manufacturers of sporting equipment, I agreed that it would be a pleasant partnership. Immediately, MacGregor went to work and came up with a set of Don Cherry Golf Clubs to include in their signature line with other big names in the field. They gave me three sets, and I sent them back home where my mother (and brother Paul) put them under my bed for safekeeping.

I wore their special line of clothing and gloves in photographs that ran in almost every golf publication on the market. I was even honored to have my own autograph-stamped golf balls in stores for golfers across the country to buy and play with. I don't know how many sets of clubs or balls were sold back then, but to this day, I have seen very few of those sticks. I wonder if any collectors have packed them away in their collections, along with a Don Cherry bag that held them.

Bo Wininger and I played as partners at La Costa the last year they had the Haig & Haig Golf Tournament in Carlsbad, California. The following week was the last official PGA event that season. The Greater New Orleans Open was to be played in Lafayette, Louisiana, the home of Lionel and Jay Hebert, who had their own golf course. Since I was driving my car to get there and Bo was flying to Oklahoma City on business, he asked if I would mind taking his clubs with me.

Charlie Applewhite, a Milton Berle protégé who had a few hit records ("Ebb Tide," "No One but You," "I Could Have Danced All Night"), owned a nightclub there in his hometown. As always, I was to play golf during the daylight hours and sing at night. Leaving right away, I arrived in Lafayette about noon on Tuesday and found a message to call Nita, Bo's wife, immediately. I called and she informed me that Bo had suffered a massive stroke. He had only lived three more days. Nita called and told me that his funeral was to be on the following Tuesday and asked me if I would sing at it.

As I reflect back now, I would say it was one of the hardest things I've ever had to do in my life. I asked her if I could just be a pallbearer, and I will never forget her answer, "I think he would rather hear you sing!" On Tuesday morning, I arrived in Guthrie and found Nita. She let me know that I should go to the church and give the organ player a chance to rehearse with me. I had decided to sing "Faith of Our Fathers" and "The Old Rugged Cross." I told the organist that we would rehearse "Faith of Our Fathers" first. I was so emotional, I could barely make a sound.

The preacher who was to perform the service was standing nearby observing the proceedings. We then started to rehearse "The Old Rugged Cross," and by this time I had regained some of my composure. I was singing and sounding a little better. When I finished, the preacher came over to me and said, "May I make a suggestion?"

At that point, I welcomed any conversation to get my mind off what I was to do later. I said, "Yes."

He suggested, "I think you should open with 'The Old Rugged Cross.' You seem to know it better."

Even at a funeral, you can resort to showbiz. As I sang, I looked at Bo's casket, which was within hearing range, and murmured, "Bo, we got it made." It wasn't easy getting through that day. Later, Nita gave me Bo's golf driver. We both agreed that it was his favorite club. It's still in my possession at home. His death wasn't easy on me, and it wasn't the last funeral I attended that year. The worst was yet to come.

I was playing in a tournament in Sweetwater, Texas, and was leading when I was informed that my mother was going into the hospital for a gallbladder operation. I wanted to get home to see her, but Mom told me to go ahead and finish the game. She said it would be just routine, and that she would see me when I arrived. I stayed on to win when I received a call from Dr. Powers. He told me that my mother's kidney had locked up during surgery, and ended by saying, "They don't usually survive this."

I left in a hurry. Driving through shortcuts I knew, I battled a fierce sand and hail storm. I could barely see the road in front of me with hail the size of golf balls coming down all around. My two sons, Stephen and Sean, were there already. Mom had been watching them for a while during the summer to give Sharon a chance to get away. When I arrived, I went to visit her in the hospital. She didn't look good. It was all I could do to hold back the tears in front of her and the boys. Both boys got a chance to talk to her for the very last time on the eighth day. Within a matter of hours, God took Mom, and left us with emotion-filled memories.

At the funeral, my brother Paul did not look well physically. He sauntered up to me and said, "Okay, Don, she's gone . . . now you can take a drink."

I remember answering, "That's just a body lying there. She's still with me." I shook his hand, but realized that Mom was the one in the middle who kept Paul and me in contact. After the funeral I took both boys back to Grand Island, Nebraska, and left them with Sharon's parents. From there, I drove straight to Chicago to record the second set of Mr. Clean commercials that I was contracted for. I heard a while later that Paul was in need of money and took my only three sets of Don Cherry Golf Clubs to the pawn shop.

Nineteen sixty-four was the year of the British Invasion, the summer Olympics in Tokyo, and the warnings about cigarette smoking. It was also the year that one of our own pop singers, Dean Martin, succeeded in knocking the Beatles off the charts with a song called "Everybody Loves Somebody."

Dean's passion in life wasn't his celebrity status or things he owned—his love was simply playing golf. That was his obsession and escape from the people that surrounded him. Golf was Dean's sanctuary from the maddening crowd. I guess that's the profile of many golfers. The quietness of just being one with that little ball. Everything is in your control, not a dozen other people.

I'm not too sure how it came about or when the actual day was when Dean and I met, but somewhere along the line, we started playing golf together. It didn't take long for us to hit it off, and we became good friends. So good, in fact, that Dean Martin became one of my five best friends.

Now, before I tell you a little bit about our friendship, I have to tell you about the day Bing Crosby (Dean Martin's childhood idol, and mine, too) and I were playing together at Pebble Beach in Monterey. We started discussing how many number one hit songs Bing had recorded. It took a few minutes, but he came up with about 20 or 25 titles that were million-sellers over the years.

It had been more than five years since I had a record company putting anything out. I told Bing that I just signed a contract with Roulette Records, and they wanted me to record a whole album. A thought came to mind, and I asked Bing if it would be all right if I could record some of his songs for it.

"Do as many as you want," replied Bing. "I'll write the liner notes and explain how and when I came to do each one originally. Tomorrow we can take some pictures on the course, and you can call the album 'Don Cherry Swings with Bing.'"

I was so flattered that I could hardly speak. Right away I contacted Roulette Records, and they too were more than excited—more than I was, if that was possible! Roulette had an arranger by the name of George Sharibo. His arranging was a bit different than most, using only saxophones and clarinets with a rhythm section. We started to work on the project by recording a few songs in the studio.

The history of Roulette Records was something unknown at the time. Morris Levy ran the record company from its inception. Born poor, Levy went into the nightclub business and eventually owned several big nightclubs in midtown Manhattan. That helped put him in business with disc jockey Alan Freed and promote his famous rock and roll shows, including those at the Brooklyn Paramount Theater. It was at Birdland (a club he also owned) that Levy began his phenomenal rise to the top of the music industry by acquiring the rights to songs written and performed by legendary jazz artists. It was also rumored that Levy had connections with the underworld and the famed Genovese crime family. Nicknamed "the Jewish Godfather," Levy lured many pop singers to his label (Jimmie Rodgers, Dinah Washington, Sarah Vaughan) before the U.S. government intervened to bring him to justice. Facing legal problems (before being convicted and sent to prison), Levy's record company, Roulette, slowly abandoned many artists and projects they had planned on. I assume one of those was mine. If I had been able to save the pictures, liner notes, and the few recordings we had started making, it might have been worth a fortune.

The Motown sound from Detroit had now started making waves all across the country with groups like the Supremes and the Temptations. Detroit was also equipping all of their brand-new automobiles with AM radios to listen to the current hits while driving. Kids were also making waves on the beach, with their transistor radios tuned to their favorite AM stations. Here they would find their favorite disc jockey playing Motown and rock and roll records. CDs didn't exist back then. Neither did cassettes or eight-track tapes. Satellite radio was only used by the U.S. government, and FM radio wasn't even available on most dials. That had begun to change. Appealing to the older audiences who wanted to hear their favorite artists not being played on the top 40, rock and roll stations, an undercurrent was starting. FM had begun finding a home for jazz, popular, and easy listening music to be played.

A very special friend of mine was one of the first to discover a new plan that paid to have artists record new songs for them to play on the air. Owned by Darrell Peters, the company was called FM-100 and encompassed more than 200 FM outlets coast to coast. I might classify my special friend (I could be wrong) as my biggest fan. His name is Vito Farinola—"Vic Damone" to you. Vic has always had nothing but praise for both my singing and my golf.

After recording a few songs for FM-100 himself, Vic stuck his neck out and insisted that FM-100 let him produce an album with me singing. There was a little resistance, but Vic told them, "If you don't like the album, I'll pay for it myself." They agreed, and we went off to Chicago to record about a dozen songs that we carefully chose. I put my trust in Vic. I remember he had instructed me to sing one of the songs with a little more rhythm. I told him that it sounded too "country" that way. Vic responded, "If you don't do it that way, I'll do it myself, you son of a bitch!" I did it his way and he was right. After FM-100 heard our first number, "Sweet Memories," we didn't have a problem—they were very happy.

In January I started with the Crosby Invitational and played right on through to Cleveland in June, just one week before the U.S. Open. After Cleveland, I quit the tour. My interview to Bill Connors quoted me as saying, "Playing regularly certainly helped me. I was able to concentrate better, and from tee to green my game was good. But that isn't where they pay off. You have to putt. If I could putt, I could make a lot of money in golf. But I couldn't do it." I was called a "street putter."

Continuing my singing obligations, performing for crowds at a hotel in Ligonier, Pennsylvania, I watched my pals Dave Marr, Ben Hogan, and Arnold Palmer play. Like always, singing brought in better money than I was making on the pro circuit.

From there I made my way to sing and play in Portland, Oklahoma City, and Ponca City, where I got to play a little golf with Ken Venturi before we went off to Miami to compete in the National Four-Ball. After that I proceeded on my way to Bay Hill, where Dave Regan, Jack Nicklaus, Arnold Palmer, and I played in a charity match.

ıııııııııııııııı

In 1953 a man by the name of Fred Foster started out writing words to songs that music publisher Ben Edelman was putting out. Foster's first effort was recorded by the McGuire Sisters in 1953. Although Fred never produced a record before, he was allowed to supervise a session by Jimmy Dean with his group, the Texas Wildcats. It did so well for Fred Foster that he took a job as a promotional man for Mercury Records and, in 1955, went to ABC/Paramount Records to become their regional promotional representative.

Tired of all the traveling, Foster took his life savings and decided to start his own record label. Named after the Washington Monument in Washington, D.C., where Foster was living near at the time, Monument Records was formed. The first record Foster released was by a former member of Jimmy Dean's Wildcats, Billy Grammar, which shot up to number four on the pop charts. From here, Fred opened a second office and recording studio in Hendersonville, Tennessee, a suburb of Nashville. With Fred Foster's guidance, hand picking producers and musicians, he was responsible for launching the careers of many artists. To give you a few names—Billy Walker, Larry Gatlin, Dolly Parton, Boots Randolph, Willie Nelson, Roy Orbison, and Kris Kristofferson (with whom Foster cowrote "Me and Bobby McGee").

Steve Poncio, a record producer who worked with Monument Records, brought me to the attention of Fred Foster. Steve, himself, worked his way up the ladder in the business. Starting out as a stock boy for Macy Records, Steve learned quickly, and by 1951 owned and operated his own distributorship, United Distributors. Through his association with many of the different record labels, Steve also sidelined as a producer to many of the artists he had met or discovered along the way. Many important artists, such as Lester Williams and Jimmy Nelson, put their trust in Steve Poncio to produce them because of his honesty and trustworthiness. When I signed with Monument Records in 1965, after a six-year hiatus from having a record label, Steve was my producer on everything I recorded over the next 13 years.

Our first two singles, "More I Cannot Do" and "Sweet Sugar," had such a wonderful sound to them. Fred always used Nashville's musicians and arrangers, but had his own way of doing things. Competing with Motown, who cranked out three or four songs in a one-day session with a house band to back every one of their artists, Foster slowed the process down.

Fred, along with Steve Poncio, carefully chose the material in advance and would spend a whole day on just one song. Inviting rhythm-and-blues musicians from nearby Muscle Shoals, Alabama, and Memphis, they got the sound they wanted. At times, the musicians in Nashville were angry and had voiced their opinion that Foster was ruining Nashville by not doing business as usual with local musicians. Actually, Fred was putting Nashville on the map with all the talent he developed on his Nashville-based label.

The public gave their approval for my next two singles. "The Story of Life" and "A Thing Called Sadness" were released in the latter part of 1965, with "I Love You Drops" and "Don't Change" coming out in January of 1966. Monument thought so highly of "I Love You Drops" that they also included it on my first LP for them, *Don Cherry Smashes.*

What a thrill it was to turn over the album cover and see a letter handwritten by Dean Martin and signed by both him and Frank Sinatra:

> *We think that Mr. Don Cherry sings the Country and*
> *Western music better than anybody in the business, but how*
> *he can do it so well and not "DRINK" is something we can't*
> *figure out. But he is great!*
> *—Dean Martin, Frank Sinatra*

Dean Martin, Jack Benny, and Number Three

MY ROOMMATE, MARTIN MILLS, WHOM I LIVED WITH a number of years in New York, introduced me to a young lady named Joy Vera Blaine. When he first told me about her, I remember him saying, "This is the kind of girl you end up marrying." I called her, talked a bit, and we made a date to go out. The day came, and I arrived at her door and rang the bell. One of the prettiest ladies I had ever seen opened the door. I was to learn later that she had been a showgirl at the Tropicana in Las Vegas, had won the Miss Nevada title for the Miss Universe pageant, and had been voted the most beautiful showgirl in Las Vegas history. She also turned out to be one of the kindest and gentlest people I had ever met.

We dated for a while and then decided to get married. Dean thought a lot of Joy, and he was so happy for the both of us. He told us that he would consider it an honor to be my best man. To make it convenient for Dean, we decided to wait and get married in Lake Tahoe, when I was booked to sing in the lounge while Dean worked the showroom at Harrah's.

Now it's confession time. I guess most people would not want to tell this story, but baring my soul in a book, I feel I have to.

Over the period of time I had been courting Joy, I was away, working in a nightclub in Tulsa, Oklahoma. I managed to get involved with a young lady named Jan. So I won't embarrass her or her family, I won't give her last name. About six weeks later, I made my way to Portland,

Oregon, to sing in a nightclub there for 10 days. Right before the show on the third night, I received a phone call in my hotel room. It was Jan's mother informing me that her daughter was pregnant and that I had to be the father because she had never been with another man. She also stated that if I would send them $1,000, they would have everything taken care of.

It was a difficult position to be in. I barely knew this girl with whom I had had a brief fling. About three weeks after I mailed the check, I received a phone call from a lawyer in Tulsa stating that by sending the check, signed by me, I had admitted that I was the father. He also informed me that there was a way that this could be handled. He told me that in order to give the baby a name, I should marry Jan. Then he explained how it could be done.

It seems that in Claremore, Oklahoma, during that day and age, you could marry someone at 10:30 in the morning and have it annulled by 2:30 in the afternoon. The baby would have a name, and I would be required to pay a reasonable child support. I don't know if you will find this funny, but Claremore was the hometown of Will Rogers. Rogers always said, "I never met a man I didn't like." I felt that I was putting him to the supreme test. With that 10:30 marriage and the 2:30 annulment, the divorce would be final before the photographs could arrive.

Booked back into the nightclub in Tulsa about five months before the baby arrived, we went to Claremore and had the ceremony performed. The baby arrived as a very handsome little boy named Christopher. I saw him once when he was about two years old. There was no doubt where he came from.

Back to Joy . . . About two weeks before our wedding day, I told Joy about what happened in Claremore. It wasn't the best news to spring on her, and our pending nuptials were called off.

When I got to Tahoe, I told Dean what transpired. He was a bit upset with what happened, but went along with our decision. At that point, the only thing I knew about Joy was that she had returned to New York, but I didn't know where.

Dean was staying at one of Bill Harrah's houses on the lake, and was kind enough to let me stay there with him. Thursday night we opened.

The next night, after the last show, Dean and I went back to the house and sat there watching Johnny Carson on the television set in the living room. One of the guests on the show was a well-known comedian named Phil Foster. You might remember him in later years as the father of Penny Marshall in *Laverne and Shirley*. Phil did his spot on the show, then went and sat down next to Carson. Johnny started to compliment Phil on his performance when Phil stopped him midsentence.

"I brought a girl with me tonight. She's sitting in the audience and is not aware of what I am about to say, but here it is: if she will say yes, I will marry her tomorrow!" Phil exclaimed. Then he went on to tell Johnny, "She used to date Don Cherry."

Johnny came back with, "It must have been a hell of a Nassau!" as he asked for the cameras to show the girl in the audience. (A "Nassau" was a popular, Saturday-morning match-play competition in which points are awarded for winning the front nine, back nine, and the overall 18 holes.)

To Dean and my surprise, it was Joy! Dean turned to me, and with a lot of authority in his voice said, "You can't let that girl marry that man. I don't care what problems you two have, I'm going to find her, have her meet us in Odessa, and you're going to marry her!" Odessa was where we were going to play in a pro-am golf tournament after we finished our engagement at Harrah's.

Dean worked his magic, and Joy met us in Odessa. Bobby French's wife, Marcia, flew Joy in their private plane to Dallas, bought her a wedding dress at Neiman Marcus, and we were married the very next night. That was in the spring of 1966.

Houston, Texas, has been known for its abundance of rainfall over the years. I had been scheduled to appear at the Shamrock Hotel there during the month of May. That year they had even more than the usual amount. For days the water just sat on top of the ground with no place to go.

The reception at the Shamrock was wonderful, and the audiences could not have been more gracious. Of course, I still hadn't quite overcome my shyness on stage. It was still a long time before I felt comfortable performing. Actually, Dean was the one who helped me more than anyone else to improve my self-confidence.

After my final appearance at the Shamrock, Buddy Hackett called and asked if I would open for him at the Palmer House in Chicago during the last half of June. It was still six weeks away, but working with Buddy was always a blast, so I said yes.

Having opened for Buddy Hackett, Shecky Greene, and Don Rickles in the past, the opportunity arrived before Buddy's job to open for one of the most famous comedians of all time, Jack Benny. Without a doubt, he was one of the classiest human beings I have ever met. When we were booked together, Jack would sometimes come out to introduce me before I went on stage. The only other person who did that was Buddy.

Little did I know that Jack loved to play golf. He approached me one day, letting me know that he would like to play with me, but had forgotten his clubs. MacGregor had just made a new set of ladies' clubs for my wife, Joy, at the time. The next day when I took Benny to the Las Vegas Country Club, I brought along Joy's clubs for him to use. Halfway through the round, Jack told me that he enjoyed playing a lot and that he hadn't hit a golf ball that well in a long time.

Later on that got me to thinking, so I called MacGregor and asked if they could make a set of clubs for Jack just like the ones they made for Joy. More than happy to do just that, McGregor went to work on them. As soon as they were finished, I had them delivered to Jack and forgot all about it. About a month later, a small package came for me with a beautifully engraved money clip that had Jack's character engraved on it. I didn't call or write him a "thank you," which was not too smart on my part. Then, two weeks later, I received a call from his wife, Mary. She asked if I had received the money clip that Jack sent. I told her that I never had a money clip—especially like the one he sent. Mary told me, "Take care of it, Don. He has only given five of them in his whole life." Picture that!

In a Coma

THE TIME HAD COME FOR ME TO MAKE MY WAY to join Buddy Hackett in Chicago. We played a lot of golf the first week at a course in Lake Forest, Illinois. To get back to Chicago, we would take the toll road, which cost 35¢ to travel. As we did the first evening, we found the entrance, but realized that neither of us had any change. Buddy rolled the window down and proceeded to throw a Titleist golf ball into the toll machine. It went crazy, clanking and grinding itself away! The guy running the toll booth came running out screaming, "Are you crazy?!"

Buddy, with a self-satisfied look on his face, said, "The toll is 35¢. The ball cost $1.25. It seems you owe me a total of 90¢."

Thank God the man recognized him and let us go. We made our way to the Palmer House in time for the first show. Being first to go on, I started off with one of my current record releases, "Story of My Life." As I kept singing, I found myself becoming a bit confused. Little did I know that "Story of My Life" was going to be a perfect title for what was to happen.

I left the stage and had no idea where I was. Very confused, I started trying to find my way to my room. My first stop was at the bottom of the stairs leading up to the showroom. I had started taking off my shirt and shoes, when Joy found me, thank God. She helped lead me up the stairs, but by then, I was totally lost. Joy sat me down, where I began taking my hairpiece off, laying it beside me and struggling to get my tuxedo jacket off. Joy had no idea what was happening, but she knew something was very wrong.

As soon as Buddy finished on stage, Joy called him and he came up immediately without even giving an encore. Seeing that I wasn't right, Buddy called the doctor. Next, he started asking me questions to figure out what was wrong. "Who is the lady in the room?" was his first.

Things were very cloudy. I answered, "I don't know."

Buddy's comment was, "Best you know your wife. You have only been married six weeks."

The hotel had these little folded advertisement cards in each of the rooms, calling attention to who was playing in the showroom. One side had my photograph on it, and the other side was Buddy's picture. Buddy snatched it off the nightstand and held it up, showing me my picture. "Do you know who this is?"

I mumbled that I didn't know who it was, so he turned it over and asked who was the picture on the other side. For some strange reason, I recognized his picture, and mumbled, "Buddy Hackett."

Buddy turned to the doctor and said, "That's no test, everybody knows Buddy Hackett!" Then Buddy asked me, "What year is it?"

I responded, "1967." (It was 1966.) Buddy said, "Mark that one right. . . . It is probably as close as he's going to get." Other than remembering that he had asked me some more unrecognizable questions, there wasn't much else I could recall for nearly five days.

They took me to Passavant Hospital, and I was examined by Dr. Rovner, one of the most respected neurologists in the field. He proceeded to figure out what was wrong, first thinking I might have contracted spinal meningitis.

Aware that there had been an outbreak in Houston, and realizing that I had been performing there six weeks earlier, Buddy suggested I was infected with encephalitis. People were affected in many different ways, and some even died. Learning that it takes about six weeks for the disease to incubate after being bitten by a Culex mosquito, they moved me into a quarantine ward. Only the female mosquitoes carry encephalitis (figures), better known as "sleeping sickness." I was given a spinal tap, which confirmed that Buddy was right in his diagnosis.

Then ... the horror happened. I lapsed into a coma. I could hear people talking, but I could not answer. You could not imagine my thoughts and feeling during the next five days. It was like being in a dream state—quite restful—unable to wake up or respond. Five days had passed—to me, it was an eternity.

If I could only remember the words to "Gentle on My Mind," was the thought going through my head at the time, *maybe it would wake me up.*

At 3:00 in the morning I started to sing it. The nurse on duty ran down the hall and into my room. Stunned at what she was hearing, she called the physician who was on duty that evening. The door to my room banged open as the doctor charged through it to catch me still belting out the lyrics, " ... ever smiling, ever gentle on my mind."

The next morning, Dr. Rovner told me what had happened to me. Not giving a thought to how severely I had been clinging to life in a coma, all I could ask was, "When can I get out of here and go home?" He turned and left, but returned a few minutes later with a large book in his arms. Opening it to a certain page, he asked me to read what it said. I read one paragraph and quickly laid back down. He then told me that I was a very lucky man. "Many people in Houston have died fighting off the same case of encephalitis that you contracted. We gave you a spinal tap and your virus count was well above 130. A count that high could have been fatal or left you in a vegetative state. Until it comes down under 35, you will have to remain in the hospital. We'll have to do more spinal taps to monitor your status."

In my life, I have never experienced such pain as with those spinal taps. They would stick a hollow needle into the spinal cord and let it drip for 30 minutes. In the meantime, Buddy Hackett was still performing at the Palmer House. Almost every day Buddy would visit me with a friend of his, Joe Kellman. They would always needle me about faking my own illness to get a rest. One day Buddy and Joe showed up carrying clipboards, dressed as doctors with white coats, masks, and stethoscopes.

Ensuring that I was all right, and knowing the hospital food was lousy, Shecky Greene showed up one day and brought me a complete Chinese dinner. Later, after he left, I went to eat my dinner only to discover that Shecky had eaten most of it himself while visiting me.

A few minutes earlier than normal, the duty nurse arrived with an ear-to-ear grin on her face. I thought the doctor had signed the papers to let me go, but no such luck. Then I saw that she was staring at the box she was carrying. "To Don Cherry from Dean Martin" was printed across the front. "Here, they delivered this for you." Standing there, she just stared at me, waiting to see what was inside. I looked for something to open the box with when she grabbed the dinner knife off my plate to use. Inside was a beautiful full-length robe embroidered with "Don" on the front. A note—"Get Well, Pally"—from Dean was also inside the box. Later on, Dean called on the telephone to see how I was and told me that his mother, Angela (once a seamstress), made the robe especially for me. "Take good care of it, she never made anything like that for me!" Dean laughed as I reassured him that I was going to be okay.

The final spinal tap came 18 days later. They informed me that it had dropped to just above 30, and turned me loose two days later. Yahoo! I got in the car and drove straight for Seattle to start singing at another nightclub again. On the way, two cows had jumped the fence and were standing in the road. I pulled over, jumped out, and proceeded to run them back into the pasture. It was then I realized that I had been very ill. As I have said so many times before, "I never played the game." With death on my doorstep, clinging to life in a coma, I was grateful to be given another 18 holes to play in the game of life.

Second Act

Caddies

|||||||||||||||||||||||||||||||||||||||||||||||||||||||||||||||||||||||||||||||||||||||||||||||||||||||||||||||||||||||||||||||||||||||||||||||||||||||||||||||||||||||||||||||||

So FAR IN LIFE, I THINK I DID BETTER THAN PAR. Well, I survived and made the cut. As I begin my second round on life, it's about time for some lighthearted tales. What better stories are there than those about caddies? In my humble opinion, caddies are one of the most necessary ingredients in the game of golf. We who have played the game know and realize this. They have saved many a good player a lot of grief. Most of them, in their own way, have a fabulous sense of humor. The caddie story I would insist close the show would be about Herman Mitchell, better known as "Mitch." Mitch caddied for a lot of people, including some best-known names like Miller Barber and Lee Trevino.

I was playing a practice round with Miller and Gay Brewer at Rio Pinar. One of the holes on the back nine had a shallow lake off to the right of the fairway with a lot of cattails and thick moss growing around the bank. Miller pushed his ball to the right, and it rolled to the edge of the lake. He teed up another one, and hit it in the fairway. Gay and I hit our balls, and we all left the tee and started down the fairway. Mitch was tagging along as we walked about 20 yards. Miller turned to Mitch and, with some concern in his voice, said, "Aren't you going to see if you can find that first ball? It just barely rolled into the lake."

"No, I ain't going over there!" Mitch shot back.

Miller asked, "Why not?"

Gay and I heard the question, and neither of us wanted to miss the answer. Mitch replied, "Mr. Bob live over there!"

As if it were rehearsed, all three of us said in unison, "Who's Mr. Bob?"

"Mr. Bob is a water moccasin about 20 feet long," answered Mitch as if we should have known.

Miller reminded him that it was cold water and snakes don't come out in the winter.

Very emphatically, Mitch replied, "As big as Mr. Bob is, he can afford himself an overcoat!"

Another story about Mitch happened at La Costa, when I walked out of the pro shop and overheard a discussion he was having with some other caddies. The subject was George Bayer, who is 6'7" and weighs 260 pounds. The gist of the conversation was how big George was and how hard he would be to whip. Mitch said it would be no problem. Again, I couldn't wait to hear his solution:

"I don't care how big he is, there ain't nobody can handle an ambush!"

A fellow who caddied for me quite a lot, named Raydel, also had an excellent sense of humor and dressed better than the golfers did. Paired with Ben Hogan, I had been playing in the Colonial Invitational in Fort Worth. It was the second day and I was 3 under par going into the 12th hole. Raydel, who was carrying my bag, always prided himself on having the exact yardage. Not just to the green, but also to the hole.

I hit my tee shot down the fairway, and we walked to where the ball had stopped. Across the river, a very heavily traveled railroad track paralleled the 12th hole. Asking Raydel how far it was to the green, he stopped, looked to the right, said a few cuss words, and gave me his answer: "Yesterday there was a green boxcar sitting right over there, but you can see that it's gone now. From that boxcar, it was 176 yards. I think you should hit a 5 iron."

"That boxcar is probably in Memphis by now!" I said looking at the track.

"Then you should probably hit a little more club!" he shot back. That was the first time I heard Hogan laugh out loud.

Then there was Donald, caddie at the Champion's Country Club in Houston, Texas. He was of a very slight build and always dressed as if he had just come from church. He and all the other caddies had a nickname for me, "Banda Gold," referring to the hit record I had in 1956. I came around a corner where Donald was holding court, and today his subject was Cassius Clay, who had just changed his name to Muhammad Ali. Donald was very upset by that fact, and I could tell. He looked up at me and said, "Banda Gold, did you read about that in the newspaper?"

I told him I had, when he replied, "I ought to go and whip his ass!"

I said, "Donald, you're not very big," knowing he only weighed about 115 pounds. "What weight do you fight at?"

He reached into his pocket, pulled out a switchblade, and very direct and loud said, "Ain't nobody ever weighed this knife!"

I remember a story that Danny Kaye told me about playing golf in the mid-1950s at Carnoustie. Being a friend of Hogan's, who had just won the British Open there the year before, Danny called and asked Ben if there was anything special he should know or be aware of. Ben told him to be sure and use the same caddie that he had because he had a famous Scottish sense of humor. Danny told me that he did just that. He went on to say, "I kept waiting for the caddie to talk to me, but for 10 holes, he never did. Then on number 11, I decided to start a conversation, so I looked at him and asked, 'Is this a par-4?'"

The caddie said without glancing, "For 400 years!"

Jackie Burke had a caddie at The Masters who gave a once-in-a-lifetime answer. You see, the 14th hole has a big hump in the middle of the green. For some reason, they had placed the pin very close to the hump, almost on top of it. Jackie hit his 2nd shot left of the pin about 15' and right on top of the mound. As most of us do, he consulted his caddie about the break.

The caddie walked behind the ball, knelt down, looked for a second, and said, "It looks like it breaks about a foot," and very hurriedly took off.

Jackie stopped him and, with some concern, inquired, "Which way?"

The caddie stopped, turned around, and said, "Well . . . now I got to go look again!"

Caddies come in all shapes and sizes. Let me tell you about the biggest one I ever had and the most effective.

Every Fourth of July, the Abilene Texas Invitational was held. It was probably the biggest tournament in West Texas, and I made it a point to play in it every year. Every tournament would have a Calcutta pool (that is where the players are sold to the highest bidder) on Thursday night before the game.

The game then consisted of 36 holes a day with two matches on Friday, two on Saturday, and the 36-hole final on Sunday. The defending champion was always seeded number one in the top bracket with 16 players. The fellow who shot the low qualifying round was given the number two seed and paired in the top of the lower bracket with 16 players.

Billy Maxwell was the defending champion, so he seeded first. I shot the low qualifying round, so I was seeded second and in the lower bracket. In that lower bracket was a fellow by the name of Charlie Tims, who had won a tournament the week before. Charlie was of very slight build, about 120 pounds soaking wet. He had black curly hair, dressed very colorfully, and always carried a comb to make sure that a hair was never out of place. He also had the misfortune of being paired against a fellow named Jerry Stovall, who was a better-than-average player.

Jerry Stovall always smoked a cigar and looked the part of a defensive football player. He weighed about 205 pounds and played defensive back for the St. Louis Cardinals. Stovall had bought himself in the Calcutta pool. The next morning on the practice tee, he calmly walked over to Charlie Tims and very quietly but directly informed him, "Don't beat me!" Charlie didn't (out of fear, I assume). I had won two matches at that point, and realized that I was to play Stovall next.

That Friday night, as always, the country club held a dance for the guests. I was asked to get up and sing with the band, and I obliged as always. Finishing my first song and starting into the second number, I glanced into the crowd and caught Stovall coming up. He didn't say a word—just gave me a sinister stare and danced away. I realized at that point what Charlie Tims must have felt.

I looked, and another football player happened to be in the crowd at the dance. It was Clyde "Bulldog" Turner, a good friend of mine who played for the Chicago Bears. Bulldog weighed even more—270 pounds I'd say—and was such an athlete that he was inducted into the Pro Football Hall of Fame later in life. When I told Bulldog how apprehensive I was playing Jerry Stovall, especially after what happened when he intimidated Charlie Tims, Bulldog looked at me and said, "Don't worry about anything, it will be handled." I had no idea what he was going to do, but I still went to bed that night a bit uneasy.

The next morning I was called to the 1st tee. Alongside me, carrying my golf bag in his right hand, was Bulldog Turner. He sat the bag down, gave me my driver, and in a very loud and confident voice said, "Play away, please." I guess if we were at Indianapolis, it would have sounded like, "Ladies and gentlemen, start your engines!" I got my engine started first and beat Mr. Stovall 5 up and 3 to go. One thing I learned about caddies, it pays to have a larger-than-life one by your side.

Telling stories about caddies, you must know by now that I spent many hours, days, and years caddying myself. I used to walk and sort of caddie for a man who completely changed the attitude and appearance of Las Vegas—Jay Sarno.

Jay started with Caesars Palace and then moved to Circus Circus. He loved to play golf and gamble on just about everything—mostly golf (after all, it was Las Vegas). Men from all over the world would fly in just to play golf with him, and needless to say, he didn't win his bets very often.

Sarno used a golf cart, so I didn't have to carry the golf bag. Thank God for that! Sarno's golf bag was huge. It was specially made for him. Most people carried 14 clubs with them, which were the rules of the game. But that didn't affect Jay's way of thinking. I know this is going to be hard to believe, but at last count, before Jay passed away, I personally counted 126 clubs in that huge bag of his. Now the reason I brought up Jay Sarno wasn't because of the huge golf bag he had—it was really the greatest question and answer I received in playing the game of golf.

We used to park his golf cart in the rough, to protect the fairway. Then we would walk to where Jay's ball had stopped. He was actually very good, and managed to hit the ball into the fairway most of the time. On the 7th hole at the Las Vegas Country Club, Sarno hit the ball into the fairway. As we walked to where it was, he asked two questions: "How far is it to the pin?" and "What club should I use?"

I had forgotten to bring any of his clubs with me. "It's either a 5 or 6 iron," I answered, not being sure of myself.

He thought for a second and replied, "Why don't you bring them both. They're not that heavy."

The Dean Martin TV Shows

PEOPLE APPROACH ME ALL THE TIME WITH APPREHENSION. Not because they remember my terrible disposition on the golf course. Heck, unless I'm at the golf course, most don't associate my looks with that of the golfer they may have heard of. I have been told that I have aged gracefully, but still, people know that they have seen me someplace, but aren't sure. Actually, it's mainly because of my singing and the many different television shows that I have appeared on over the years. This is especially true with the baby boomers of today. Between the late '60s and all through the '70s, talk shows and variety shows were the main staple of television. I was lucky to have been invited to appear on many of the most popular ones.

My first appearance on *The Dean Martin Show* came in December of 1966. December was a good time when most families were relaxing around the TV with their families, enjoying and preparing for the holidays. Dean's show was one of the highest-rated programs, constantly making it to the number one spot. *The Dean Martin Show* was done very differently than other TV shows I was accustomed to. Basically, Dean never rehearsed. His producer/director Greg Garrison saw to that. If Dean was happy, then it reflected on the show. Dean was happiest playing golf. Sure, he took pride in his work, and spent a lot of energy making it look easy. But Dean had this magical way of preparing in a very short amount of time. Even when it didn't look like it, Dean was always in control.

While most of the other guests on the show that week were at NBC studios rehearsing with his stand-in, Lee Hale, Dean and I were on the Riviera Golf Course in Los Angeles, acting like grown kids—playing golf, laughing, telling jokes, and generally having a good time. Many mornings a couple of "pallies," as Dean would refer to them, would ask to join us for 18 holes. On TV taping day, which was usually Sunday, Dean would finish up a little early to make it to the studio right after lunch.

Garrison, his producer, had a closed-circuit TV installed in Dean's dressing room, so Dean could watch a run-through of what they had planned for him all week. Amazingly, Dean would absorb everything by just watching it once. That way, when they walked him on stage, he basically knew what to do. Sure, he flubbed up, not quite remembering what came next, or where he had to stand, but that was all part of his mystique. Dean's fans loved his easygoing charm, and what you saw on his show was what Dean was really like in person—easygoing.

The first time I appeared on his show, I came pretty much prepared, not needing much assistance from the makeup artist. Well, except one thing. Dean took one look at my hairpiece and made his observation: "Don, you gotta get a new one!" He asked someone to look up the address of Max Factor in Beverly Hills and write it down for me. "Here, I want you to go to this place. I'll have it all set up for you when you get there."

When I arrived at the big Max Factor building on Wilshire Boulevard, they took me into their back room area and showed me some of the hairpieces they were making. I spotted one that I liked very much and asked if I could try it on. Adjusting it a little, I took one look at it in the mirror and thought, "Yes—this one is perfect!" I asked them if I could "borrow" it to show Dean.

Allowing me to leave with it turned out to be one of the worst mistakes Max Factor ever made. I went back to the studio and walked into Dean's dressing room with the hairpiece in a bag. "Okay, put it on," Dean instructed. Taking one look at me, Dean picked up the phone and dialed Max Factor. "Okay, we'll take this one," he told the person in charge at the other end.

Being told over the phone that they couldn't sell him the hairpiece because it belonged to John Wayne, Dean shot back, in a rather stern voice, "It used to belong to John Wayne!"

If only I had kept it after all these years, that hairpiece would now be a tremendous conversation piece. You can see how much Dean meant to me.

My good friend, Vito (Vic Damone) was also a guest on that same *Dean Martin Show*. He also mentioned how good I looked, but I don't know if he recognized it was the Duke's hair or was just being nice to me. I told him with a laugh that I always looked as good off the golf course as I did on it. The duet Dean and I sang of "The Glory of Love" and "Gotta Travel On" was a lot of fun to do. Response from the audience was so good that I was asked back to be a guest on his show five more times.

When Phil Harris (my fourth best friend), Dean (my fifth), and I were golfing together one day, the subject of Dean's show had come up. I had suggested to Dean that Phil might be a fun guest to have on his show. Dean agreed, and before I knew it, Phil had made a couple of appearances on Dean's show. It wasn't a surprise that when a couple months after my first appearance on his program, they decided to have us appear together on the next episode. Dean, Phil, and I sang a good old Texas song together, "San Antonio Rose." We then sang a medley of saloon songs. I guess the first choice was for me, and the latter, for the other two lushes. Actually, the only real drinker was Phil. Dean only had the image of being an imbiber of the vino, but whenever Phil was around, Dean could be found having a bit more than usual. I was the "designated driver" of the group.

Dean and I had become as close as friends could be at this point. To give you an example, whenever we would play together in a golf tournament, people would constantly follow us around the course. They begged to eavesdrop on our conversation, and occasionally some would come up to get an autograph or ask a question. John Sliney, a writer for the *Odessa Times*, captured the following:

> *"Boy! This is the biggest sand trap I've ever seen," as Martin looked over the country club layout. The fans loved it.*
> *Martin and Cherry were on the course today taking their*

last warm-up before tourney play. Thursday, Martin is the amateur partner of Cherry. "Now bite!" Dino roared as his tee shot sailed off the fairway and 25 yards into a rough out-of-bounds. "If I find a dead rabbit out there, I'm going to keep it," he cracked as the crowd laughed.

Martin and Cherry whistled, hummed, and harmonized together as they toured the course. Martin cracked several "inside" jokes to Cherry about Don's pending marriage to a former Miss Las Vegas. Dino is to be best man. "If you get the girl there, and I'm not sure you will, I'll stand up," Martin laughed.

"You just make sure you can stand up," retorted Cherry.

"What do you shoot?" one woman asked Dino. "Oh," smiled Martin, "rabbits, deer, snakes."

"Did you have a handicap?" asked someone else. "Yes, getting here," replied a good-natured Dino.

"Dean's a pretty good golf player," said Cherry, but he added, "This is a course you must play more than once."

"Would you believe 30 times?" chimed in Martin.

"It's sure nice to have you back," Cherry told his partner after Martin had been flailing about in the boondocks for a while. "Where have you been?"

"Oh, just out visiting with the other guys," replied Martin.

Cherry literally split his britches on the 11th hole. The tragedy occurred as Cherry squatted down for a brief rest under a shade tree. "What do I do?" he asked with a bemused look on his face.

"You can play, just don't putt," laughed Martin after surveying the damage.

Driving on a trip across eight states, I began by singing at the Victoria Terrace in the famed Hillcrest Hotel in Ohio. Seymour Rothman, a reporter for the *Toledo Blade*, came to see my show and interviewed me for an article in the May 9 edition. He reported that I philosophized to him, "A bit that is a new aspect for Don Cherry—one of a hundred or more wonderful new things that have been happening to him since Dean Martin."

The article went on to quote me at the time, "I sang and I played golf, but I never really felt at home doing either—publicly, I mean, I didn't like people—strangers, that is. I could sit around and talk and kid and laugh and get laughs with people I knew, but once I got up, I was a bundle of temperament. If a drunk heckled me, I wanted to quit. I didn't like my audiences. I'd think of something else or funny to say because I was so afraid of bombing. I guess the truth is I never bombed, but only because I would never risk bombing. Well, I eventually fell into Dean Martin's sphere, and it was absolutely the greatest thing that ever happened to me. He is such a warm, kind, helpful individual that he makes you want to be what he is. I unconsciously adopted his philosophy. I learned to like strangers, to enjoy entertaining. What the heck, if someone heckles me, I can't be doing a job of entertaining him. I try harder."

Thinking back about the first time I sang in the lounge while Dean headlined, I confessed, "Dean and I first worked Lake Tahoe together, then the Sands. I watched him with people. He'd spend 20 minutes signing autographs when he really wanted to play golf. But he'd do it graciously, and in good humor. Just being with him gave you warmth. Watching Dean's relationship with people around him helped me climb out of my shell so that I could enjoy the life I led." I would get kidded a lot because any kind of conversation I got into seemed to work its way back to Dean Martin.

It was only seven weeks later that I was asked to appear on Dean's show for the third time. Three more pals were booked along with me: my good golfing buddy, Bing Crosby, Dan Rowan, and Dick Martin (no relation to Dean). Dick had known Dean since way back in the years he was teamed up with partner Jerry Lewis. I've also considered Dick a good friend of mine, finding that we had a similar outlook on life. In a duet with Dean, they had us seated on a big country porch, whittling wood and singing "Hick Town" to a bunch of farm girls in skimpy clothes. Isn't it funny how I became so closely associated with country music by now? Not that I have a bad word to say about it—heck, I love country music. You gotta remember, I started out with the big band sounds of "Vanity" and "Thinking of You." Ten years after that I was singing pop standards like "Wanted, Someone to Love Me" and "There's a Place Called Heaven." Then 10 years later I was turning out songs like "I Love You Drops" and "There Goes My Everything." Other artists were even covering my songs now.

Some covered versions became bigger hits than their originals. Take for example, my version of "There Goes My Everything." It was later recorded by Engelbert Humperdinck and became a huge hit for him. I even think Elvis Presley covered it. "Between Winston Salem and Nashville Tennessee" was recorded three years after mine by the Mills Brothers, and "I Love You Drops" was covered by the legendary Bill Anderson, who scored big success with it.

Of course, I also covered other artists' songs as well. "When You Leave That Way You Can Never Come Back" was a song written and recorded by a group called Confederate Railroad. My version started climbing the charts, when it caused a bit of a ruckus with some religious advocates. There was a line toward the end of the song that went, "I told the preacher man to go to hell." When the complaints started mounting, radio stations across the country stopped playing my record. Confederate Railroad changed the ending to "I told the preacher man to leave me alone." Their song picked up steam and took off down the tracks to become an immediate hit, while my version went to a place where the vinyl was melted.

Back to the show—Bing, Dean, and I sang a three-part medley to a song that both Dean and Bing sang in the movie *Robin and the Seven Hoods*. It was called "Style," and they had us decked out in Alpaca golfing sweaters, driving a golf cart on stage with our clubs in the back. Who would have ever dreamed, as a kid sitting in that Chinaberry tree singing Crosby's "Pistol Packin' Mama," that I would one day be singing with Bing and Dean in front of millions of people?

After finishing the show and my engagement at Studio City's Spare Room (near NBC in Burbank), I made my way back to The Champions Golf Course in Houston, where I retreated for a little breather. Awaking to my doorbell ringing, I heard the sound of a wooden crate being delivered. The truck driver pointed where he wanted me to sign as I noticed the name "Dean Martin" on the bill of lading. Prying the large crate open, I found a beautiful white golf cart inside with a message from Dean. It was the very same cart that we used on Dean's show, and he wanted me to have it. After using it for the week, I didn't have a way to transport it with me, so I left it behind where Jackie Burke sold it for $1,000. How stupid could I have been?

Before Dean's TV series began its third season on TV, I was honored to be asked to be one of the regulars on his summer replacement series that starred none other than my pal Vic Damone. Carol Lawrence, Dom DeLuise, and Dean's daughter, Gail, were also signed to star in it. Getting to know Gail would have been payment enough for doing the show. It was a blast to do. Dom DeLuise has got to be one of the funniest people in the world.

By now, my face was becoming pretty well known. Donald McClair from the *Los Angeles Times* wrote: "Like Sinatra, Elvis, Dino, Marilyn, and DiMaggio—Cherry has become a one-word household name." Who would have ever thought? A household name? Listen—up until now, I thought when people took to their feet for a standing ovation, they were standing up to leave. The friendship I had with Dean really improved my confidence tremendously.

To further build my budding confidence, another person paid me one of the greatest compliments that I think I ever received. It was during a taping of another show, *Nashville Now*, that I was asked to sing on. I chose "Out of My Life, Out of My Mind," a romantic ballad that I recorded years earlier. Halfway through my song, I caught the eye of the great Minnie Pearl standing offstage. After finishing and taking a bow, Minnie walked out and whispered during the applause, "If I come back this way again . . . and I will . . . I hope the Good Lord gives me your voice." What a huge compliment!

One more, then I won't bug you with compliments again. I was singing in a night spot in Greensboro, North Carolina, called the Plantation Club when Tony Lema and Gay Brewer came by that evening to hear me sing. After the show, they got into a discussion about a golfing rule. Neither one could figure out when the rule for out-of-bounds was changed from

1 to 2 shots. I happened to walk past their table when they both looked up and told me how much they enjoyed the show. Tony then quizzed me, "Don, you've been playing golf a long time, maybe you can tell us when the out-of-bounds rule was changed."

Before I could answer, Gay said to him in a loud voice, "Hell! What are you asking *him* for?! He ain't never been out of the fairway!"

Shouting the Words

I RETURNED TO THE RECORDING STUDIOS in Nashville to put together more songs for a second album. By this time, every pop singer around was jumping on the country music bandwagon. Barbara Mandrell once said in a song, "I was country when country wasn't cool." In 1961 there were 81 radio stations in America devoted to country music. By 1966, there were more than 350. Believe it or not, one out of every two American records was produced in a Nashville studio.

Fred Foster called me to tell me that they were looking to score a new movie soundtrack in Hollywood called *Will Penny*. On my trip out to the West Coast, I stopped to lend my voice to the song "The Lonely Rider." Studying the words, I was ready when the tape rolled and the orchestra began. "No, no, no!" came over the monitor. Cam Mullins, the conductor, instructed me that this was going to be played over the credits as the movie ends, and that I needed to sing it with everything I had.

"Shout the words!" he instructed. "Approach it like an opera singer!"

I did just that. If you ever catch *Will Penny* late at night, wait until the end and you'll hear me with the best operatic tenor voice a Texas boy could muster.

Through my shouting, my ears picked up the sound of fantastic guitar playing among the musicians. When we finished that afternoon, the young man who played guitar on the session came up to me and introduced himself. "I'd like to play golf with you sometime," he said, but in my sometimes brash demeanor, I brushed him off. Two months later the nation was taken by storm with a new country song called "Gentle on My Mind." The young man I brushed off came out to Las Vegas soon afterward. I approached him and said, "Hi, Glen!" His response: "Get out of here!" We both laughed. He got even—in more ways than one. Within two years, Glen Campbell starred with John Wayne in *True Grit* (winning Wayne an Academy Award for Best Actor), hosted his own highly successful country TV variety show (*The Glen Campbell Goodtime Hour*), and topped the charts with a string of country songs—"By the Time I Get to Phoenix," "Galveston," "Wichita Lineman," etc.

Before striking out on his own, Glen Campbell also played guitar on many of Dean Martin's country recording sessions. Dean, once known for his Italian numbers, such as "That's Amore" and "Non Dimenticar," was now himself recording hits such as "Houston," "Detour," and a cover version of my earlier recording, "The Tip of My Fingers."

During the recording session, a fellow sitting behind the drums made his way over to me and introduced himself. Strange as it may sound, he said that his name was Hal Blaine—my third wife's first husband. Hal Blaine, Glen Campbell, and some of the other musicians comprised a group of the most sought-after studio musicians in Hollywood. They were even dubbed "The Wrecking Crew"—a name also associated with a series of spy movies that Dean Martin had made during this time.

After recording "The Lonely Rider" in Los Angeles, I met Dean for a game of golf the following morning. Mispronouncing the word "album," Dean said to me; "Don, I just listened to your last a-blum . . . if it weren't for you, I wouldn't have given much thought to doing country songs."

Fred Foster, who helped create the cycle in country music, also liked the pop hits that many folks remembered me singing. Nestled in between the country standards "Lucky Old Sun" and "There Goes My Everything" on my new album were re-recordings of my own pop songs "Band of Gold," "Vanity," and "Thinking of You." If you were a fan of the originals, you would be delighted to hear these versions in a more soft, serene arrangement.

The Sons of Katie Elder had been released in 1965 and was a huge box office success. This was the second, and last, movie that John Wayne and Dean Martin made together (the first being *Rio Bravo*). Dean had a Western script that he wanted to make after completing a costarring role with Frank Sinatra in *Marriage on the Rocks*. He just loved Westerns, but the plan was to alternate between dramas, comedies, and Westerns. "Don, I've got this great script and it involves the mean character who has a terrible personality. With your record, I think you'd be perfect for the part," Dean sprung on me.

Knowing he was ribbing me about my reputation for having a terrible temper, I knew Dean wasn't kidding about a role in his movie. I asked him a little more about it, and he said, "Don't worry about a thing. Well, there is one thing . . ."

"Yes?" was my question.

"You'll need to grow a beard for the part. After all, this is a Western, and the bad guys never shave."

That was it. I went home and threw away my razor. Days went by . . . then weeks . . . then a couple of months. I was quite destitute looking by now. Then one morning, the phone rang. It was Dean. We were supposed to meet at the country club to go golfing when he told me that his most favorite horse, Tops, had died. I told him I was sorry and that I understood. Tops was Dean's good luck charm. I don't think he ever did a Western without his favorite horse. After Tops passed way, Dean didn't have the heart to make the movie without him. The next time I saw Dean, we were heading out to Atlanta to play in the Atlanta Open.

Going out to the practice range before the event, Dean spotted the Reverend Billy Graham hitting practice golf balls. Not wanting to disturb him, Dean whispered to me, "That's Billy Graham . . . we should leave him alone and to his own business."

We didn't get three feet before the Reverend spotted Dean and came right over. Graham kept going on and on about how much he loved Dean's singing. Not knowing quite how to respond, Dean put his index finger to his lips to keep the Reverend from gushing on and becoming too embarrassed. He said, "Thank you," while I jumped in, adding, "We're up next and should get going."

When Dean and I got to the 5th tee, I noticed that he was playing great. He turned to me and said, "Don, it's funny, but you know, after talking to Billy Graham, I'm hittin' those golf balls much harder and better!" We both laughed so hard for the rest of the morning over that.

My fourth appearance on Dean's TV show brought Phil Harris, Dean, and me together once again with a song called "Pass That Peace Pipe." Yeah, right. Like I smoked too. I wondered if they were trying to change my image. As strange as it seems, the five best friends I ever had—Mickey Mantle, Bobby Layne, Jimmy Demaret, Phil Harris, and Dean Martin— were known as the five most famous drinkers that ever walked. I loved each one of them—I just never dove in. Actually, Dean's image was bigger than his real drinking. His glass was always filled with Martinelli's apple juice—obviously Italian! I remember the time Dean even offered me $500 to drink a pineapple daiquiri. I looked at him and said, "It ain't gonna happen!"

Before the week was over, both Dean and I were booked to sing at the Riviera Hotel in Las Vegas. I played the lounge room, while he sang in the main room. I sometimes think Dean just wanted someone to play golf with, but he was the boss. No one would argue with Dean. He had a 10 percent share in the Riviera at the time, and I was having the time of my life.

My next two appearances on Dean's show in 1968 were with more moderate guests. Dean and I did more Texas songs with a medley of "Eyes of Texas," "Yellow Rose of Texas," "Houston," "San Antonio Rose," and "Deep in the Heart of Texas." I guess Lee Hale, the show's musical director, had done his homework. I also got to meet Dean's uncle, Leonard Barr, who was also on the show, as well as Mickey Rooney and Minnie Pearl. Then, later that year, Dean and I sang a duet to "Oh, Lonesome Me."

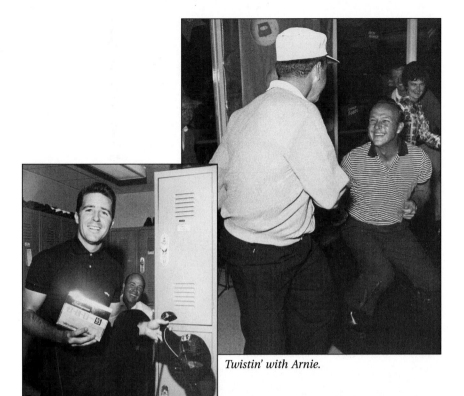

Twistin' with Arnie.

With Gary Player in the locker room.

Dinner with Jack Nicklaus.

Our 1961 Walker Cup Team.

Good friend and Las Vegas legend Shecky Greene.

Top left: My sons Stephen and Sean holding onto the Walker Cup.

Top right: Singing while looking debonair in my tux.

Appearing for MacGregor in its ads.

Dean and I having some fun.

*Whittlin' wood
with Dean.*

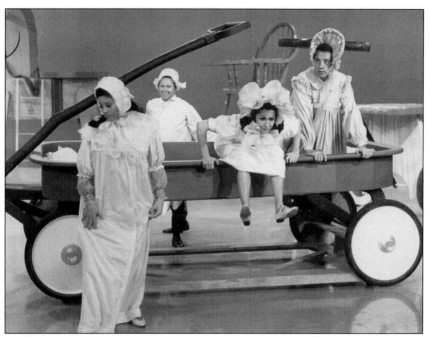

Dean's summer show: Gail Martin (left), Carol Lawrence, and Vic Damone.

Dean and I having a day of fun—again.

Mean Joe Green, Mickey Mantle, and I.

My sixth best friend: Willie Nelson.

With Phil Harris and Francine.

With Francine.

With Mohammad Ali.

Stephen and Sean walking Francine down the aisle.

President Bush and I inducted into the Hall of Fame.

Living Las Vegas

I HAD RETURNED TO MONUMENT STUDIOS, ready to put together more songs for a third album called *Let It Be Me*. Again, Fred Foster let me redo a couple of my pop hits from years earlier—"Because of You" and "Country Boy," which had been the beginning of my association with country music. I was thrilled to see the front cover of the album when it came out. It featured a hand-sketched drawing of me by artist Terry Smith. The artwork was eerily similar to that of Dean's album cover for *The Dean Martin Show*. I considered it a small tribute to my pally.

I had been calling the glittering/gaming mecca of Las Vegas home. Ever since Dean and his Rat Pack friends Frank Sinatra, Sammy Davis Jr., Peter Lawford, and Joey Bishop took to appearing at the Sands in the mid '60s, Vegas was becoming a hot spot for tourism and entertainment. Living right there in town, I found myself quite busy with offers to sing at many of the large hotels on the strip. I also found myself playing less and less golf because of my emphasis on singing.

The Riviera Hotel offered me a job, but not to sing in their showrooms. Because of my association with golf, and the popularity I had with the public, they courted me to act as their golf director, a position that resembled a casino host. Knowing that many high rollers wanted to stay at a place where they could relax and play a little golf, I would be the one that could attract them to stay and play at the Riviera. My new job was fun for a while, but I grew weary of the amount of time it took.

Wanting to play golf and sing in other spots of the country, it became hard to find the time to do all three things.

I was a bit worried that I wasn't playing enough to have my PGA card renewed, when a very important letter and phone call came from the PGA's Southwest Office. Appearing on the date they requested, I was thrilled to be awarded the ultimate honor of being chosen a lifetime member of the PGA. Out of all the awards and trophies I have accumulated, the centerpiece of my collection is the framed document they presented me. Golf has truly been part of me and my life.

As I moved from showroom to showroom on the strip, my name became a constant fixture for tourists at any time of the year. Many nights, different celebrities would come to my show, and it was thrilling for me to see who might be in the audience (that's what made lounge shows a bigger entity back then than today). Dean, of course, would come over after his show (if he were doing only one show per night) to catch my midnight show. Friends like Jerry Vale, Sonny King, Vic Damone, Kelly Smith, and even Dean himself might jump up on stage to sing or kibitz with me. The audience never knew what extra entertainment they might get for their cover charge that evening. That was actually the fun of lounge shows back then.

While audiences had a good time at the shows, Dean and I were having our own fun on the golf course. The time I took Dean with me to Odessa, it was as if God Almighty himself had shown up. Folks there weren't use to seeing many celebrities in Texas, and they went all out. They managed to have a huge house for both of us to stay in while we were there, along with transportation and just about anything we would need or want.

The first morning out on the course, Dean had a shot over on a par-3 hill, and the ball was in the dirt behind the sand trap. Dean shook his head and said to me, "How am I gonna hit this one?"

I told him there was nothing to it, that it was an easy shot. "You should just hit it kind of easy."

"Yeah, then show me!" Dean snapped back.

I laid my ball on the ground next to his and bladed it. The ball hit the top of the pin and dropped into the hole. Without a pause,

I looked over at Dean and said, "Now, that's the last time I'm gonna show you!"

"Oh, yeah. You're gonna show me!" he muttered. I didn't tell him how I skulled it after telling him to hit it easy.

There was another time at the Edgewood Course, when Dean and I were performing at the same place in Lake Tahoe. Golfing buddies Tony Frabile, Minnie Cardello, and Myron Freedman would come up to play with us. This one day we were on the 12th hole, and I had put the ball in a bunker. This bunker was deep—almost as deep as I am tall. I stood there, thought for a minute, then swung. The ball went up, hit the lip of the bank, bounced off, came back, and hit me! I was so mad that my temper got the best of me and I began to lose it. By the time I got finished hitting the dirt with that sand iron, the ball was another three feet deeper. I looked up to see Dean lying on the ground. They say it was the funniest thing they ever saw. Dean was laughing so hard that he could hardly get up.

Dean and I were staying in the same house there and were singing in the evenings. One night after we finished both shows, I started coming down the stairs when I heard the television set on in the living room. There I found Dean sitting in a big chair, just staring at the TV screen. Nothing was on except snow and lines. The station had gone off the air, but Dean was going on with this elaborate story, describing in detail what the snow and lines were doing. I was laughing so hard. He had such a fantastic sense of humor! We were so close. I remember once telling Dean that I liked the sweater he was wearing. The following week there was a knock on the door. Dean had the department store deliver a dozen of the same cashmere sweaters in every color imaginable. Dean Martin was so good to me, it's unbelievable.

My records were selling very well, which made Monument very happy. So happy, in fact, that they had me in their studios to record a whole album of new songs, and wanted me back just a few months later to record more. One of the songs they selected was a tune from the 1958 movie *Thunder Road* called "The Whippoorwill." The movie starred actor Robert Mitchum, who himself wrote both "The Whippoorwill" and the title song. Released on a 45 single, and also included on my fourth album for Monument, *Take a Message to Mary*, the song did well in a time when the Beatles were trying to "Get Back," and Elvis Presley had "Suspicious Minds."

Dean had invited me to visit him in Durango, Mexico, while he was on location shooting his new movie, *5 Card Stud*. As soon as I got there, Dean grabbed me around the neck and pulled me over to where his costar was, announcing out loud, "Hey Pally, I want you to meet a good friend of mine."

His costar turned around, took one look at me, and said, "Oh, hell, I already know this guy! He just recorded a song of mine!"

The fellow was none other than Robert Mitchum. Needless to say, all three of us had a great time. I was also glad to find out that Mitchum liked my version of his song. That album had many memorable songs included on it. Two of my favorites were, "Love Me with All Your Heart" and "Take a Message to Mary." Equally as delightful were the liner notes that Buddy Hackett wrote for the cover. The way the public envisioned Buddy's comedic ability, this seemed out of character. If you were lucky to know Buddy personally, this was really him—intelligently and prophetically written, and with love:

> *So much makes up America. Parallel with the inequities of various struggles for recognition and a decent life, is a world of entertainment and sports.*
>
> *Personalities in these fields ofttimes are filled with tenderness and compassion for the suffering of their fellow man.*
>
> *Such a man is Don Cherry. If you were ever fortunate to play golf with him, or watch him play, you are aware of his unblemished record.*
>
> *If not, you can feel the warmth and feeling in his music—listen to him, and feel the basic quality of the country grown boy, and the sophisticated man of his urban world of today.*
>
> *On the golf course, or on the stage, or on the pulpit of living—I love him.*
>
> *—Buddy Hackett*

Monument only released 15 albums by their other artists before they wanted to have me record more songs for a new album simply called *Don Cherry*. This just might be one of my favorite albums, if you don't take too long looking at my picture on the cover. I was posed near a hill filled with weeds outside, wearing a buttoned-up single-breasted suit in the hot sun. If that wasn't bad enough, the suit was at least two sizes too small. If you ever find a copy of the album, turn it over quickly—the back is better. Here you can read the note singer/poet Rod McKuen wrote:

> *Dear Don,*
>
> *I wish you would ease up on your golf and sing more of my songs. Even though Dean Martin thinks your golf game is tasty, I'd rather hear you singing my songs, or anybody's songs.*
>
> *That you've chosen two of my favorites for this album is especially nice, but then I can't remember you ever singing anything I didn't like.*
>
> *Stay well . . .*
>
> —*Rod McKuen*
>
> *P.S. Have you ever wondered why Dean tried to keep you on the golf course?*

Besides McKuen's two songs, "Ain't You Glad You're Livin' Joe" and the hit "Jean," the album featured 10 other songs that were some of the finest ever written. Every one of them told a complete story. From standards like "My Romance" and "My Foolish Heart" to the nostalgic homesick feel of "Green Green Grass of Home" and a beautiful saga about love and life, "The Days of Sand and Shovels."

I made one more appearance on Dean's TV show, and this time it was with Shecky Greene. Dean and I sang a song together, "Gotta Travel On." That title was more true to life than I knew at the time.

HOLE
23

The Football Greats

I RECEIVED WORD THAT MY BROTHER, a craftsman and one-time instructor for Arthur Murray, had passed away. I prefer to remember Paul as my talented brother who helped me with golfing lessons as a kid. He lost much of his spirit after his discharge from the service. Then life hit a low point for him when his wife perished in that fatal car accident 15 years earlier. Drinking and tobacco abuse became a crutch he used to deal with his dark depression. His misuse of alcohol combined with chewing raw tobacco took Paul's life at such an early age. Officially it was listed as cancer of the stomach. Being older than me, I have often wondered what led to his painful demise. Maybe Paul's upbringing by Mom had affected him differently—only God really knows why we are all so different and how we handle what life deals us in our own way.

The news on TV was filled with images of our soldiers in Vietnam. Sugar-coated life at home was portrayed in shows like *The Brady Bunch* and *Love, American Style*. Talk shows were becoming very popular too. After Paul's death, invitations to appear on these shows kept coming. *The Merv Griffin Show* had me singing and laughing about the way the music business had changed, while on *The Joey Bishop Show*, Joey and his then cohost, Regis Philbin, bantered about the subject of my playing. Joey replied, as the audience took it all in, "Don Cherry is awesome, simply *awesome!*" That made for an impressive introduction to his audience. It was nice to sing many of my new songs and talk about the things I was passionate about. My appearance on his show was in

October, and before I knew it, in the blink of an eye, the decade had come to an end.

Up to this point, my records were selling briskly, and I knew that television was the medium giving me the greatest exposure one could hope for. Monument had me record a dozen more songs for a new album to start off the 1970s. *I Love to Love You* was the name of the collection, but the song selected to be a single release was "Between Winston Salem and Nashville, Tennessee." It did reasonably well, although five years later a jazz-harmony vocal group, the Mills Brothers, would give it a stab. Reviewers said, "The full tones of the Mills Brothers combined with simple melodic structure allow the singers to convey deep emotion." Never having recorded country music before, the Mills Brothers scored a hit. Two other selections, "Statue of a Fool" and "Everybody Else," were then pulled from the album and released a couple months later as I prepared for fatherhood again.

In 1970 we named our new baby daughter Jennifer Joy Cherry. I was blessed watching J.J. grow up and make her own family. J.J. named her son Adam Ross Golden. What a wonderful tribute to give to my mother.

The Dunes gave me my own nickname too, "A.P.," which stood for "assistant pro." Like the duties I performed for the Riviera Hotel, my new part-time job was greeting and playing host to big-time golfers and sports enthusiasts. It would fascinate folks to see "Don Cherry" in lights on the marquee, come to my show, then be able to play a little golf with me the next day. The hotel reaped the benefits from all the money they would leave in the slot machines during their stay.

As audiences became more and more acquainted with coming to my shows, so did the reviewers and columnists. It was something that I talked about with Johnny Carson when I appeared on his enormously popular *Tonight Show*.

During the month of September, fellow Las Vegas performer Totie Fields was the other guest on a Johnny Carson appearance I made. She was not only an immensely funny comedienne, but was very cordial to me, expressing her love for my singing as well. It's nice to be liked by one's own peers in show business. Ooh, ooh—there's that phrase again—"show business." I still didn't play that game. With all the positive accolades coming in from every direction, I am surprised my head didn't swell up to the size of a horse.

Rodeos were becoming as popular with the country music crowd as disco dancing was going to be with the younger generation. I would travel and perform at quite a few, with many of them in my home state of Texas. In 1972 I was invited to appear and sing at the granddaddy of them all, the Jasper Lions Rodeo. Another popular event was the annual rodeo in Jacksonville, Texas. Many new roping and riding records were broken that year, as the event began with a parade prior to the show held in their weather-covered arena. The committee asked me right before the parade was to begin if I would mind riding on a horse. I had ridden horses before, but not dressed in a full western tuxedo. Besides my cumbersome apparel, I also told them that if a strong wind came up I was afraid of losing my hairpiece.

To my surprise, a gentleman was listening in on my conversation, and with a little smirk in his voice said, "Don't worry, I'll ride behind you on another horse and make sure if it comes off that no horse will step on it." That fellow was a football player with the Dallas Cowboys, Walt Garrison—one of the great fullbacks of all time. In a strange way, we became, and have been, very good friends since.

The greatest running back in football history, without a doubt, was a fellow by the name of Jim Brown. He used to come to Las Vegas and play at the Las Vegas Country Club. One day, I walked over to introduce myself to him. He was very nice and we started playing golf together. He was a very good player—in fact, Jim had a 7-handicap. Back in those days, I was called a "scratch player." In golf that means I had no handicap at all. So when Jim and I would play together, I would have to give him 4 shots on the front nine and 3 shots on the back, to make it more balanced and fair. Sometimes we would only play nine holes, but I would still give Jim 4 shots on the first nine. I wasn't too smart sometimes.

For example, I would constantly pick up heavy objects, never giving a thought about getting injured. That stupidity led to two hernia operations. My doctor both times, Tommy Armour, warned me over and over to take it easy and quit hurting myself. I guess I was too bull-headed to listen. Tommy's father was actually one of the top 10 golfers during his lifetime, and his son Tommy picked up an interest in it too.

I had just finished recording an album with Willie Nelson, and a song on it was a story about The Masters called "Augusta." I had given Tommy a copy of the CD about two weeks before I had to have my second operation. As he began to put me to sleep in the hospital before the operation, he put the CD on the stereo and I very peacefully fell into a deep sleep.

As I began to wake up, I realized that I was in the recovery room. Looking down, I saw the bandages and knew all had gone well. Three days later, not wanting to stay any longer, I began getting dressed. In my mind, I only lived six blocks away from the hospital and I wanted to walk home. Knowing my determined attitude, Dr. Armour informed the staff to try to talk some sense into me, that it would be hard for them to stop me. They finally relinquished, and said that they could not hold me, but had to wheel me to the front doors in a wheelchair.

Being the understanding person that I was (and still am), I let them do that. I signed the form and began to walk home. That's when the painkillers wore off, and when I made it to the front door, I headed for the bed to lie down and fall asleep. Awaking the next morning, I decided to walk over to the golf course about six blocks away.

The first person I spotted was Jim Brown. He invited me to play golf with him, but I had to explain about my operation. Wanting to play, Jim said, "I'll play you even on the front nine for $25," meaning I didn't have to give the 4 shots he had been receiving. I thought for a minute, then grabbed a golf club. The first swing I took somewhat easy, not knowing if anything would rip open. I didn't hurt very much, so I thought, *What the hell?*

We teed off, and it started hurting a little more, but I wasn't going to say anything. To make a long story shorter, I beat him 1 up in nine holes. With a beaten look on his face, Jim began to take the $25 out of his wallet. Before he handed it to me, he said, "I want to see your operation." I unzipped my pants to show him. He looked—then he asked again, "That's the bandage—I want to see the scar!" My feeling at the time, looking at the size of Jim Brown, was, *Thank God it's there.*

Jim had a great sense of humor, and it was a real pleasure playing golf and getting to know the man. He was one of a kind.

My Sixth Best Friend: Willie

THE NEXT FELLOW I AM GOING TO TALK ABOUT is one of the three most intelligent and creative people I have ever been exposed to in my life—and I have no idea who the other two are! His name: Willie Hugh Nelson, better known as just "Willie."

Willie and I have two things in common. We both sing and we both play golf. Willie does have one advantage over me when it comes to golf. He owns his own nine-hole golf course, the Pedernales Golf Club, in Spicewood, Texas (about 26 miles west of Austin). Unlike most other clubs, where par for the course is usually listed on the scorecards (usually 70, 71, or 72), Willie is right up front about it. Larry Trader, a close friend of Willie's who helps maintain and run the club, erected a little sign that everyone sees entering through the front door. It reads: "Par: Whatever Willie Shoots."

Now enough about golf, let's talk about singing. Not only is Willie a wonderful singer, his phrasing is especially unique. He also writes words and music with the best of them. By now, you pretty much know how lucky I feel about being able to play golf and sing. The same goes for Willie.

Willie has been gracious enough to do three albums with me. The first one, titled *Augusta*, tells a beautiful story about one of the great golf tournaments of all time, The Masters, in which I was invited to play in nine times. To me, and I'm sure to Willie, our title tune, "Augusta," is almost like a love song.

The second album we did was called *It's Magic*, produced by Fred Foster. It had two very famous musicians playing on it with us, Boots Randolph, one of the best saxophone players of all time, and Charlie McCoy, in my opinion the best harmonica player of all time.

Our third album, *The Eyes of Texas*, was done for Lady Bird Johnson's Wildflower Charity. As one would expect, it's an album comprised entirely of Texas songs.

Now, a little about Willie's sense of humor: Willie was born in a town called Abbott, Texas—a few miles north of Waco. On occasion, he would drive to Abbott from Austin to play poker with his friends. Usually playing into the early morning hours, Willie would stay there overnight. In the morning, when he was refreshed, Willie would drive back to Austin. One morning, Willie didn't get much sleep and began his drive back. Becoming sleepy on the road, he decided to pull over and rest somewhere between Waco and Hewitt, Texas. Closing his eyes, he fell off to sleep when a knock on his window startled him awake.

It turned out to be the local sheriff, who recognized Willie immediately. As Willie rolled down the window of his high-priced Mercedes, the officer spotted one of those things he smokes lying on the seat next to him. The next thing Willie knew, he was holding a ticket for sleeping and smoking. He also received a lot of publicity over that.

The next time I saw Willie, he told me of the incident. I told him, "Willie, as famous as you are, that is one of the dumbest things I ever heard of—especially with that cigarette by your side!"

He answered, "I'm wanted for sleeping in 17 states!"

Whenever Willie would come to Las Vegas, we would always play golf together. Not too many years ago, the Orleans Hotel and Casino invited Mr. Nelson to help celebrate their grand opening. Wanting to play golf, I drove over to pick Willie up in my brand-new Mercury Mountaineer. It had all of 300 miles clocked on it at the time. It wasn't hard finding where Willie was, because his big tour bus was always parked in the parking lot where he was.

As you entered the private parking area, you had to go through an entrance that had spikes in the ground. Obviously, they were put there to make you leave through a different exit. I pulled up and Willie loaded his clubs in the back of the car. As we started talking, guess where I exited from? Yep, the entrance with the one-way spikes in the ground. We traveled about 300 yards before the car stopped and wouldn't move. I had blown all four tires. I didn't say anything. It was quite obvious that I had taken the wrong exit.

Willie called his bus, and one of his men picked us up and took us to the golf course. On the way there, Willie looked at me and said, "I always wanted to see if that shit worked."

We had arrived and played about six holes, when without looking, Willie turned to me and said, "I guess we can forget about me sleeping in the car as being the dumbest thing you ever heard of." Reading this, Willie may become my first best friend!

The Break-Up

IT'S TIME TO TELL YOU ABOUT ANOTHER OF MY BREAK-UPS. Since I have been confessing about my terrible record with the women in my life, you'll probably think this is about another of my marriages. No, not exactly—that's still coming. This time it was the break-up with one of my five best friends. I don't know how to rate the mistakes I have made in life, but this has to be one of the worst.

When Dean Martin and I would get out on the course to play golf, I would usually play him for a $5 Nassau. You golfers out there will know what that is—that was $5 bet on the front nine holes, and a $5 bet on the back nine. Five more dollars were wagered on the full 18, with a press on the back nine, for $5 more. Not much money was involved. It was more for the fun and sport of it.

As with the story about Jay Sarno, people used to fly in from all over to play golf with Dean Martin. The other players who would come in would tend to play Dean for a $100 or $200 Nassau. I remember this one gentleman from Pittsburgh who would fly in and play with us from time to time. He was a very good player, but would never give Dean enough strokes to make it an even match.

For nearly a year, I watched him take advantage of Dean when I just couldn't stand it any longer. I confronted the guy and called him an asshole for being unfair and benefitting off of Dean's good nature. I even told him in no uncertain words that he should be barred from the course for taking advantage.

I don't know exactly how or what he said to Dean. He informed Dean what I had said to him, and somehow, it didn't set right with him. Dean asked Tony Frabile (a friend who played with us) to tell me that he could take care of himself.

From that point on, I really didn't talk to or see much of Dean for nearly two years. When we finally got together to play a game, Dean never mentioned the past incident to me and acted as if nothing had happened. Although we got back together, it just wasn't the same between Dean and me after that. From then on, the number of times we played together, I would never accept his money if I would beat him at a game.

Dean's own course in life seemed to be shifting for him in many areas. His once hugely popular TV variety series that started in 1965 had all but run out of gas by 1974. The successful star that he once was had now turned him into an emcee to showcase the talent of others with his celebrity roasts.

Dean was one of the very few who beat the odds when music had changed back in the '60s. But now, his records weren't selling much either. Dean's voice for singing and his appetite for life didn't seem to be there anymore. His last few movie roles were in titles most people never heard, and finally Dean was resigned to playing a caricature of himself in the *Cannonball Run* movies. I hated to see him disappearing from my life, but more importantly, his own. Dean's love and attention, and all the things he had done for me, were more than anyone in my life had ever done.

The title of my 1975 recording, *The Good Old Days Are Right Now* fit so well at this point. Even though Monument had still been putting out my records continuously, as I said, the music scene had really changed again. Monument was having a hard time competing with the emergence of musical monoliths like Polygram and WEA. Being an independent company, Monument's founder, Fred Foster, did what he could. First he took advantage of using isolation booths in the recording studio; next, laying down recordings in pristine multitrack presentation; and finally signing Polygram to handle distribution of its product to compete against the giants. A few more records were released, and by 1978, *Play Her Back to Yesterday* was the last recording of mine for Monument.

A gentleman with whom I had started my career, Jan Garber, also marked a period of ending with his passing before reaching his 83rd birthday. His daughter, Janis, who sang lead, and took over as bandleader in later years, called to give me the news. In our conversation, she wanted to relay to me what her father once said. After seeing my success following "Band of Gold" and Mr. Clean, Jan Garber said matter-of-factly, "That Don Cherry—I knew that kid could sing!" Those were the good old days.

HOLE
26

Bocce Ball

LET ME TELL YOU ABOUT ONE OF MY MOST UNUSUAL VICTORIES
in the world of sports. In Italy they have a game called "bocce." It is
considered to be their national sport, much like baseball is in the United
States. Wanting to gain more exposure in this country, the bocce council
decided in 1975 to stage the Celebrity Bocce Ball World Championship
Tournament in Las Vegas, Nevada. Caesars Palace was chosen to host
the event with a first place prize of $5,000.

If I can remember correctly, there were 12 teams, each consisting of
two men per team. It was a celebrity tournament, and everyone they
invited had some sort of Italian heritage to them. At the last minute, one
of the teams withdrew, and they needed to find two other players.

Foster Brooks, the comedian best remembered for playing a drunk
on many Dean Martin shows, was working at one of the showrooms
in town. Obviously, he wasn't Italian, but they needed to fill the spot,
so the committee asked him if he would like to play, and if he could
find a partner. The next thing I knew, my phone rang asking me if I'd
volunteer. Thinking it would be fun, I accepted, even though neither I
nor Foster had ever played the game before. I advised the sponsor of
this, and they informed us that nothing was expected of us.

My first thought upon arriving at the Caesars Sports Pavilion was of
how many world champion fights, tennis matches, and other competitions
had been held there. I started to become a bit apprehensive, when I
remembered them saying that nobody expected us to do much good

anyway. Foster and I met and had a few minutes together before meeting the other players—Joe DiMaggio, Ralph Branca, Paddy DeMarco, Jerry Vale, Sonny King, Rocky Graziano, and others I just can't remember—but all Italian.

Ralph Branca was kind enough to take Foster and me over to one of the bocce courts, explain the game to us, and show us how it was played. Here's the scoop—the court itself is usually 60' long. If it is a two-man team, each team is given four balls, different colors, of course, and usually red or green (Italy's colors). The main target is a little ball called the "pallino." A coin is tossed, and whoever wins the toss gets to roll the pallino, and it must go past midcourt. He then gets to roll the first bocce ball as close as possible to the pallino. The game is usually played to 15 points, and you must win by two. After you have rolled the bocce ball, your opponent gets to roll his ball, trying to get closer than you, and so it goes.

Foster and I lost our first match 15–13. We never lost again! We played Joe DiMaggio and Paddy DeMarco in the finals, and by some miracle, we beat them 15–13 and won the Celebrity Bocce World Championship! They never held another tournament after that. I wonder why.

One interested spectator was Ernest Borgnine. Ernie realized what underdogs we were, and as a result, he pulled for us in each match. When we beat Joe and Paddy, Ernest was the only one-man standing ovation that Foster Brooks and I ever got!

Losing People Who Meant So Much

I guess you could say that the '70s ended on a somewhat sour note (a musical term used in show business, the game I never played). As the '80s began, that sour note fermented, and so did my marriage. It had been 17 years since Joy and I tied the knot, but I learned how to loosen it and make it a slipknot. I'd been slipping out, spending time with other women while away from Joy. Sometimes I think that the success of our many years together was the fact that we never saw each other. The times that we were together, Joy let my behavior slide, time and time again. We never fought—by now, I don't think I was around long enough to start an argument. I still hadn't learned the foundation for a successful marriage.

On September 8, 1981, we were officially divorced and finally went our separate ways. As time passed, I realized that the one who suffered the most in our break-up was our own daughter. Never seeing us fight or understanding why her father was no longer in the picture created animosity and disillusionment for her. I never understood what repercussions my actions had until the years passed and I began to see what I had done to all my children. I was selfish. If I could do anything over again, it would be to try to be a better father.

Heading for Reno, I opened the Headliner Room at Harrah's for Mr. Warmth, Don Rickles. We played during the week of October 22 to packed houses. At least the reviews that came in were something positive . . .

Two Standing Ovations for a Performance!
Rickles Did and Does!

Opening the evening is singer Don Cherry, certainly one of the best choices possible. He's got a wonderfully smoky whiskey baritone which is free, fluid, flexible, and the ultimate in listenability. The man himself is easy, warm, totally unpretentious, and thoroughly delightful, and the combination is dynamite. He opens with Kenny Rogers' "The Gambler," after which he introduces himself by saying, in part, "For those of you who may not know me, I'm a professional golfer, had a couple of hit records back in the '50s, and I'm wearing a very expensive hairpiece!"

He's so dry, the room is his and he proceeds to lock it up with a program of songs which are obviously favorites. There are no glitzy introductions, no glossy segues from song to song . . . he just intros them and proceeds to sing the hell out of each, best of the bunch being "You Always Hurt the One You Love," "Sweet Memories," and "Watermelon Wine."

The only nit I'd pick is his musical arrangements . . . they are unnecessarily repetitive and monotonous and deserve some attention, but even so, Don Cherry is a welcome addition to the area and I hope he'll come back . . . often!

—Howard Rosenberg, KTVN / Reno

The wonderful experience of appearing on *The Merv Griffin Show* came next. A man of his stature, Griffin was a uniquely charismatic and, simply stated, a very nice person. Merv would listen with attention to every conversation we had and was truly interested in what we talked about. I appeared on his show a number of times and believe he enjoyed my visits as much as I did.

It was only a short passage of time before another voice in my life fell silent—that of my dearest friend and comrade, Jimmy Demaret. Jimmy used to tell me, "Don, I've carried you longer than your mother." In an unfeigned way, Jimmy did.

Jackie Burke founded the Champions Golf Club in Houston with Jimmy, and the two of them were best of friends. Jackie was with Jimmy on the day he died. He told me the story: "On Jimmy Demaret's last day at Champions, a club Jimmy loved, I asked him what he wanted to do that morning. He replied that he was going for a haircut at Hazel's Barber Shop. Hazel had been known to have a few beers at night. Jim said, 'I sure hope she has a light hangover,' and went down to our barn to retrieve something out of his motor home. As he got out of the cart, he fell flat on the ground. Jim didn't hang around for one old man's aches and pains. There will never be another Jimmy Demaret."

I could not have said it better myself. Jimmy Demaret's most lasting contribution to golf was creating the Legends of Golf Tour. It eventually transformed into the Senior Tour.

llllllllllllllllllll

As the mid-'80s approached, my name was appearing on the marquees of more and more places around the Vegas area. Stints at Del Webb's High Sierra in Stateline to Debbie Keller's Las Margaritas were squeezed in between my regular engagements at the Dunes. I remember Elaine Herbst once said, "Don Cherry is to Las Vegas what Don Ho is to Hawaii. You can't pull into town any time of the year without seeing above some hotel or pavilion, the name 'Don Cherry' in lights." I wish that were true, but it was nice to hear.

Here are just a few of the many reviews of my act that could be found around town:

> *With his easy style, peppered with anecdotes, crinkly smile all over his tanned face, Cherry purrs....He jokes at the beginning that his first tune is 'Purple Rain,' and when his crowd whacks away at handclapping, Cherry squints his eyes at them and drawls, 'Don't hold up the show with applause.' He starts out with 'The Gambler,' and as the response dies out, he keeps on with self-ribbing; 'That's the best number—it's all down hill from here.'*
>
> *—Bill Willard*

Listen for Don Cherry's new recording, "Free to Be," due to break nationally this week on the country music charts. A local resident in Vegas, Cherry's peers enjoy him as much as his fans.

—*"Showbiz Daily,"* Vegas Sun

I get a kick out of the recent engagement singer Cherry did at Debbie Keller's. That place looked like an auto show for Cadillacs and Mercedes. I even saw three Rolls-Royces parked there as I walked in. The fact that Cherry has been a top-flight golfer doesn't detract from his entertainment drawing power either. The man's superb vocalizing has long been a favorite, and his off-beat nightclub patter is something you've got to see. Don jokes about getting married to two beauty queens: "Don't go after the winner . . . your best bet is Miss Congeniality."

—*Jim Parker*

Fourth Marriage

FAST BECOMING A MAINSTAY IN LAS VEGAS didn't stop me from still traveling. Doug Sanders, Bob Goalby, and I were paired together in a tournament in Greensboro. After 13 holes, Doug hit the pin twice on 2nd shots at par-4s, and I had hit it three times, once on a par-3 and twice with my 2nd shot on par-4s. Goalby had hit the pin once on his 2nd shot at a par-5, then hit the pin for a second time on 14. As Doug and I stood there, Bob turned to us and said, "We've got to quit shooting at these pins!"

That same week Doug Sanders got married to a beautiful young girl named Joni and both came to my show after the wedding. I asked them what song I could dedicate to them, and they requested "When I Fall in Love," a perfect song for the occasion and one of their favorites. I never see Doug now that he doesn't sing that first line to me. I think it's become *our* love song! Sometimes I think I should have sung "The Gambler" for the newlyweds.

Damn! Can you believe it? The year was now 1986 and I was now eligible for Social Security—I was a certified senior citizen. Double damn! I didn't feel 62. Most men's midlife crisis happens a bit earlier. Well, my crisis just took a little longer to find me in the name of Rebecca Louise Koontz.

A very young and pretty cocktail waitress in the lounge at the Dunes Hotel in Las Vegas, she was 28, and I was 62. Thirty-four years is a lot to overcome. We were with each other for about a year before anything was ever mentioned about marriage. She enlightened me one day that if we didn't have a commitment to each other, she wanted to end the relationship. That's what we did. She started seeing other people, and my ego started to show. That's when I pleaded with Rebecca to marry me, which turned out to be a mistake for the both of us.

My close friend Vito Farinola (Vito to me, Vic Damone to you) was happy to act as my best man at our wedding. There's an observation I would like to make at this point: no one else ever had two of the most famous Italian singers for their best man (Dean Martin was my last one). Vic was married to actress and singer Diahann Carroll then. She was at our wedding, too. After the ceremony, Vic and Diahann took us to their dressing room at the Golden Nugget hotel for a little wedding reception. The contract with FM-100 for those songs I sang and Vic produced had expired just then. The ownership and songs reverted back to Vic, who in turn gave me all the songs and rights to them as a wedding present. Those songs all comprise an album today titled *Don Cherry Again*. I will always love and respect Vito for all he has done and been to me.

The arguing and bitterness between Becky and me became a horrendous mistake following our nuptials. About 30 percent of Rebecca's life consisted of drinking. Remember, I didn't drink alcohol at all. That would have been more than enough to split us up. Then, she wanted to have a child, and I didn't, so we ended it. I wish Becky nothing but the best always.

⋙⋙⋙⋙⋙⋙⋙

My new contract with the Desert Inn in Las Vegas called for me to perform for many weeks throughout the year, and for years to come. I was singing one night in the lounge when Milton Berle came in to listen.

Milton was not only credited with writing the hit song "Near You," but wrote over four hundred others. His tune, "Leave the Dishes in the Sink" was a million seller—actually it was the flip side, "Cocktails for Two" by Spike Jones, that sold a million, but Milton went along for the ride. Truthfully, Berle was very talented at many things concerning (here comes my favorite word again) showbiz.

After staying for the whole show, Milton approached me. "Don, I have heard from others how good a singer you are, and I heard for myself. They were right, I am very impressed. Is it okay if I ask a question of you?"

Very curious as to what his question was I immediately answered, "Yes."

"Two friends—Steve and Buddy—and myself, just wrote a new song called 'Happy Hanukkah.' It is like the songs most people sing for Christmas, except with an emphasis on the Jewish celebration. When we come to Texas, we would love to come and play it for you if that is okay," asked Milton.

Sure enough, I heard the song and thought it was very beautiful. I recorded it in the studio and gave it to him. Milton sent me a letter of appreciation, saying, "I happily received your rendition of 'Happy Hanukkah.' It's really wonderful! You did a great job. You recorded it exactly as I thought you would—simple, plaintive, and beautiful." He said he took the song to every synagogue in L.A., and the response was unbelievable. He jokingly added, "Who would know more about singing 'Happy Hanukkah' than a baldheaded gentile from Texas?"

One minute I was singing a serious religious holiday song, the next minute I was on TV, singing the words, "And [with my tongue out] phullllgh, you were gone." The indecorous transition was a-beholdin' for my appearance on the down-home country TV show *Hee Haw*. I had just finished recording a number of songs for an album financed by Ann and Jimmy Lynn. The Lynns were close friends of *Hee Haw*'s founder, and suggested that I would be perfect for the show. I don't know about being perfect—what were they trying to tell me?—but I was glad to be included, clowning around and singing on one of the country's most popular and longest-running series ever.

On a level much higher than the songs I sang on *Hee Haw*, my good friend Willie Nelson was gracious to get together with me and record the beautiful album *Augusta*. The title song tells a striking story about one of the great golf tournaments of all time: The Masters. Our song has been played countless times during the events, and we have received so many wonderful compliments from golfers all over the world.

Darrell Royal of the University of Texas—one of the best football coaches in history—was in the studio when Willie and I recorded "Augusta." He listened to us go over the song a few times, and then offered a suggestion of his own. "I think it would be more dramatic if Willie spoke the words about the golfers," he proposed. I looked at him sort of funny, but when we finished and played it back, he was right. It turned out to be a much better recording. Many say that our duet brings them closer to their dreams and feelings of one day seeing Augusta in person. That's a great feeling.

||||||||||||||||||||

I continued making Las Vegas my home, and loved the many folks who came into town that wanted to play golf. It gave me a chance to play with so many people, from celebrities to doctors.

Sammy Davis Jr., Mel Torme, and I began a fun game of golf at the Tropicana. Suddenly on the 2nd hole, something overcame Sammy. He stopped everything and looked for a place to sit down. Feeling his chest, Sammy exclaimed, "I think I'm having a heart attack!" Mel, not wanting it to ruin his whole day, looked at me and said, "Leave him. We'll play four or five holes and come back for him."

Five-time world middle-weight champion Sugar Ray Robinson, who previously won the world welterweight championship, would occasionally drop in to see one of my shows at the Sahara. We got to know each other a bit before I found out that he loved to play the drums. Finally, one evening I introduced Sugar Ray to the audience and asked him if he would like to come up and sit in. A smile as huge as if he'd won a prize fight formed on his face. I was a bit amazed that he was such a good drummer with hands that were used for boxing. When my second show began an hour later, there was Sugar Ray sitting on stage, ready to go again. I think by the time we got finished with the third show of the evening, he had one of the best times of his life. So did I.

||||||||||||||||||||

I have written so much about Tommy Bolt and how I first met him in 1938 when I first caddied for him at age 14. Now it was 50 years later, and I was singing in the lounge of the Sahara Tahoe Hotel. The Senior Open was in town at the Edgewood Country Club, and Tommy was there along with the whole gang, Arnie, Gay, Miller, etc.

We both agreed that it would not only be so much fun, but that we would set some kind of record if I would caddie for him again. So, 50 years later, I donned the official caddies' poncho with BOLT printed across the front. Not being as shy as I once was 50 years earlier, I took out my thick marking pen and inscribed CHERRY above his name. Now remember, he was known as Terrible Tempered Tommy Bolt, but there were many times in my golfing career that I was compared to Tommy. I even said that my actions often made him look like Little Red Riding Hood.

We laughed and joked a lot, and yes, I walked every step of the way for five days carrying Tommy's clubs on my back. I told him he hadn't lost a thing since I first caddied for him as we finally made our way down the course on the last day. With the cameras on us, Dave Marr, who was announcing for ABC at the time, made this observation on the air: "This may be the only time in golf history that the caddie threw more clubs than the player."

⁙⁙⁙⁙⁙⁙⁙⁙⁙⁙⁙⁙

The 1990s were ushered in when I received my January issue of *The Senior Golfer* in the mail. To my surprise, the cover had the words "Don Cherry: Swinging and Singing." Inside was a feature article called "Don Cherry of the Golden Voice and the Great Golf Swing Still Batters Par as a Full-Time Entertainer," written by none other than Tommy Bolt. A picture displaying both our golf bags hanging from the back of a golf cart had these words beneath: "Two old buddies set out for a round." Tommy said a lot of nice things about me, but I was at a loss for words when I read his ending. Speaking about me, Tommy wrote, "After a round with Don recently, he said, 'I thank the Lord for a strange kind of life.' He didn't even say he was thankful that our bets came out even. Probably wasn't. He's used to being a winner." And I am a winner for knowing Tommy.

Francine Bond Smith

‖‖‖

NOT TOO FAR AWAY FROM THE BRIGHT LIGHTS OF LAS VEGAS lies this little town of Laughlin, Nevada. It actually reminds me a bit of Vegas in the early days. I don't even know if most folks living more than a couple states away know of its existence, but for gamblers from Southern California, Arizona, and Nevada, it lies in the corner where the three states meet, divided by the great Colorado River. You get more of a feeling of the Wild West in Laughlin, even though it's full of casinos and showrooms that can rival many in Las Vegas. In 1990, after playing a week at the Las Vegas Hilton, I began my hour and a half trek to perform at Sam's Town Gold River in Laughlin. Their publicity department went all out to advertise the fact that I was appearing there, and it seemed to work. The house was packed every night. I knew I'd be back again. Before leaving, I was asked to preside as master of ceremonies over the Golden Goodies Talent Contest, held annually in Laughlin.

From there I traveled farther south—at lot farther—to Rio de Janeiro in Brazil. At the palatial Copacabana Palace, I sang to American tourists as well as the local people, many of whom only spoke Portuguese. It amazed me how warmly they accepted me. I was always told that music is the universal language, and their reception surely proved it.

Singing to new crowds became more and more fun. I was able to try new songs out to see how well they were received. The audience wouldn't let me get away without hearing all the familiar songs they grew up with. Many people, to this day, tell me how they made out with their first boyfriends or girlfriends listening to "Band of Gold" on the radio. I wonder if the necking stopped when the Mr. Clean jingle came on?

Back in Las Vegas, I hosted the 1992 Don Cherry Invitational and began a long relationship with the Desert Inn to headline in their Starlight Lounge.

Crooning into the wee small hours, it wasn't until after 1:30 in the morning when I would head home. Always wanting to get a lot of exercise and not sit idle, I walked and ran a lot. My hours were so crazy, and how I felt each day determined when and how long I ran. It was in the early part of September and the weather was hot in Vegas (when isn't it?). I tried to get out early, but no two days were ever the same. As I jogged along the way, I got to see different people and things at different times. Along my route one morning, I ran past a lady walking her dog. Nodding my head and saying, "Hello," we barely exchanged pleasantries before I was off again.

I knew who she was, and I also knew that her husband had passed away very suddenly about seven months earlier. It seemed as if we knew when each other would be running or walking, because we kept on running into each other. Finally after the fourth or fifth time, one of us (I've forgotten which one) stated, "We've got to stop—" and the other finished with, "—meeting like this." Someone must have been looking out for us, because at that time we both needed someone in our lives.

Francine is a beautiful lady in more ways than one. She appeared in 28 Broadway shows, and is a wonderful singer and the best dancer—from the Texas two-step to ballet—in the world. She starred with such people as Barbra Streisand, Walter Matthau, George Gobel, and many others. Her stage name is Francine Bond. Now she is Francine Bond Smith Cherry. Let me tell you how I trapped her...

About our fifth meeting, I asked her if she would come to the Desert Inn to hear me sing. She told me that she had to go to New York, but as soon as she returned she'd be happy to come. I must say, and I think she would agree, Francine had no idea about how I sang. The day after she returned from New York, I picked her up and took her to the Desert

Inn. She sat in the audience as I did my show, and it wasn't hard to tell how much she liked it. When I was through, I quickly went around to her table. Her first words were, "I love your voice."

With a little disappointment, I replied, "How about me?"

That had all been taken care of. You see, in that show, I sang a song written and recorded by a wonderful singer and writer named Melissa Manchester called "Come in from the Rain." The more time we spent together, the more we came to realize how much that song fit the both of us. The words of the song told a story:

Well, hello there, dear old friend of mine.
You've been searching for yourself for such a long, long time.
There is so much to say, no need to explain.
I just want to be the one to keep you from the rain.

That first year just flew by. We went to so many places and had so much fun together. The following summer we traveled to Italy and had a wonderful time. Francine and I were married on October 2, 1993. It was the most beautiful wedding I have ever seen, much less participated in.

David Hinck, a Lutheran minister and Joy's husband at the time, performed the ceremony. Norman Alden was my best man. My biggest fan outside of Francine, a young lady, aged 10, named Beth Bridgeman, was Francine's flower girl. My two sons, Sean and Stephen, walked Francine down the aisle and gave her away to me. As the piano played, I stood at the front of the church and proudly sang her down the aisle. What better song than "Come In from the Rain."

As it came time, the Reverend looked at my best man and asked if he had the symbols of our commitment. Norman delivered one of the classic lines in true showbiz fashion. Reaching into his pocket, and before he produced the rings, Norman asked, "Will this be cash or charge?"

The people sitting in the front heard what he had said, and it created a bit of a stir. David, who also has a sense of humor, said aloud, "I don't think some of the people in the back heard that."

Norman turned around to face the people seated in the back, and in a very loud voice repeated, "Will this be cash or charge?" It had to be one of the biggest laughs he ever received.

Once it became official, "Come In from the Rain" was played as we were introduced to our friends and relatives as Mr. and Mrs. Cherry. We are dry now and will be for the rest of our lives. Since that day, I have recorded another song made famous by Perry Como, "And I Love You So."

Up until this point in my life, my driver's license had always stated Wichita Falls as my address. I guess I never felt that anyplace I had lived up to now was actually home to me. The year I met Francine, Las Vegas became the change of residence I finally blessed into calling "home."

A Burt and a 'Bert

IN 1993 I MET A MAN ON THE GOLF COURSE who, to this day, has one of the largest fan club bases in the world. Women would throw their room keys and panties on stage. If they could manage somehow to get themselves on stage to touch him, they tried. He has a strange name, but that helps a lot. All you have to say is "Engelbert," and you know I'm talking about Engelbert Humperdinck.

Back in '66 I had recorded "There Goes My Everything," written by Dallas Frazier, a wonderful songwriter and artist himself. Fred Foster thought so highly of the song's potential that the album it appeared on was titled the same. Shortly after, Jack Greene had a hit with it, too, but it wasn't until the following year when Engelbert put his own signature on it that it got the notoriety that it deserved. Since that time, everyone from Faron Young to Anne Murray and Charlie Pride to Elvis Presley has recorded it, but none is remembered better than Enge's.

Francine and I were invited to one of Engelbert's shows when he came into town one Saturday evening. Given special treatment, we were seated right away and introduced by Enge to the audience who filled the showroom. In attendance was a fellow who was handling Burt Reynolds' and Engelbert's careers at the time, Alan Margulies. I told him that I was a great fan of Burt Reynolds and that "being a big moviegoer, Burt starred in my very favorite movie." Movies have impressed me my entire life. I have seen *Deliverance* a bunch of times, and will see it again. Burt's performance was one of the best I have ever seen.

When Margulies had asked if I had recorded any new songs recently, I told him that I had just cut an album called *A Tribute to Perry Como.* He looked at me as if I said some magic words. "Perry Como is Burt's favorite singer of all time!" he exclaimed.

I remembered that I had a couple copies of the new CD in the car out in the parking lot. After the show, I went outside and grabbed them to give to Alan. He seemed very pleased and told me that he would give one to Reynolds. He also mentioned that Burt was putting together a show and, when he came to Las Vegas with it, he would love us to come.

Sure enough, the time came and Burt opened his show at the Orleans Hotel in town. His show started off wonderfully when, about a half hour into what he was doing, Burt paused, started humming Perry Como's song "It's Impossible," and told the people about my being in the audience. I'm not one to stand up and take a bow, but this time it felt so good. I stood up and waved to everybody.

ııııııııııııııııı

It came time to go to Austin and record an album of love songs. This time, though, the songs were written for duet voices, and I had the best partner one could hope for—Willie Nelson. Most people who attempt to sing love song duets usually go at it as man and woman. I wasn't sure how this was going to be done, but before I finished the first song, "What a Wonderful World," I knew it was going to be a hit.

Studio time for musicians can be expensive, so it was decided that only a simple rhythm track would be used to keep costs down. In this day and age, a lot can be added at a later time. Paying only for the studio time, we wrote a check for a whopping $335 and walked out the door with master tapes!

Right away I sent the tapes over to my close friend, Fred Foster, to listen to. The next thing I knew, he got every major musician I worked with—Boots Randolph, Charlie McCoy, etc.—at Monument to fill in the tracks with music. I could hardly wait to hear the final mix. It turned out so damn good that I had to call Willie right away and tell him.

I was left speechless when I later learned that all the musicians who added their musical talents to the tracks would not accept any payment for their time. It was that kind of close-knit family of friends that Fred Foster had made among us. Thank you again, guys.

On April 13, 1994, a birthday celebration was given in Phil Harris' honor. Born in 1904, his 90th year was a big one to celebrate. Held at the Thunderbird Country Club, the committee in charge of the event went all out to make it a special and momentous occasion. Jim Vickers was appointed master of ceremonies, and all of Phil's closest friends were invited to attend or, as in my case, perform. Reminiscent of a Friar's Club Roast, the jabs and barbs were poked (in fun) by the lineup of invited speakers. I, along with Billy Barty, Jay Bedsworth, Joey Bishop, Pete Fountain, Dolores Hope (Bob's wife), The Three Meatballs, Buddy Rogers, and Enzo Stuarti all ribbed, kidded, and sang, but nobody was more entertaining and funny than Phil himself.

The next year, after his 91st birthday, Phil sang his last song and told his last tale. Francine and I were on the road heading north to Reno for an upcoming singing engagement of mine. Turning on the radio, I heard the announcement that Phil Harris had passed away. The news hit me like a ton of bricks. The thought that I couldn't make it back in time for the funeral was difficult. I mourned the fact that I would no longer see my wonderful comrade in this life again.

Now, whenever I hear the song "Watermelon Wine," I'll always remember the day I first discovered that tune. Phil had heard me sing on stage in Brownsville. The lyrics were about children, old dogs, and watermelon wine. I thought the song was perfect for him, and said he should sing it in his act. From that point on, with Phil's own special style, his audiences stood up and applauded every time. I am also blessed to be left with this poem that Phil wrote:

How beautiful it is to be alive.
To see, to hear, to have the longing to survive.
Now a dog at 12, he's in the twilight zone
Still content with one friend and a bone.
While we who could if we would give thanks to
Him who calls the shots, the man.
And just to say you're with him or simply say you're not
But when the roll is called up yonder and he's ready

To spring the trap,
There ain't gonna be nobody around but you that's
gonna take that rap.
And when he's got his finger on the trigger I'm gonna
lay you eight to five
that you're gonna look up at
him and say . . .
How beautiful it is just to be alive.

—Phil Harris

Double punched—mourning over Phil's passing was only the half of it. More bad news came. Two days later, on August 13, I learned that Mickey Mantle had also passed away. Two of my five best friends were both taken within a week. There are no words to describe the empty feeling that formed in the pit of my stomach.

Nothing could hold me back the following year from attending the Mickey Mantle Charity Golf Classic held in Oklahoma on the one-year anniversary of his death. I fought the tears when the tournament director, Marshall Smith, led me and five other close friends of Mickey's (Tom Tresh, Stan Musial, Hank Bauer, Moose Skowron, and Yogi Berra), out to the 14th hole at Shangri-La's Golf Course. There, erected for all to see, is a memorial plaque dedicated to the memory of Mickey Mantle.

While thinking about how my best friends were all traveling on and writing these words, I received calls from two people in the past three days—Vic Damone and Jimmy Dean. What timing! Just like the golfer I am—always thinking of how everyone else places on the scorecard—I'm gonna put them both down as tied for 7th place.

I will say, though, that there really isn't any special order to my friends. I truly cherry-sh my friends more than anything in the world. Each one is number one to me!

The Great Hunt

THERE IS SOMETHING THAT I AM HOOKED ON and will be for the rest of my life: hunting and retrieving golf balls from the water. You may think this is a little overstated, but it's a fact. There has never been or never will be anyone close to me with this gift. I guess it all started when I was 10 years old. My brother Paul caddied for a wonderful golfer and man by the name of Rufus King. In later years, Rufus won the National Amateur Championship. He was beaten by one of my closest friends, Charlie Coe, my playing partner in the Americas Cup and the Walker Cup.

I would walk with my brother when he caddied for Rufus, especially in tournaments. This time, it was in the Wichita Falls Invitational. Paul would walk up to the green to help Rufus read which way the putt would break, and also determine the speed of the green. Paul would hand me the golf bag and ask me to take it to the next tee. I loved it.

At the Wichita Falls Country Club, on the 15th par-5 hole, there is a very wide creek about 300 yards from the tee. It's not very deep, but has a strong flow. Rufus hit a bad shot, and his brand new Spaulding T tournament golf ball went straight into the flowing stream. Paul told me that if I could retrieve that new ball, he was sure Rufus would give me a tip, "most likely a quarter."

Back in 1934, a quarter to a 10-year-old meant a lot. Now came the excitement. Because the water was clear and shallow, I spotted it immediately. Wading into the water to recover it, I wasn't aware of how

231

fast the stream flowed. Every time I reached for the ball, the flow would take it away from me. I must have followed that ball for 50 yards down that stream. Instead of trying to grab it with one hand, I decided to dive into the water and use both hands. This was one of the smartest and wettest moves I ever made. I took the ball over to Rufus, and as Paul predicted, I received a new shiny quarter and a smile from Mr. King.

Now, who wouldn't want to spend the rest of their life hunting golf balls? I can see in the water better than anyone. I go where no one else will go, because that's where most of the balls are. I don't know how many balls anyone else has found, but it ain't even close to my record.

There are a lot of guys these days who scuba dive and wear masks that provide them with air. To me, that's cheating. I do it all with one homemade ball retriever and my two bare hands. Let them do it the way that I do it, and it won't even be a contest.

Okay, I must name three other guys who are quite good at it. They are all famous golf pros. In the order of their golf ball–hunting ability they are Lee Trevino, George Bayer, and Al Besselink. I, myself, also have a PGA card, but I'm the only pro at retrieving golf balls at the Las Vegas Country Club.

I once played golf with a very famous writer by the name of George Plimpton. He wrote books—*Out of My League, Paper Lion, Open Net*— about every sport that he was allowed to participate in. There are nine lakes on the country club that we played, and as usual, I did a little fishing—being very successful, I might add. Plimpton didn't say a word about it until we finished. Sitting in the grill room, very quietly, so no one else would hear him, he whispered something to me. "I have always had a fetish about hunting golf balls, and did not know a lot of famous people who did that sort of thing," he said, slightly embarrassed.

I gave him a few names of players who liked to hunt, too. He then replied, "With your experience and ability, maybe we should write a book about it."

We never did.

At one time I lived on the 7th hole of the Las Vegas Country Club. I would get up early in the morning before anyone started playing. How does 5:00 AM sound to fish for balls? That's when I'd start out with my retriever and sack to put the balls I collected into. After being very successful one morning, I started my trek back home with my golf ball–filled sack. Noticing there was a lot of mud on my running shoes, I saw a little stream of water by the curb. Thinking it would be a good place to clean off my shoes was a bad decision. As I stepped into the curb, I slipped and fell backwards. My first thought was not to let the bag of balls hit the cement. The bag would break and the golf balls would be all over the street. Then came another bad decision—as I came down, my left leg wound up under the upper part of my right leg. As a result of my fall, I ruptured the quadricep muscle in my left leg. I could barely move. My wife took me to the hospital immediately. I don't recall how many stitches it took to close the incision, but I still have the scar. It measures over 7".

Two weeks after that happened, I was supposed to play in a golf tournament in Houston. The doctor had taken the first cast off and put a lighter one on my leg. I then flew to Houston one day before the tournament and played on one and a half legs. The main reason I went was because I was guaranteed $1,000 for playing. I figured it would help pay part of the doctor bill.

P.S. I still hunt balls.

Quite an Honor

|||||||||||||||||||||||||||||||||||||||||||||||||||||||||||||||||||||||||||||||||||||||||||||||||||||||||||||||||||||||||||||||||||||||||||||||||||||||||||||||||||

MANY PEOPLE HAVE SPECULATED on what could have been achieved if I had simply given up one career and concentrated on the other. I've given a lot of thought to this question, but I have never been a fan of hypothetical questions. Which career would I have concentrated on more?

I'll do it one time, but I hope I don't ever have to do it again. My answer is singing!

My reason: there are so many beautiful songs that I get to sing, written by all the greatest songwriters of all time. The words and the music had such an influence on my life and especially my mind.

Golf: I could have done much better if I had possessed a better attitude on the course. I could hit the ball long and straight, but I never seemed to be satisfied. I guess that's the nature of the game—competing, trying to be better, and always having yourself to blame if you weren't. I was my own worst enemy, throwing clubs and kicking lots of grass and dirt. I eventually stopped my tantrums as time went on, playing in major tournaments.

Singing: I always thought I was a good singer. Be that as it may, all singers needed help. That help was given to us by all the radio stations and the disc jockeys who played our songs. In my case, there was one man who did more for my career than any other—Paul Berlin. For 52 years, he has played my music. He is one of the first disc jockeys who played good music, and is recognized as an inductee in the Texas Radio

Hall of Fame and the Rock and Roll Hall of Fame in Cleveland, Ohio. I was honored to sing with over five hundred guests in attendance. The occasion was to celebrate Paul Berlin's 50 years in broadcasting. Paul, my dear friend. I will always be grateful.

A letter arrived in my mailbox on the last day of spring in 1995. It was addressed from the Texas Golf Hall of Fame. They were preparing for their next Gathering of Eagles event, and apparently Dan Jenkins had nominated me, along with former President George Bush, to be inducted into the Texas Hall of Fame.

What was a wonderful honor to have been selected, but to be perfectly honest, I never realized the full magnitude of what was being bestowed upon me. Just a few years earlier I had been sent a copy of a book titled *Texas Golf Legends* by Kurt Sampson. I always find it humbling to find my name included alongside others that I consider legends myself. In my own mind, I try not to take anything too seriously, which probably helps me from developing much of an ego (remember, I'm quite shy).

In August, I received another letter that was a press release from the Texas Golf Hall of Fame. It read:

> *The Texas Golf Hall of Fame at The Woodlands has tapped author Dan Jenkins and Houston radio personality Paul Berlin to present the 1995 inductees, former President Bush and former Walker Cup Team member Don Cherry at A Gathering of Eagles on November 13, 1995.*
>
> *Jenkins, who has authored several bestselling sports novels, including* Semi-Tough *and* Life Its Ownself *will present Houston resident George Bush. Jenkins states without reservation that he is Bush's "favorite author" and that he plans to leave his work on a long-awaited novel titled* Rude Behavior *just to honor Bush.*
>
> *Paul Berlin, the well-known voice of Houston's KQUE Radio, will present Don Cherry. The owner of a record store and two Houston nightclubs has been a friend of singer Cherry's about as long as he has been a top-rated radio personality. Berlin is the first recipient of the American*

Woman in Radio & TV Award and was a Major Market
Personality of the Year Marconi Award nominee.
A Gathering of Eagles includes the Hall of Fame Pro-
Am, a cocktail reception, and banquet, all to be staged on
November 13.

Before I knew it, the day had arrived. At 6:30 PM I walked into the ballroom of the Woodlands Country Club with Francine and my two sons, Sean and Stephen, by my side. Stephen had flown in earlier and we played a round of golf the day before. One of the first things that I noticed were all the Secret Service men who were walking around. They blended in with the huge number of people already there. You could spot them by the little earpieces running up from their coats.

Folks ran over and started greeting me all at once. I can't remember who was first or whom I said "Hello" to. I do, however, remember being asked for autographs and having my picture taken before we were shown to our table. Dinner came, and everyone else found where they were sitting. That gave me a chance to look around the huge room. I spotted so many friends whom I had known or played golf with over the years. Then I glanced across the floor from where we were seated and saw President Bush wave and flash his big smile my direction. It then hit me how important this evening was.

Between golfing and singing, I had met many presidents before, including Mr. Bush. But for some reason, a thought came over me while I sat there waving back to the President of the United States. Here I was, a poor kid from a small dusty Texas town whose only desire was to sing and play golf. I never took a singing or golf lesson in my life. I never went on to college, and I carried a terrible temper for the better part of my being. Yet, here I was, Don Cherry from Wichita Falls, preparing to cut into a filet mignon, surrounded by so many important people from all walks of life, all waiting to honor both the 41st president of the United States . . . and me.

Jim Nantz, the great CBS Sports announcer, emceed the evening. His comments were very much on the mark, and he had the audience (whoops, there's that showbiz again, I meant to say "guests") all revved up when he brought Paul Berlin to the stage. Paul had no trouble keeping the momentum going with his quick wit and funny anecdotes about me. I didn't have anything written down or prepared when it was my turn. Paul introduced me and I just spoke from my heart. I thanked the people there and those who followed and supported me throughout the years. After throwing in a couple of golfing jokes, I thanked the good Lord above for giving me golf and the talent to play it. Still looking for the words to convey what I felt, I thought of the words to "Augusta," and did what came to mind.

I began to sing.

Without a piano or musician to accompany me. The whispers of voices and tinkling of wine glasses stopped. Everyone felt the importance of those lyrics echoing throughout the silent, unmuttered room. After President George Bush received his own induction, we stood and hugged for pictures. The knowledge I had sung before the President of the United States hadn't even registered in my mind until it was all over. What an honor that evening was.

The following year I attended the Gathering of Eagles, where Paul Berlin was once again invited to serve as the master of ceremonies. Jack Valenti, president of the Motion Picture Association of America handed the stage over to both Harold Weisenthal and me. We were to introduce the newest inductee into the Texas Golf Hall of Fame—Tommy Bolt. When Tommy got a chance to thank everyone, he was quoted as saying, "Don't be fooled by Don Cherry's rough exterior. He's just as ugly on the inside."

IIIIIIIIIIIIIIIIIIIII

Sam Snead's Grand Champions Tournament at Panther Woods in Fort Pierce is just one of the many places I continued to play the game that honored me. Still singing my heart out, I was booked once again at the Gold River in Laughlin, Nevada. This was now 1998, and like always, they had my upcoming appearance spread all over the billboards and magazines in the area. Francine and I took the car since it was less than two hours from Vegas. I pulled into the parking structure and began taking all our luggage out of the trunk. Not realizing we had overpacked, I didn't have enough arms to carry everything, so I just pushed one of the bags under the car, not telling Francine.

We checked in and rode the elevator up to our room, where I dropped the bags on the floor and proceeded to go back down to get the bag I left. Francine asked where I was going, and I muttered something about being right back, not wanting to tell her that I couldn't manage all the bags at once.

Making my way down the elevator and through the lobby to where the car was parked, I reached under the back end and couldn't feel anything. Reaching farther, I had to get down on all fours. I raised my head up to look at the license plate number, making sure this was the right car. Then it sunk in: someone had taken our luggage bag. Making my way back to the room, I didn't say a thing. It couldn't have been her purse—nah, I remembered it was bigger than that. Maybe she wouldn't notice. Notice she did, it was her toiletry bag, filled with her makeup and brushes. That wasn't a good weekend for me. People say I'm too trustworthy. I came from a time when people knew their neighbors and trusted each other. It was a generation of hard times and camaraderie. The effects of the Depression and the war brought folks closer, as we looked out for each other—something that is sorely lost today, along with Francine's bag.

||||||||||||||||||

Peggy Lee had been battling her own health problems for a few years, but kept the nature of her illness away from the public. Francine and I had attended one of her final concerts given at the Hollywood Bowl in Southern California. Then, in 1998, a stroke left her unable to sing with that beautiful voice of hers. Over the years, we would talk to each other on the phone almost every month, swapping new stories and reminiscing the old ones. Ten days after my 78th birthday in 2002, Peggy suffered heart failure.

> *Never are we more aware of the importance of family and friends than at a time like this. Your kind thoughts and prayers have been a great source of comfort to us. Thank you so much for honoring our beloved Peggy's life.*
> *—The family of Miss Peggy Lee*
> *Nicki, David, Holly, Michael,*
> *Teagan, Caleb, and Carter*

|||||||||||||||||||||

The new millennium was right around the corner. For the last three years, since the country celebrated its 200th birthday, patriotic songs were becoming more prevalent. Out of about 16 or 17 songs, my lineup on stage usually included "The Wind Beneath My Wings," "Without a Song," "Country Roads," "Green Green Grass of Home," and of course "Band of Gold." But now, in the state of Texas, I added "Red and Rio" and "(Waltz Across) Beautiful Texas" to the show's set. The same with other states I performed. We took the Don Cherry Show to Florida that February and played places such as Fort Pierce, the Palladium Theater in St. Petersburg, and the 7,000-seat amphitheater at Rock Crusher Canyon in Crystal River. It was wonderful to see so much patriotic spirit in the folks who came out.

Back in Vegas, most of the hotels were planning their New Year's Eve 2000 extravaganzas well in advance. Being a resident of the fastest-growing city in America, I would run into just about every entertainer who came into town to perform. Jerry Lewis was no exception. He had asked me a couple of times if I would drop by to sing on one of his annual telethons against muscular dystrophy. His event was broadcasted from town that year, and it was impossible to say "no." I sang on the air, in the early hours of the morning, to do what I could to help raise money in a fight against the dreaded disease.

I sent the new tribute-to-Perry-Como CD I had just finished, along with a note, to President Bush. In the note, I kidded him that he could sing harmony anytime he wanted. The president wrote back, "Dear Don, 'Without a Song' is wonderful! You're doing just fine yourself, my friend; so if it's okay with you, I'll skip those singing lessons." Little did I know that soon our letters would be in acknowledgment of another nature.

|||||||||||||||||||||

"The United States Golf Association cordially invites you to a reception and dinner Thursday, August 9, 2001, at The Cloister in Sea Island, Georgia." That's how the invitation went out to us former Walker Cup players. Twenty-five past U.S. team players and 11 past Great Britain/Ireland team players made it for the four-day celebration and event. Tee times began at 7:30 AM on Thursday, while the spouses' tour left two hours later, to give the wives a break and a tour of Jekyll Island. The reception and dinner began at 6:30 and ran until the wee small hours. We had a ball, and with little sleep, it wasn't hard to get up for tee time again on Friday morning.

In the afternoon we had a flag raising ceremony on the 18th green of the Ocean Forest Golf Course, with a singing party in the clubhouse that evening. The final two days were set aside for the new players in the 2001 biennial Walker Cup match. What a blast everyone had. As the four-day gathering ended, we got in our cars and boarded airplanes to head home. Less than 30 days later, our fond memories were soon clouded with pain. Airplanes, just like the ones many of us boarded for home, would be used as weapons of hate.

9/11

I HAVE WRITTEN A LOT ABOUT MANY OF THE PEOPLE whom I have met and been involved with. Here is one name that I can't wait to share with you: Stephen Patrick Cherry. He was born September 25, 1959, at the Mount Sinai Hospital in New York City. He left us on September 11, 2001. Stephen was working for Cantor Fitzgerald in a towering high-rise that was struck by an airplane. It left new meaning for the numbers 9-1-1.

He was my son... and he still is. I may be prejudiced, but I never met anyone quite like Stephen.

As a baby, Stephen would cry a lot, especially at night. As a result, I would pick him up and carry him. He would stop almost immediately, but as soon as I put him down, he would start again. Not having any other way to silence his tears, I would carry and rock him three and four hours at a time until he could fall asleep. After many months (nine or ten if I recall properly) we discovered that he had a double hernia. After it was taken care of, Stephen never cried again. This may sound a little strange, but I think this is one of the reasons we became so close for life. Even though his nightlong crying ended, I still loved carrying him as much as I could.

In Wichita Falls, my mother watched over Sean and Stephen quite often. Even though, as a seamstress, she would sew all day long to make a living, her main mission in life was taking care of those two boys. Every day the three of them had a ritual. They would go to the store and buy Poly-pop, a drink similar to Kool-Aid. Strawberry was the flavor that all three loved. Mom would take a quart-sized fruit jar, dump in the Poly-pop powder, add water, and put it in the icebox until it got cold. Then, a short time later, she would take the jar out, put three straws in it, and all three would drink it at the same time.

While the boys were staying with her one summer, Mom fell ill. She was told that she needed to have her gall bladder removed. During surgery, complications occurred and her kidneys shut down. Mom survived for nine days after that happened.

The doctor wouldn't allow me to take Sean and Stephen up to see her on the third floor of the hospital. The boys knew that their grandma was very sick and wanted to see her. So I would put them into the car, drive over to the hospital, and park in front of the building. There, I'd put the boys up on the top of the car's roof and tell them that she was waving to them from the window I had picked out. Naturally, they would wave back. The doctor took notice as to what was going on with us. When the eighth day came, and Mom's condition worsened, the doctor broke the rules, giving me permission to take the boys up to visit her.

As you know, people in the condition that Mother was in often have breathing tubes in their noses to help them breathe and stay alive. As we walked in, Sean followed Stephen, who was sucking his thumb. Innocently, Stephen walked up to her side of the bed. He took one look at Mother and removed the thumb from his mouth. Seeing the breathing tubes in her nose, Stephen informed her, "Gand-ma, you got the straw in w-w-ong place."

Another memory—a time somewhat earlier, when we were visiting Mom at home—Sean had his own bed to sleep in, and Stephen and I would sleep in a double bed set up in the screened-in porch area. Even though there were a few inches of space between the wall and the bed, I had Stephen on that side so he wouldn't fall out. Within moments we all fell fast asleep.

In the middle of the night I awoke to find Stephen was gone. Stumbling around in the dark, I called out his name, "Stephen!"

A muffled voice came back, "I'm Daddy's baby!"

Seems he fell into the small crack and stayed there until he was rescued. That memory has never left my mind.

Stephen had such a colorful life. I could write a whole book about him. He was a pretty good golfer and, boy, could he sing! Before he had a chance to complete one of his dreams, Stephen went to Nashville with Joe Sherman, a very famous record producer. He cut what they refer to as a country/rock album. Some of the songs on it were titled "I Will If You Will," "One Man Woman," and "More Than Words Can Say." The album was simply but aptly called *Steve Cherry*.

I mentioned Stephen's brother Sean, whom I love and respect with all my heart. Sean graduated in the top 10 percent of his class at Brown University. A master of the Russian language, Sean spent two years in Russia as an interpreter for two American oil companies. He now teaches school and is living a very good life. Sean, I am very proud of you.

There also happens to be another wonderful young lady whom I spent a lot of time with growing up. She is my daughter, Jennifer Joy Cherry, otherwise known as "J.J." Jennifer is such a beautiful, slightly eccentric, very talented woman who is blessed with two great kids of her own, Adam and Alexia.

Arm-in-arm, Sean and Stephen walked Francine Bond Smith down the aisle and gave her away to me on that special day of ours. I recall with a smile, as all four of us attempted to serenade "Band of Gold" to Francine. Sean and Stephen tried to keep their composure, while Jennifer was the only one who could remember all the words. Just remember, little girl, Daddy loves you very much.

The Sunday before the World Trade Center tragedy, my son Stephen and Francine had a long and wonderful conversation on the telephone. How lucky could a father be? Everything seemed so good, but how fragile life can be, changing with the blink of an eye. The moment that plane hit that tower that day, Stephen left behind four very handsome boys of his own—Jeremy, Peter, Brett, and Colton.

As I have stated, I could go on and on about my precious son, but I don't want this to be the main focus of a full and wonderful life. I hope that most of us remember to cherish each day, each hour, and each minute much more than we have before. After that blink of an eye, you'll wish you had said "I love you, son" more often. I try to feel good in knowing that Stephen and Mom are probably sipping their Poly-pop out of a quart fruit jar. You can rest assured they have the straw in the right place.

IIIIIIIIIIIIIIIIIIIII

September 11, 2001: The twin 110-story World Trade Center towers were targets of an attack. Using hijacked passenger-filled U.S. commuter airplanes in flight, terrorists flew the appropriated jets directly into the buildings. Terrorists became murderers hitting the buildings straight on. Dozens died upon impact, hundreds died trying to flee, thousands were injured or missing, thousands more were among those who perished, and millions were adversely affected by its aftermath.

News of what had happened to the skyscrapers in New York hit radio and TV airwaves within moments. Confusion ensued, then chaos and panic set in. No one knew immediately if this had been a terrible accident or if we were being thrust into a war of mammoth proportions. It was war, but of a different kind. A war of symbolism and terror. The symbols were the people killed working in their offices. Innocent, decent people who toiled at their jobs to put food on the table for themselves and for their loved ones.

In Las Vegas, Don and Francine woke to the sound of the phone ringing. It was a little after 6:00 AM when Don picked up the receiver to find his son, Sean, in Florida on the other end.

"Dad, you're not going to believe it, but a plane just hit the building where Stephen's office is located!" Sean exclaimed feverishly.

Francine turned on the television set as Don sat down on the edge of the bed, staring at the images of smoke and destruction. The flickering screen replayed over and over what terror they had captured on tape.

"I had a feeling when I saw that plane hit the first tower that something was wrong, something deep inside me felt unnatural. I knew that Stephen had been working for the large firm of Cantor Fitzgerald, but I had no idea where his office was located in New York," recalled Don.

Stephen's office was located in the southern end of the 104th floor of the north building with a view of the Statue of Liberty.

The first commandeered jet plane hit the tower four-fifths of the way up, at about the 90th floor, sending smoke and debris up to the floors above. People were trapped. Stephen tried the intercom in his office, which was linked to other Cantor Fitzgerald offices all over the country. "Can anybody hear us?" he shouted in desperation. A few moments later a trader in Chicago heard Stephen's plea and said back, "They know you're there!"

Stephen's next instinct was to join the others in making their way to the conference room, huddling together in confusion. Many people on the floors below made it out with their lives. At last count, 2,572 did not escape.

One day before 9/11, Stephen sent an email to his boys. Dated Monday, September 10, 2001, 13:16:53, it read:

> *"You guys really made me so proud yesterday, not only the way you played, but the way you conducted yourselves. Your golfing etiquette is wonderful and it's nice to see you guys not goofing around as much. We can have lots of fun out there, and lots of laughs as well, while remaining gentlemen. Keep it up and we can play all the time. Thank Gramps for teaching you as well. Love, Dad."*

The next day, on 9/11, only 30 minutes prior to what would occur, Stephen called home for the last time. Not a common call for Stephen to make, he just wanted to tell his family how much he loved them. They never got a chance to hear him say those words again.

—Neil T. Daniels (coauthor)

Dear Don,

Barbara and I were so very sorry to hear about Stephen. We, more than most parents, can identify a lot with the hurt in your heart, and the great grief you feel.

Stephen is in heaven now, and we can't bring him back. But someday, Don, I am confident that we will bring those

*responsible for this senseless act of terror to justice. I pray
for that, and I will say a little prayer for your beloved son.
Barbara and I send you and Francine our heartfelt
condolences and our family love.*
  Sincerely,

        George Bush (October 8, 2001)

Sadness and anger filled my soul for the months following September 11. I questioned myself: Could I have prevented anything by being a better father? Why didn't I give my children more time? All the thoughts that could run rampant through my mind, did. The loss of a child is something that should never be experienced by any parent.

I remember when I heard that my friend, Dean Martin, had lost his own son in a plane accident. He was never the same after that. I saw Dean, as the rest of the world did, simply give up on life. I didn't want that to happen to me. That's when music pulled me up. I decided it was time to get in the car and do what I could to make others forget the terror and pain, if only for a short amount of time. Singing always seemed to make me feel a lot better.

The first place I headed for was Clearwater, Florida, to help raise money for a memorial honoring the victims of the 9/11 disaster. It was my tribute to Stephen and the other victims who were involved. The two-day golf event also raised money to help the American Lung Association build their new Healthy Building. From there, it was weeks of driving. I did a lot of shows—many of them for charity. I needed to sing as much possible.

Lately ... Busier Than Ever

ⅢⅢⅢ

RECORDING "THE EYES OF TEXAS" came at the right time for me. This was the third album that I was fortunate to have Willie Nelson share the words with. It was even more important when we donated all the proceeds from the CD sales to a wonderful and deserving cause.

Invited to the Lady Bird Wildlife Center by the former First Lady herself, I was honored to host the 2003 Wildlife Center Pro-Am Golf Tournament. Many members of Lady Bird Johnson's immediate family attended. Showing their sincere gratitude, I was hugged and kissed continuously. Because of her health, the former First Lady was not able to attend. They taped the event and showed it to her later. I was given the Licensing Appreciation Award along with a letter of appreciation. Mrs. Johnson also gave her gratitude to Willie and me for making our new CD available for their environmental cause. That attests to the true heart and generosity of Mr. Willie Nelson.

The year 2003 seemed to mark a change in an upbeat direction. The correspondences with President George Bush Sr. helped bring calm after the brutal loss of my son, Stephen. In the president's handwritten letters, he'd always make mention of how much he enjoyed my music. It got me to thinking more about how good my own life had been despite all the losses.

Dear Don and Francine,
   Barbara and I are in Maine now, far away from Houston.
But The Eyes of Texas CD is here, so we feel like we are at
home—a terrific collection of music and a marvelous tribute
to a great lady. Incidentally, I was at the LBJ School for their
commencement in May, but I did not get to see Lady Bird.
Barbara and I have spoken with her since.
   Warmest regards and thanks again,

George Bush

||||||||||||||||||||||

Links magazine came out with a wonderful cover story in their January issue that surprised even me. Again, I was realizing how full my life had been by reading what others would write. Then, another milestone came when I was asked to be an honored guest of the Walker Cup's 50th Anniversary celebration at the Kittansett Club in Marion, Massachusetts. Seeing and swapping stories with all the guys was a pleasure most of us had missed from our days on the Walker tournaments.

While I serenaded everyone that night at the reception, E. Harvie Ward mentioned to Francine, "I just can't believe he can still sing like that!" Harvey kept telling everyone, "I just wanna be around in 2005 when we'll get to go to Chicago for the next Walker Cup affair!" Sadly, he passed away before his wish came true.

My wife Francine is involved with so many projects of her own, I wonder how she manages to keep so many of my things in control. Not only does she manage the Don Cherry Website, but she prepares materials for interviews and oversees so much of the business end of everything. She's a real go-getter.

Remember how I keep telling you that I didn't play the game? By now, you know that the game I didn't play was the game that goes along with golf and show business. With my attitude, I walked out when I felt like it. I never pushed to get better representation. I never gave up one career to concentrate on the other. I don't play that game, but Francine now helps me keep up.

Through longtime friends Phil and Nancy Bridgeman, Francine worked in helping Neil Daniels put together an article for his *Dean*

Martin Magazine publication. As the deadline came closer, Neil informed me that he wasn't able to run his article in the upcoming edition. Over the course of three months, he informed me once again that his article wasn't going to be ready for another three months. Finally, a half year later, I discovered the reason why. The whole issue from cover to cover was a spotlight on my career. I could not have been more humbled yet thrilled.

In the back of my mind for about the last 12 or 13 years, I began writing down little notes, much like keeping a diary of thoughts. I guess everyone at some point in their life has the thought of writing their memoirs, if only to hand them down to their children. Maybe it's a way to make room for more thoughts, maybe it's just a way to explain why one makes the decisions they do along the way. Whatever the case, I was now doing much more reflecting about life in general. The thought of writing a book was much more real when Neil called me on the phone and asked if it was something I had thought about. That's how dozens of visits, hours of phone calls, zillions of emails and two years later, you're able to hold these words in your hands.

I turned 80 on January 11, 2004. Where do you think I was? Performing on stage—where else? Folks filled the room at the Sands in Houston, when Francine surprised me by having them roll out a huge birthday cake. Then, I was even more surprised when the audience all stood and sang "Happy Birthday" to me. Telegrams from Jack Nicklaus, Arnold Palmer, Willie Nelson, and Sonny King arrived. A few were read to me on stage. It was a great birthday, and Francine took care of everything, as always.

Sonny King has delighted audiences with songs, jokes, and comedy routines since he was 15 years old. He can surely entertain a crowd and he has definitely played a part in the evolution of Las Vegas. Sonny's real name is Louis Antonio Donato Schiavone, and back in those golden days, we would often visit each other's shows. We still do even today.

As kids, Sonny palled around with a young and then-unknown Dean Martin, often sharing rooms and staging "punching matches" to make a few bucks. Sonny would set the bets up, and Dean would take the hits. It was Sonny King that introduced Dean and Jerry Lewis to each other on the corner of Broadway and 54th in New York way back in 1945. At the age of 23, Sonny along with entertainer Jimmy Durante formed a partnership that lasted an incredible 28 years. More recently, members of the Nevada State Senate set forth a resolution commending Sonny for his lifetime contribution in entertainment in the state of Nevada. As the main attraction at the Bootlegger, many entertainers, from the up-and-coming to huge celebrities, drop by unannounced to perform for their peers and responsive audiences. Sonny welcomes them all and has paved the road for many.

ıııııııııııııııııı

During one of my visits with Don, he and his wife Francine took me along with them to the Bootlegger. The ambience of the place was a magical experience. The tables filled with guests and celebrities were crowded together. Sonny King was first to appear on stage. After singing a couple songs and welcoming everyone, he prompted a few people to get up on stage and tell their jokes or sing their songs. The band seemed to know every song thrown at them unprepared.

It wasn't long before Don was picked out of the audience. We had a table up front and off to the side, when Don stood up and walked to the stage. This was the first time since I had begun cowriting our book together, that I fully absorbed the magnitude of what Don Cherry possesses.

It took a while for thunderous applause to subside as Don told the band what key he was going to sing "When I Fall In Love" in. As Don began, he slowly waltzed over to the table where Doug Sanders was seated and winked his eye at him. That was the song Don serenaded to him many years back when Doug first married. Sonny prompted Don to sing another song. Glancing at the band, Don said he wanted to do "My Way." Sonny left Don to sing, while he walked over and sat down in Don's empty chair where Francine and I were.

I took my eyes off Don to glance around the room. It was so quiet, you could hear a pin drop. Then I reached for my glass of water, when I looked at Sonny sitting there. Right then, two tears rolled out of his eyes, as he brushed them away so no one would see. I saw it. I looked back over at Don singing. Here is a man in his eighties who unbelievably sounds better today than ever before. The power of the gift that God had given to Don Cherry showed in the emotion that was on Sonny King's face. I was easily becoming emotional myself.

—Neil T. Daniels (coauthor)

ıııııııııııııııııı

Sonny hasn't been doing too well lately and unfortunately is in the hospital as I write. I pray that he recovers quickly.

ıııııııııııııııııı

During the summer months, I played in the Walker Chiropractic Celebrity Classic and sang for the Junior League of Houston. I played golf in Marvin Zindler's Golf Tournament in Lake Conroe and sang at the DejaVu in Houston. I played in Dan Jenkins' Tournament at the Walden Course in Fort Worth and sang the national anthem at the Las Vegas Country Club on the Fourth of July.

PBS had called and asked if I would appear on a new television special saluting the songs of the '50s called *Magic Moments*. The special would run during pledge week so that all the public broadcasting stations could help raise money for their nonprofit funding. I thought it was for a great cause and decided to go. We boarded a plane and arrived in Atlantic City the day before in time to have a quick rehearsal.

The special was taped before a huge live audience in the beautiful Trump Taj Mahal palace. Many of the stars and celebrities I knew were there also—Patti Page, Wink Martindale, Pat Boone, the McGuire Sisters, Mel Carter, and Gogi Grant—as well as folks I hadn't had the pleasure of meeting before—members of the Four Lads, the Crew Cuts, the Diamonds, and the Four Coins. A member of the group that backed me on "Band of Gold" was there, a fellow by the name of Paul Evans. Paul had a hit himself many years ago ("Seven Little Girls Sitting in the Back Seat").

The week it aired around the country brought more attention than I had seen in recent years. I have heard that our show has become the highest-rated special in PBS history. Raising more money than any show before, they keep airing it every few months still. I am so thrilled to see that the great music of that generation, of which I am included, is so embraced by the public today.

Comin' Down the Final Stretch

NOW FOR SOME STRANGE REASON, I can't wait to tell you about this guy. I'll give you some clues that you probably aren't aware of: he is a great jazz singer. He plays piano and guitar. His golf game is even more surprising than his musical talents. I met him at the Las Vegas Country Club when he was playing with a good friend of mine, Jimmy Muladore. Jimmy is a very good golfer and a great clarinet player, specializing in jazz, although he can play anything. It was there that he introduced me to Joe Pesci.

The first thing Joe did was start singing "Band of Gold." Jimmy and Joe invited me to join them in playing golf. I wound up playing with them for seven days. I hadn't played that much golf in a long time, but I enjoyed every yard of it.

I have met so many singers and actors in my life, but nothing compares to Joe Pesci. In my opinion, Joe's roles in *Raging Bull* and *Goodfellas* are at the top of my list. *My Cousin Vinny* wasn't bad either. My favorite question is, "You talkin' to me?" and my favorite answer is, "Forget about it." If you've seen his movies (and who hasn't) you'll know the meaning of that.

You may wonder why this is a 36-hole book. That's because all the major golf tournaments, up until a few years ago, were completed by playing

36 holes on the last day. The British Open and the British Amateur were the first, then along came the U.S. Open and the U.S. Amateur.

Golf, as we know it now, was allegedly started in Scotland. Both the Opens and the U.S. Amateur now play four days, with 18 holes a day. The reason for the change is simple: money and the physical stress it would put on a player. The two amateur tournaments still play 36 holes, if needed. The Opens are medal play, and the Amateurs are match play.

I would like to give my opinion about the difference in golf between then and now. Like everything else in this world, money has taken over this sport. All the good amateurs turn pro as early as possible; therefore, amateur golf has lost a lot of its meaning (and importance). For example, winning one pro tournament now can earn a player more in a week than a player like Sam Snead did in his whole lifetime. But, I guess that sums up just about every sport today.

One other thing that turns me off about today's golf players. Can you imagine Ben Hogan, Sam Snead, or Jimmy Demaret running across the green pumping their fist, jumping up and down on the green, the way players do now? Could it be something more than the game—perhaps money?

Something else that has bothered me for so many years was when a lot of people stated that I was the only person who could sing and play golf better than anyone else could. I guess I didn't like hearing it. It doesn't bother me anymore, because I finally realize that they were, and still are, right. That's not ego—that's the truth.

Now to singing . . . thank God I can sing! You've heard me address and express my feelings about golf, now let me say a little something about singers and the kind of music we are all exposed to today. Simply put, can you imagine Perry Como or Bing Crosby having to listen to Rod Stewart sing their songs, or the so-called rock and hip-hop stars of this era? Blame the radio stations and money again.

I'm so very grateful for the memories I carry with me. They take me back to my sister Anna Lee and how beautiful she was. My brother Paul and how good he was to people, and how he loved life. That little house that I grew up in and always called home. Those first golf games, where I met the legends and the others who shared my passion. Even though my nerves got the best of me, the exciting and sometimes elusive world of show business—the game I never played (now, I'm not too sure if it's too late to join in.) I remember my own loves and losses. Mr. Clean and "Band of Gold," the tune that will be played when I'm long gone. Even when I'm such an ass, the people who care about me and *especially those whom I care about*—my children, my friends, and my wife. I am positive that Ross Alma Cherry and James Newton Demaret will watch over and take care of Stephen Patrick Cherry, just like Francine will over me. Finally, I thank God for giving me golf, a song, and two roads to follow in case I needed a back way out.

The biggest lesson in life that I have learned, I will now share with you . . .

HOLE
36

Another 18 Holes to Go

THE GAME ISN'T OVER YET!

So far, my life has been a "jubilee" to me. I have two last sentences I want to add before the cover gets closed and this gets put on a shelf. I want to thank each and every dear friend for writing to (and about) me in this book. It has been a wonderful life all because of all them. Here are their comments:

⁙⁙⁙⁙⁙

I WOULD OFTEN INVITE DON TO COME ALONG to parties and gatherings. Most of them would have something to do with show business, but Don didn't feel comfortable. He was very shy and uncomfortable.

You've got to remember, Don came from this small town in Texas and is such a down-to-earth person. Once in New York, he was like a fish out of water. People had other agendas and seemed, at first, so artificial to him. If someone would walk up and begin talking about golf or music, then he would open up and feel more at ease.

I would play little jokes with him, like the time I pretended actress/ model Terry Moore was on the telephone. I was saying things like, "Yes, Terry . . . and you have a friend for my buddy, Don? What does she look like? Five-foot-seven, with a huge chest and tiny waist? And she would love to meet Don?"

Then I'd have him get ready and pretend to get ready myself, only to drag him out for the evening. It was my way of needling him while introducing him to new people.

Honestly, Don didn't do too badly with the girls we did meet either. I think his shyness and quiet nature worked well with the gals.

—MARTIN MILLS

||||||||||||||||||||||

I FIRST HEARD OF DON CHERRY IN 1949 when I was fooling around playing the PGA winter tour as an amateur, and also playing in a few amateur events in the South. Everyone knew how great Don Cherry hit the ball, and what a putter he was . . . and they were right!

In 1952 I ran into Don again when we played in Seattle, in the U.S. Amateur. I played Don in the fifth round, and he beat the hell out of me, 4 and 2 as I recall. He made every putt he looked at (probably the best putting round of his life). He should have won that tournament, but his putter came back to normal on the last nine against Al Mengert, and he lost at the last hole.

In the early '60s, I was director of golf at Meriwether Golf Club in Beaverton, Oregon. We decided to have a big amateur tournament, and I invited Don to play and entertain at our dinner. The night before our dinner he told us he was going to turn pro. The next day was awful—cold, rainy, and windy. Only those players who drank brandy or coffee had a chance, and Don didn't do either. He shot 87, but afterward put on a great show in a leaky, cold tent for our guests. When I took him to the plane the next day, we both agreed that the 87 definitely set him up to turn pro.

I remember playing nine holes before the Houston Open with Don as my partner against Chick Harbert and Vic Ghezzi, two very fine players. Don hit the flagstick three times with long drives, and we got the money. An amazing feat!

To cap off my little story, here is something I'll never forget. We were playing in Akron and staying at the same hotel. Don met a pretty lady that week and spent a lot of time with her. After Sunday's round, Don left immediately for Seattle, where we were playing next and he was singing at the Wyatt Howard's Town and Country. It seems that he left his toupee in the girl's bedroom and didn't realize it until he arrived in Seattle—and Don had to have that toupee to go on stage. I had a very early flight on Monday, so I called the young lady at 2:00 AM with our problem. She must have liked Don a lot because she met me at 6:00 AM at the airport, and the hairpiece arrived in Seattle in plenty of time for Don to perform.

Looking back over 50 years of friendship, I think that understanding each other has been the key. Don and I are both very hard on ourselves in both life and golf, but we respect each other. Some people have trouble understanding how Don and I are, but that's the way it goes in life.

—BOB ROSBURG

IIIIIIIIIIIIIIIIIIII

WELL, MY FRIEND, IT HAS BEEN OVER 60 YEARS since you and I first met. Much has happened in both our lives during that time. We both married lovely wives, raised our families, and now enjoy our grandchildren. In all those years, we have traveled many courses and done some crazy things that young men do. I still think Bing Crosby had to have a sense of humor when he paired up the two of us. He must have realized you and I, being so much alike, would bring out the best in each other or sometimes, to our chagrin, the worst!

In fact, just the other day I was telling friends of mine about some of our antics—like the time you drew back that putt halfway to the hole and took a stroke on the hole. Well, you just about gave me a real stroke that day, my friend, with that surprise move.

All kidding aside, Bing did us a favor all those years. You know, my friend, we were an awesome twosome in tournaments. We led the pack on numerous occasions, but it seems like the final day of rounds Terrible Tommy, also known as Thunderbolt and Cherry, would let loose and, as they say, the rest is history.

You know there is not enough time or paper to detail all you and I have done over these 60-some years, but my friend, it has never been dull! So I close this letter for now, remember me as fondly as I remember you. God bless and keep you, my friend.

—TOMMY BOLT

IIIIIIIIIIIIIIIIIIII

I FIRST MET DON AROUND NEW YORK CITY while I was still playing for the New York Yankees. I used to go see him in clubs around New York, because he was about as close to country as you could get in New York City.

Then I moved to Dallas and used to see Don every New Year's Eve in Big D. He became a good friend. We spent a lot of time together, playing golf and kicking the football around. He was a pretty good athlete for a golfer *and* singer.

I had the Yankees put a "Happy Birthday" message on the scoreboard for him one day when he was at the stadium. Once in Las Vegas, where I would see him a lot, he introduced me at one of his late-night shows. I was asleep at the table and he thought I was kidding . . . but the show wasn't really that good.

I have always enjoyed him, no matter what anybody says. He is okay and I am proud to call him my friend.

—MICKEY MANTLE

|||||||||||||||||||

DON IS A NATURAL! He's a natural everything—except dancing. He's good-looking, but he can't dance. He's a great golfer, but he can't dance. His voice has a beautiful, full, round, mellow quality, with warmth, and I suppose it doesn't matter if he can't dance. Eh, Don? Keep on singing, you know I love you. P.S. I think you write pretty good too.

—LOVE, PEGGY

|||||||||||||||||||

DON CHERRY IS A BIG TALENT—singer, par golfer, a fur trapper, and sometimes a miserable bastard. But I'm telling you up front: I love him. Jimmy Demaret, who he calls his second father, introduced Don to me. He looked about 20 at the time and was bald as a bat. Still, we had our work cut out for us when it came to a good-looking chick. Look at the odds he was giving us. Don never drank or smoked, and had an impediment in his reach—he could put a dollar on any counter and stay all day.

Don has traveled all over the country playing every type of club, for practically nothing. Just to play golf and try to prove to people that he could really sing with the best of them (and believe me he can!). I could tell you a lot of stories about Don and Demaret and myself, but I'm sure they will be in his book. I've known Don for a long time, and during all these years he has worked his ass off, trying to make people see his talent and believe in him, and give him the break he deserves. Don is doing well now, with big hit records behind him and playing the top spots in Vegas and top hotels around the country, and he is always ready to do you a favor. He's the first one to volunteer for a benefit, and best of all, he's a great guy to be around. His personality has completely changed.

That's right, Don has found himself! He's a solid guy. He'll give you a golf lesson, sing you a song, run an errand—you name it. He hasn't hit a home run yet, but he's batting .300. I love him!

—PHIL HARRIS

||||||||||||||||||

Don was a unique, carefree talent, and I happily recorded with him—and we had a wonderful time!

—MITCH MILLER

||||||||||||||||||

When he sings, the vibrant tones of his voice make you know that this is someone singing because he can't help it. Sing the song, man!

—JOE WILLIAMS

||||||||||||||||||

A few words about Don Cherry:

For sure, he's the real thing.

One of a kind—a true original.

What you see is what you get.

He is an upfront, out there, open guy.

He'll always be a country boy, with a strange sense of right and
wrong, good and bad, full of heart.

He's a true *natural.*

His talent is a birthright.

Music and golf are his territory.

He's always had both gifts, and years later, Don Cherry remains
a straight shooter with a voice and heart richer and truer than
ever.

I shout it loud:

I love this clown.

—HOWIE RICHMOND

DON CHERRY WAS HIS OWN WORST ENEMY. He had the innate ability
to irritate people with his personality. I got along with him very well,
but he could get to some people. Even with this, he could really play
golf. He was one of the best ball-strikers I ever saw.

At the 1955 Walker Cup at St. Andrews, he had one member of the
team in tears. That was Cherry. The captain of the team, Bill Campbell,
came to me and said, "Harvie, Don is playing better than anyone on
the team except you! I have to use him in the foursome matches, but
no one wants to play with him." That's what Bill thought of his ability.
We won our match—Don played great.

Thanks for the memories.

—E. HARVIE WARD

I STILL REMEMBER OUR DAYS ON THE WALKER CUP in 1953, and then
we were on the PGA Tour when we played in the Four-Ball Championship
together. I'll always remember you holing out of the bunker on the 18th
hole.

Then we go back to the days at Indian Wells and other steps along
the way when I was playing drums with you, Murray Arnold, and Lionel

Hebert on trumpet. Also, you and I singing together, and the only time we ever got out of beat was because Palmer was conducting.

You've always been a great friend!

—KEN VENTURI

iiiiiiiiiiiiiiiiiii

"BAND OF GOLD" MIGHT HAVE BEEN DON'S BIGGEST HIT, but my own favorite is a lively number written by George Marion and Richard Whiting called "My Future Just Passed." I swear that when you play this track, a smile will break out on your face that will continue for days.

Knowing Don, and thinking back about what he might have been like in those days, this song conjures up pictures in my head. From the moment he states, "Hello, there. There goes a girl, I think I'll follow her . . ." you can actually see Don smile, as he runs up and down the bouncy scale with a vivacious prowl in his voice.

—NEIL T. DANIELS

iiiiiiiiiiiiiiiiiii

GOODNESS, I'VE KNOWN DON ALMOST 60 YEARS. He was sure something back then—probably the best darn amateur golfer in all of Texas. He was a hothead too. I never saw Don throw any clubs, but I sure saw him break a few over his knee. One time at the Odessa Pro-Am, Tommy Bolt commented that Don broke so many clubs that all he had left to hit with was a 2 iron.

I had this piece of property in Churchill County, Texas, and invited a dozen or so folks to go hunting during deer season. Everyone stayed at this dormitory-style house, so we would all start out together in the mornings. When Don arrived, his suitcase was filled with the finest-looking shirts you have ever seen. His mother was a fantastic seamstress and made them by hand. Don took out what he needed, folded the rest, and put the rest back inside.

I had this fake 6' rubber snake lying around, when a couple of us decided to curl it up, unzip his luggage, and put it under one of his shirts. I can't begin to tell you the look of panic when Don opened his suitcase and the rubber snake jumped out. I think he ruined two or three of the shirts in the fight to get rid of it!

Another time comes to mind when we were both playing in the Abilene Invitational. It was a day before the Invitational started, and we went out to practice. Another fellow joined us that neither one of us knew, but had heard rumors about. People were suspicious that he was the one who had been robbing the slot machines at all the courses in the Texas area. That didn't stop Don, though. We played a couple of holes before Don started needling him about his playing.

Then we got a little further, and Don badgered him a little more. A couple minutes later this fellow dropped his clubs and began to go after Don. Don started to run, and I stood there watching them chase each other around two holes before Don came back and this fellow cooled down. I don't think it fazed him at the time, but after we finished the game and went back to the clubhouse, it dawned on Don that the fellow he provoked could have been a mobster or even a killer. That was Don—always fun to be around.

—BOBBY FRENCH

||||||||||||||||||||

DON CHERRY? DON CHERRY? Oh yes, the name does ring a bell.

Seriously, I have known Don for a long, long time. I consider him a good friend, which right up front tells you what little taste I have.

Don is and has been one of the best singers around for a long, long time. As opposed to many of the singers you hear nowadays, when Don hits his first note, you know immediately who is singing. He has a great sound and, to me, more importantly, he doesn't sound like 17 other singers.

Don Cherry, I feel, is his own worst enemy. He does not, nor has he ever, taken crap from anybody, which in all probability is a quality that endears him to me.

Don Cherry is one hell of a guy and I am glad to call him a friend.

—JIMMY DEAN

||||||||||||||||||||

I HAVE KNOWN DON FOR MANY YEARS and I call him "the Combination Kid." Don is not only a fine golfer but an outstanding singer. Don has always had a friendly disposition and is very much a people person.

—GARY PLAYER

mmmmmmmm

I HAVE KNOWN DON CHERRY SINCE HE HAD HAIR, and that was a long time ago. As most people know, Don was one of the best amateur golfers this country ever had. He is also an outstanding singer. But what I never understood was how he got all the good-looking ladies.

Years ago at the Crosby in Pebble Beach, the organizers suddenly realized with Don, Tommy [Bolt], Bob [Rosberg], and Jim, that they would have lost half the gallery. In spite of our explosive personalities, I have always enjoyed playing golf with Don. His swing is a beautiful thing to watch. When I see Don coming, I always smile.

—JAMES GARNER

mmmmmmmm

DON CHERRY—A WONDERFUL MAN, good friend, and above all, a hell of a man with the tubes (singer, that is). He was more than a stick man, with any club in the bag. I remember playing in Milwaukee in a PGA tournament with Donald, who was leading the Milwaukee Open at one point. With the pressure and a bad shot, he was getting upset, grumbling something awful. At this time, he was an amateur. It upset me just a little, so I scolded him: "Knock it off, Donald. You are just playing for a salad bowl, anyway, and I am playing for the loot."

I have known Don for 100 years, it seems. We have a little sing-along every now and then, which brings back happy memories. He is still a guy I have admired all these years and enjoy seeing him more each time.

Keep singing, pal, you're the best!

—SAM SNEAD

mmmmmmmm

DEAR DON,

Everyone should know someone like you—talented, ambitious, kind, gentle, explosive, and a friend of the great Tommy Bolt. You're an outstanding singer whom I never tire of hearing sing. You also have an outstanding way of presenting your singing and have a great choice of songs.

Maybe, like so many people we have both met, you'd rather be a great golfer like Tommy or many others you know. You certainly have the talent for golf, but maybe you didn't have the patience for long hours of practice, especially around the greens. As someone once said, "It isn't the arduousness of the task—it is just the monotony of the procedure." You surely have enjoyed your association with the greats of golf.

Personally, I have always admired your talent, enjoyed and respected your friendship, and know you as a really caring person—one to go out of his way to help.

Thanks for being my friend all these years.

—JERRY BARBER

||||||||||||||||||

DON CHERRY HAS BEEN A GOOD FRIEND OF MINE for well over 40 years. We've played a lot of great golf together and have always had fun needling each other along the way. Barbara and I used to catch up with Don absolutely every place we could listen to him sing, and we still love his music just as much today. We play his CDs at home, in our cars, on the boat, and in my airplane—we even fight over them!

While everyone knows that Don is an accomplished entertainer, perhaps his friends and fans don't know just what an accomplished golfer he is. I recall the 1960 U.S. Open at Cherry Hills when I played as a 20-year-old amateur and finished second to Arnold Palmer by 2 strokes, and Don finished just 2 strokes behind me. Not bad for a kid and a singer! We played together on the Walker Cup team and the Americas Cup teams too.

He is certainly one of the funniest guys I know. I will never forget the year Barbara and I invited him over for Thanksgiving dinner. We had been married about four months and I was in Columbus for a show.

Barbara was making biscuits, but Mother had accidentally turned off the oven. Let's just say that the biscuits turned out a little undercooked. Don decided to toss his at the wall, and it stuck!

As you can tell, Don and I go back a long way together. Unfortunately, our busy lives don't allow us to get together with Don and Francine as often as we'd like. I am fortunate to count him among my friends. He has known a lot of people, made a lot of friends, and done a lot of things in his life.

—JACK NICKLAUS

iiiiiiiiiiiiiiiiiii

THIS NOTE IS TO THE MILLIONS OF PEOPLE reading this book:

Next to high school football, Donald Ross Cherry was the greatest thing ever to come out of Wichita Falls, Texas. God gave him a double dose of talent. He said, "Take this dinky little golf swing and show 'em what you can do with it." So for many years he played as an amateur and a professional on the PGA Tour with the likes of Hogan, Nelson, Demaret, and Bolt—and on one weekend over 45 years ago, he led Arnold Palmer going into the final round of the U.S. Open.

Then God said, "You're gonna talk like Texas, but you're going to sing like the world. You're gonna sing and play golf." Now, that's perfect. Then God thought a bit, "Hey, that's breaking my rule—nobody's perfect. How about a little attitude problem?"

So now you have a great golfer and a great singer with a bad attitude. I call him "Venom Man." I have known and hung out with him for over 50 years. He doesn't know the meaning of the words "humble" or "humility." He doesn't know the meaning of the word "compassion"—there must be a thousand words he doesn't know the meanings of. But he is my friend, and I know that if I keep digging, I'll find a pony down there someplace.

P.S. Don't tell him this, because I'm sure he doesn't want anyone to know, but he's kind, he's considerate, and above all, he's caring. So from then 'til now, us two good ol' boys from Texas have had some laughs.

—"WARM NORM" ALDEN

||||||||||||||||||||

I'VE KNOWN DON CHERRY FOR A VERY LONG TIME, and I would have to describe him as a very unusual and great guy. Don is such a fine person—he gave his own mother a new home, which shows you just what a fine person he is.

Not only did Don have a beautiful voice, but he was an outstanding athlete. He was an All-State halfback at Wichita Falls High School and one of the fastest men in the country. Don was also an outstanding golfer. I have a lot of experience playing with him, and he is a delightful man and a very emotional man, as most good athletes are.

I remember playing the Walker Cup in Rhode Island, and Don played extremely well. Don is just a fine player. Another time we were playing at Seattle Country Club, playing alternate shots. We were paired together, and he still teases me about the fact that every time I drove, I would put the ball six inches in the rough and give him a miserable lie. We had a lot of fun.

—CHARLIE COE

||||||||||||||||||||

FOR YEARS I HAVE BEEN READING articles in *Reader's Digest* called "The Most Unforgettable Characters I Ever Have Known." I won't say that Don Cherry is the most unforgettable character I have ever known, but I will say he is a character.

I believe that Don is looking to find himself, and has been all his life. Sometimes what is perceived as a negative personality is only someone who is suffering from tremendous insecurities. God gave Don Cherry tremendous talents for playing golf and for singing.

I have worked with Don, and each time I try to figure out why he sets up this wall between himself and people. There is a little-boy quality that Don Cherry has that makes women gravitate to him. Doctors would say that it is a maternal thing, but what I have watched over the years is not the maternal thing they are doing with Don—lucky guy!

266

I am happy to say that Don and I are good friends, but may not be after he reads this personality analysis I have written. I may add that I am studying Psychology 101 at a junior high school now.

I have to go now because the two men in white coats are going to take me for a ride again. Fore!

—SHECKY GREENE

IIIIIIIIIIIIIIIII

I HAVE KNOWN DON FOR MORE THAN 50 YEARS, and I have always thought he was a very special individual—crazy, yes, but special. Don is really misunderstood. He gives you the impression that he doesn't give a damn about anything, but he really does—especially if he likes or respects you. He just doesn't know how to let you know. He is really very shy—hard to believe, shy!

As far as his singing, I am his biggest fan. I think he's as good as he wants to be. Singing country music is really his forte. I have so much confidence in him. I produced an album for him, and it turned out to be one of my proudest achievements.

As a golfer, I'll never forget when I met Don. We were in San Antonio, Texas, and I was in the army. I was stationed at Fort Sam Houston and he was playing in the Texas Open. He was playing a practice round with Doug Ford and Mike Souchak and some others I can't remember. They were having a friendly money game. I had just started playing golf and was really impressed with golf players. I asked if I could walk along with them and watch and learn. Well, Don and I were really involved talking about singing and music as he played the match.

After about six holes, Mike Souchak (Don's partner in the round) told him to start thinking about golf and the game. Don turned to me and said to please excuse him, that he had to get his mind back on the game. He proceeded to birdie the next five holes—so much for his talent as a golfer.

Another time there was this 16-year-old kid who would follow Don around. Don, in his own pleasant way, would yell, "Get away from me, kid!" A few weeks later, the teenager got sick and went into the hospital. When Don found this out, he made it a point to visit the 16-year-old.

Wishing him well, and hoping he would see him back out on the golf course soon, Don left. When the boy's parents came in a short while later, he told them of Don's visit and added in a stressful state: "Now I know I'm going to die! Don Cherry was nice to me!"

Yes, he's quite a guy and a great friend.

—VIC DAMONE

ıııııııııııııııııı

I'VE KNOWN DON PRETTY WELL SINCE 1953 when we were both playing in the U.S. Amateur at Oklahoma City Country Club. Don had just lost a very hard-fought match to Curtis Person in the first round. We had become pretty good friends, and I remember in the locker room afterward, Curtis was singing, doing a thing on Don. I thought it was rather amusing. But I don't think that Don, who had a bit of a temper, liked it too much.

Some years later, in 1965, Don and I played in what turned out to be a very significant exhibition match in Orlando, Florida, at a new course called Bay Hill. Don, Jack Nicklaus, Dave Ragan, and I played in the match, which was a benefit for the Orlando Chamber of Commerce. As I remember, Don and I played Jack and Dave, and I had a good day—shot 65. I was so happy about that, I ended up buying Bay Hill not very many years later.

Through the years, Don and I have remained good friends. We've had a lot of good times together, playing golf and doing other things. I have always enjoyed his singing, even though he never took my advice on how he should be presenting his music to the audiences. But I guess he's done pretty well ignoring my advice, so I'll just let it go like that.

—ARNOLD PALMER

ıııııııııııııııııı

IT WAS THE SAME OLD STORY. He could have been one of the half-dozen best athletes in his sport—but he couldn't give up nightclubs.

He did what Walter Hagen was supposed to have done—walked directly toward the 1st tee in evening clothes. He was wearing an alpaca or a tuxedo. He spent all day in the sun—and all night in the spotlight. He spent the day smelling the trees, the flowers, and the greens—and he spent the nights smelling perfume and booze.

Girls threw themselves at him. Some he caught. But he preferred birdies to birds. He didn't have much time for courtship. The minute he finished a round of golf, the band would strike up in some roadhouse nearby, and he couldn't afford to miss that.

He came out of Wichita Falls in the '40s, and, raised by a mother who took in sewing, he was that offense against nature: an introverted Texan. He played baseball because, as in golf, you didn't have to depend on anybody else.

He began shagging on the practice tee for Jimmy Demaret and, as a baseball player, he thought you had to *catch* the 2-iron shots. "I only missed three out of 24," he tells you. Which tells you something about Demaret's accuracy in those days too.

He says he held the peaches– and butter bean–canning championship of North Texas, and, when asked how you can peaches and butter beans, he answers: "Well, first, you go pick 'em . . ."

The tragedy of Donald Ross Cherry's life was not that he couldn't play golf, it was that he could sing. By the time they found that out, the reason he wasn't setting records was probably because he was making them.

He never had a lesson in his life—golf or voice—but he was too good at golf to give it up for singing. And vice versa. God gave him a swing and a beat.

Nobody has enough concentration to be both a Frank Sinatra and a Ben Hogan, but Don Cherry made the cut in both professions.

He chased Arnold Palmer to Arnold's first big tournament win, the U.S. Amateur in 1954, when he had Arnold 3 down and 6 to play. Don Cherry was one of the first victims of the soon-to-be-famous Palmer charge. He was a Walker Cupper. He played tense matches with the likes of Gene Littler, Bob Rosburg, Frank Stranahan, and won his share. When he turned pro, he led the Dallas Open after one round. He was one of five players who still had a shot at Palmer when Arnie won his Open in 1960. The course, fittingly, was Cherry Hills, and Cherry went over the hills at 3 under par until the 17th of the final round where a 7 put him out of contention at 284.

Meanwhile, back at the recording studio, Don had started out too bashful to sing in front of a band—or even in front of a curtain. Jan Garber didn't know this when he picked Don up, but seven days later he gave Don $39 to go back to Wichita Falls with the observation that he didn't want a band singer who was going to phone in his solos.

Don had (and has) a range of 2.2 octaves, which puts him up with the big hitters of that game too. When you can wander 18 notes up and down the keyboard, that leaves you, musically, with an easy wedge to the green.

He scheduled club dates to coincide with tournaments. So it was a good thing he wasn't a ballet dancer. He got $35 for his first 800,000-seller record. But he didn't need the money in those days. Not when there were so many guys out there with fast backswings who didn't think a guy who sang that good could play that well.

Don is the only guy in Las Vegas who was starring in the Sahara Open during the day and the Sahara Lounge at night. Get him to sing you "Green Green Grass of Home" and shoot you a 67 with two 3-putt greens, and if you don't get goose pimples, then you wouldn't be impressed if Caruso went 3-for-4 in the World Series in the afternoon and brought down the house in *Pagliacci* at the Met that night.

—JIM MURRAY,
PULITZER PRIZE–WINNING
SYNDICATED SPORTSWRITER

IIIIIIIIIIIIIIIIIIII

I WASN'T AROUND TO HEAR OLD THOM MORRIS SING, but I did hear Jimmy Demaret, Bing Crosby, Dean Martin, and other singing golfers— and golfing singers—perform on the stage, and I saw them perform on the golf course. As a one-man combination plate of singing and golfing talents, nobody would ever come close to Don Cherry.

This is a guy who nearly won the U.S. Open, who played in The Masters nine times as an amateur, and who turned out hit records like "Band of Gold" and "Country Boy," singing in that distinctive Cherry voice, which is as smooth as polished ivory. Using his homemade Wichita Falls backswing, which appears to stop waist high, he won the driving distance contests on the pro tour often, and was cited by Ben Hogan as one of the straightest iron players ever.

Don would book his singing act into nightclubs along the pro tour route and then lay in the tournaments as an amateur. People wondered how Don could do it, night after night, singing in clubs until way after midnight in a haze of cigarette smoke and the constant tinkle of booze splashing onto ice cubes, and then arrive early in the morning on the 1st tee with clear eyes, ready for a wager.

He has never smoked a cigarette or tasted an alcoholic drink. One result is that he remembers everything that happened to him. A long time Don Cherry fan!

—BUD SHRAKE,
JOURNALIST
SPORTSWRITER,
AUTHOR OF *LITTLE
GREEN BOOK* AND
LITTLE RED BOOK

||||||||||||||||||||

THE FIRST TIME I MET DON CHERRY, I didn't like him. I didn't like him the second, third, or fourth time either. He's kind of a blister on your butt. In time you get used to it.

Don is sarcastic, but only if he likes you. He must love me, because he's been rude to me for more than 30 years.

Don is a great entertainer and truly a good friend. My life is a lot better because of friends like him.

—WALT GARRISON

||||||||||||||||||||

DEAR DON,

It seems like we go back to the days of the first pages of the Bible! Not only do I know you as a friend and golfer, but a supplier of golf wardrobe and equipment to make a 300-handicapper look good.

I've always found you to be a great entertainer. The times when that thought has slipped my mind, you've always made sure to remind me. Your sense of humor is special. You seem to do particularly well in coffee shops and country club locker rooms. Now if you could only put that together and make it happen on stage, then there's a chance you could star in all the rodeos in Texas.

Don, I wish you good things for the years ahead, because honestly, your personality could use some work . . . but I will always remain a loyal fan. As ever,

—DON RICKLES

WHEN I THINK OF DON CHERRY, I think of a man who has so many talents. His singing voice is striking and leaves a lasting impression on all who hear him. His physical strength is excellent, and he can run like a deer.

Don joins the ranks of the singing cowboy—Roy Rogers, Gene Autry, and George Strait. However, Don is the singing golfer, and what a golfer he is! His swing is short and impressive, and gets the job done in seemingly effortless effort, making him the envy of golfers worldwide.

It takes a dedicated man, a man who can concentrate and achieve the goal he sets. So I write with my heart about one of my closest friends, the man, the legend: Mr. Don Cherry.

—DOUG SANDERS

YOU MAY HAVE BUMPED INTO DON CHERRY one time or another and found him pretty difficult. Don doesn't waste time telling you how he feels at the moment. My experience with him has been mainly a pleasant one, but I have caught him on a down day now and then.

Don has the temperament and personality of many artists, since his main livelihood has always been singing. I have found him entertaining as hell because golf and his voice have carried him many places, and he has lots of tales to be told in this book.

Born in a storm and peace, "I do despise" seems to be Don's way of life. If he seems to be mellow and smoothed out, just stick around and you will find that he will change into a storm.

Of all things you can say about Don, I know for sure that he is not a bore.

—DARRELL ROYAL

IIIIIIIIIIIIIIIIII

I HAVE TO INTERJECT A FEW MORE WORDS about the people Don has met while singing and swinging. Many have been mentioned already, but the list of names is phenomenal. There would not be enough pages to list all the names, but I thought you'd like to hear just a few:

On the golf course—Glen Campbell, Johnny Bench, José Ferrer, Howard Keel, Pete Rose, James Caan, Mickey Rooney, and Johnny Carson, who played his last game of golf at the Hilton Las Vegas Country Club with Don.

Others include "Mean" Joe Greene, Eugene Cernan, Dale Robertson, Lee Trevino, Jack Palance, Bob Hope, and Louis Prima, to mention a few.

Prima had purchased 54 acres outside of Las Vegas in about 1964 or 1965. It's located just east of where the Bootlegger is now located. Here Prima built his own golf course and had it laid out in a dog-leg pattern engulfing two lakes. Playing Prima, Don scored a 65 on the course. To this day, a sign still hangs in the entrance of the club which reads, RECORD: DON CHERRY—65.

On stage, Don was always surrounded by his friends and peers. Name-dropping (a practice I'm not fond of doing) includes Joe E. Lewis, Buddy Greco, Steve Rossi, Bob Newhart, Sergio Franci, Rich Little, Tommy Smothers, Ella Fitzgerald, Rosemary Clooney, Mac Davis, Tim Conway, and Jack Lemmon.

While playing at La Costa, Don was seated with his wife and actor Jack Lemmon. Lemmon commented on how he liked Don's music, leaving Don feeling somewhat humble. (He really feels uncomfortable when people gush over him.) He thanked Jack for his words, then hesitated, and finished with a thought that entered his mind, "You know, we are like a losing hand in Las Vegas. Two Cherrys and a Lemmon." Jack just about spit his drink through his nose at Don's quick wit and perfect timing.

Just a few of the other names I'll drop are Johnny Mathis, Andy Williams, Peter Marshall, Harvey Korman, Johnny Ray, Elvis Presley, Gordon and Sheila MacRae, Mary Healy, Sarah Vaughan, Patti Page, Jack Jones, Jerry Vale, and Phyllis McGuire, who would join in and sing with Don on many occasions. Even legendary Judy Garland once jumped up on stage at the Living Room in New York, eager to sing with Don.

Dennis Weaver once said, "When I first heard the song 'Streets of Laredo,' I thought that there were two people singing it. I was wrong, it was all himself singing. I didn't realize that Don had a unique ability to sing in over two octaves!"

One last note: Carol Mann of the World Golf Hall of Fame had stated an interesting fact about the great Ben Hogan: "Hogan spent countless hours looking out his window, listening to Don's records while daydreaming and relaxing to his voice. We play Don's music in our large gallery where Hogan's life is celebrated."

—NEIL T. DANIELS

〡〡〡〡〡〡〡〡〡〡〡〡〡〡

SELDOM DOES AN INDIVIDUAL COME ALONG who can rise above the norm in his chosen field. The man who can excel in two entirely different fields is an extremely rare individual. Don Cherry, for several decades, has entertained millions of people with his music, appearing in some of America's premier showcases, including, of course, the mecca of entertainment, Las Vegas. In golf he made the pro tour among thousands who tried to qualify—only a few ever made it. Don Cherry was one of those few. Singer, golfer, and now writer. Above all of this, he is a friend.

—DALE ROBERTSON

〡〡〡〡〡〡〡〡〡〡〡〡〡〡

I MET DON CHERRY FOR THE FIRST TIME in Lake Charles, Louisiana, playing in the Alvin Dark tournament back in 1965. I heard about Cherry before from all the guys in Dallas. We got to talking about some of the guys I had played with at Tennison Park, so I knew he was probably a local guy, but I had no idea what kind of golfer he would be. Since then I have known Don for many, many years and have played a lot of golf with him.

We were playing in Dallas one year and I'll never forget this as long as I live. The wind was blowing about 30 mph, and he was going up the 14th hole at Preston Trail wearing a Panama hat. All of a sudden, after hitting his second shot to the green, that Panama hat blew off toward the lake located on the right side. The hat started rolling with the wind and got closer and closer to the water. Cherry was going full blast, and I thought he would hit the gallery rope and decapitate himself. He then did the prettiest hook slide under the rope and grabbed that Panama hat before it went into the lake. I mean, I laughed . . . I was all over the 15th fairway, and I laughed and laughed.

What impressed me most, though, was the night Lionel Hebert was playing trumpet and Don Cherry was singing. He could really sing. He has been a great friend over the years, and I've enjoyed being around him.

—LEE TREVINO

〜〜〜〜〜〜〜〜〜〜

I KNOW ONE THING FOR SURE. If you are still playing golf as well as you are still singing, I would hate playing against you! It is hard for me to imagine how great it is to hear you sing the wonderful songs of our days. I also know if you had not knocked your ball into the water at the 17th hole in the 1960 U.S. Open, you might have won.

Enough of golf, I am really enjoying your singing. I have your music in my car and I do love hearing your singing every day. Keep it up and play lots of golf!

—JACK FLECK

〜〜〜〜〜〜〜〜〜〜

THERE IS ONE MAN SO SMOOTH—ever so smooth—at whatever he decided to do, golf or sing. January 11 binds us together—we share the same birthday, and the same Texas roots.

He performed any way he wanted to—his way—and you might sum Don up in one word—"talent." One more thing, he is the best putter I have ever seen!

—BEN CRENSHAW

〜〜〜〜〜〜〜〜〜〜

I TRUST YOU WILL AGREE THAT OUR GROUP'S RELATIONSHIP had been enhanced by the five-day Atlantic crossing. By the time of our arrival in Southampton, E. Harvie Ward had assigned nicknames to the entire team, including yours as "Affable" (perhaps because of your angelic disposition).

In my Walker Cup experience, spanning 24 years (1951–1975) and including three team matches (and two team wins) at St. Andrews, I can't think of any other foursome match as important under the circumstances as Harvey's and your defeat of Carr and White on the Old Course in 1955. You two did us proud on that great occasion.

Finally, in case you have forgotten or are too modest to mention it, I would like the readers to know that you have the all-time second-best record in foursome (2–0) and singles (3–0), behind only one E. Harvie Ward (3–0, 3–0), In both cases, including your timely victories at St. Andrews in May 1955. So you were both undefeated! Thanks for the memory, my friend.

—WILLIAM C. CAMPBELL

⁣||||||||||||||||||||

IF YOU KNOW DON CHERRY, you take him to raise. He loves golf and music. He could never give up one for the other. Both are better for having Don involved with them.

—JACKIE BURKE

⁣||||||||||||||||||||

DEAR DON,

I wanted to write something for your book, but what to say is very difficult—maybe I care too much.

—DAVE MARR

⁣||||||||||||||||||||

SOME THINGS IMPROVE WITH AGE, but I am not quite sure we did. Remember the seniors' competition in Vegas? You were full of surprises even then. You caddied for me at the Desert Inn's senior tourney and on this one particular hole, I wasn't sure of the break. Well, I figured since you lived there, and probably played this course often, you would give me some really good tips on this one. Well, Don ol' buddy, I looked around and you were gone! You had played this hole, did not know how it broke, and decided Tommy could handle it, and you watched from the next tee.

I don't know how well I thanked you then, but I'll tell you now: *Thanks a lot!*

—TOMMY BOLT

⁣||||||||||||||||||||

I CAME HOME ONE DAY to find the following note stuck on my front door:

> Francine,
>> With your permission
>> I would like to confirm what a lot of people seem to already know.
>> Can we get engaged and be married?
>> For further information call 1-702-555-1511.
>> I love you a lot,
>
> Donald

Our wedding was so terrific and wondrous. So many people attended. Burton Cohen, the president and chief executive of the Desert Inn even cut short his vacation to be there. It was very beautiful. Just last week someone walked up to me and said, "You're so lucky to be married to a living legend!" When Don overheard what they said, he came up and replied, "No, I'm the lucky one!"

In all the years we have been married we have always been by each other's side. I did, though, have to break him of one bad habit. Seems that when I first met Don, he had this practice of filling his bathtub to the top with golf balls. This was all part of his fascination with hunting and finding them. He had to let them soak for hours in water and then clean each as if it were a work of art. Of course, you may ask, how did Don shower or bathe? He would always use the steam rooms and showers at the country club where he lived. After we married and moved in together, we had an area set aside in the garage for his "hobby." They are not in the bathtub anymore, but our garage is filled with bags and bags of shiny white golf balls.

I should mention that, even to this day, it's hard to pry Donald from the TV or a game. He is still such a jock when it comes to sports, and not just golf. He's glued to the fights, football, well, you name it. He still goes for long walks and exercises every morning to keep in shape. That's probably what also keeps his lungs in great condition for singing.

On Don's 80th birthday, I arranged to have a big surprise party for him while he performed on stage at the Sands in Houston. The cake

278

was decorated with cherries, the place cards were all properly arranged, and the room was packed. Radio emcee Paul Berlin was present that night, when his wife collapsed while Don was singing on stage. The ambulance came and took her to the hospital (a carotid artery in her neck), but before she was taken to the hospital, another woman came up and exclaimed, "Could you imagine dying while Don Cherry was singing?" I was stunned that anyone would say such a thing, but that's Don's fans for you. To top it off, as Paul's wife was being carried out, she let out a cry, "Don't tell him to stop singing!"

Paul Berlin, ever so professional, took to the mike after Don finished and stated, "All the women swoon over Don Cherry, but my wife hit the deck!"

—FRANCINE CHERRY

||||||||||||||||||||||

UNACCUSTOMED AS I AM to reviewing the life thus far of a fellow chanteur, or my experience with him, I shall give it my best British. I shall use gloss and icing only where applicable—now don't get ahead of me. I'm talking about sweet words of praise. There are plenty, but they are at the "happily ever after" part of my story, rather than the "once upon a time" part.

I knew of Don Cherry before I came to America in 1967, but when I think back I can't quite pinpoint the moment. What I do remember is having a feeling of being a punter who was asking for the time of day from him in a punter-free zone. It was like he was Mr. Spock and we were Klingons—without big ears. After meeting him, I realized that his reputation preceded him, and I came face to face with Mr. Nasty Bugger. Now that's a real English expression for a miserable and unlikable sod whom you do not want to upset.

At that time in my early career, I was aware that I made an impact when I entered the room. I looked like a pair of walking sideburns tucked into trousers and had an unmistakable accent from across the pond, but I was still young and impressionable. So here was a man who experienced so much of life, and for some reason, unbeknownst to me, he was impressed with Humpy. When we did sit down and have a drink (soda), he would tell me some wonderful stories and business insights that intrigued me for hours.

He was, and continues to be, an amazing professional golfer who played with all the greats, and also a gifted singer. These ingredients made for a great player on and off the course. I don't know much about his personal life, but I'd rather read about it than try and spill beans I have no business cooking up in the first place.

It's a real treat to have this man on the golf course with me. He doesn't usually play, not sure if that's because he can't be bothered playing with a kid or if he just likes to follow me around and give me tips, but I have a seat in my golf cart for him any day.

I don't know what happened to him, but ever since he met Francine, it's been like Shakespeare and Cupid did a number on him at the same time. She is a sweetheart and a perfect lady, and they shine around each other. Honest to goodness "sweet talk" made sweet chops a permanent characteristic in the man. Now, when I meet him on the golf course, it's like another character, equally as colorful, just kinder, gentler shades of himself.

I nicknamed him "the Arrow" because every shot went down the middle—straight as an arrow. Just had to throw that in because only my close gumbas get the nicknames.

One thing that impresses me most about him is that he tells it like it is whether you like it or not. It may not have suited a lot of people, but I had no problem with it. It's a good trait to have in a business that can be filled with yes-men and untruths.

The last time we hung out in Vegas, we sang for hours backstage. We both tried to tell each other how to sing, swapped styles, and then gave them back and laughed our arses off. We also drank to being blessed with voices and long careers. Well, I toasted and his eyes misted.

When God finally calls this guy, and I know that's a long way off, he should be buried 12 feet down, because deep down, he's a nice guy. Mr. Nasty Bugger is now becoming Mr. Nice Bugger. Actually, it's just Don, with a Cherry on top. Thanks for being a friend to me.

—ENGELBERT
HUMPERDINCK

||||||||||||||||||||

DEAR DON,

Your tribute to Perry Como is wonderful! I've played it over and over, and like always, when I think of him, I smile. I have lost so many of my heroes the past few years—who truly can't be replaced. You're one of them, so take care of yourself, my friend. God bless and warm thoughts.

—BURT REYNOLDS

||||||||||||||||||||

ONE DAY, YEARS AGO, I WAS IN NEW YORK having lunch with an RCA promotion man when I spotted a fellow Memphian, golfing great Dr. Cary Middlecoff. I got up to go say hello and as I neared the table, the man lunching with him looked at me as if I was about to put a piranha in his finger bowl. You know, that "Can't you see we're eating? How dare you interrupt?" look.

After a friendly hello, Cary said, "Paul, do you know Don Cherry?" I shook my head no, and so the good doctor said, "Don, I want you to meet Paul Berlin. He's a disc jockey in Houston." Well, at the mention of the words "disc jockey," I was suddenly welcomed like Bill Gates at a fund-raiser—a warm handshake, a huge smile, and a down-home Texas, "Sit down, pally." We've now been pallies for more than 50 years. Thus began my friendship with the only serial bridegroom I've ever known.

His bad temper on the golf course is well known. His often cold approach to strangers I've already mentioned. And he's the same with his toupee or without. I told him he would be great on Broadway in *Beauty and the Beast*. He could play both parts.

But over 10 years, Don has mellowed. He smiles at all his fans, autographs CDs, and makes a genuine effort to be a good guy. Of course, he gets a lot of coaching from his wife, Francine, a former Broadway singer and dancer.

To me, the most amazing thing about Don is that at the age of 81, he can still sing his butt off, still has a beautiful voice, and can hit *all* the high notes. An aging Sinatra couldn't do it. Perry Como couldn't, nor could most singers who became octogenarians. Maybe it's because he never smoked or drank. In all the years I've known Don, I've never seen him drink one glass of wine.

Don Cherry doesn't throw many bouquets, but I guarantee you, if he's your friend, he'll always be there for you.

—PAUL BERLIN

IIIIIIIIIIIIIIIIIII

WHO AM I TO DEFINE A FRIEND? I'm in a business where so many people call you out as a friend, never knowing the significance of the word. To give you an idea, take Don Cherry (a success in singing as well as golf. Not too many people can lay claim to that feat). I think the reason is that although we may seem miles apart in personalities, we are not.

Don is a loner, and though I go around shaking hands with everyone, I too am a loner.

I never heard Don go boasting around of his achievements, such as having so many beautiful albums and CDs—or his world of golf, which brought so many celebrities to his side, hoping for a few tips on the game. By celebrities, I'm talking about Bob Hope, Bing Crosby, Dean Martin, and on—yet this never went to his head.

Dean Martin was very fond of Don, and the same for Don. They not only played golf, but they had fun with it. "Band of Gold" was a number one hit record, and yet you never heard him talk about it.

How he loves to sing and play golf, and he did them both so well, but I never heard him brag about it. It actually sort of embarrasses him when other people bring it up—but I know he will live through it. It's hard to admit that you love another man, but I do. I get the same feeling from him.

God bless you, Donald.

—SONNY KING

IIIIIIIIIIIIIIIIIII

I CAN'T BELIEVE DON WROTE A BOOK. I don't believe Don Cherry ever read a book . . . be that as it may, when you've finished reading this book about his singing and golfing, may we recommend "2001: A Space Odyssey"—another good science fiction story. Seriously though folks, when you've finished reading this, you'll love him like we do! Don Cherry has always had one foot on the stage and the other foot on the golf course. If he ever gets his legs together, he'll swing beautifully on either!

—STEVE LAWRENCE &
EYDIE GORME

llllllllllllllllll

DEAR DON,

I enjoyed the Texas Golf Hall of Fame event. You were terrific. If I could only sing and play golf, you and I could go on the road. It was great meeting your wife and seeing your sons.

WARM REGARDS,
—GEORGE BUSH

llllllllllllllllll

I'LL NEVER FORGET THE FIRST TIME I heard Don Cherry sing "Band of Gold." I loved it and thought he was a great singer.

I always heard people say he was a great singer, a great golfer, but an asshole. Then I met Don Cherry.

He's a great singer, a great golfer, and a great asshole. He reminds me a lot of myself when I was 35 years old. I was an asshole too!

I only hope when I'm as old as he is, that I'm a great singer, great golfer, and a great asshole like him. I love the man.

—JOE PESCI

Afterword

IIIIIIIIIIIIIIIIIIIIIIIIIIIIIIIIIIIIIIIIIIIIIIIIIIIIIIIIIIIIIIIIIIIIIIIIIIIIIIIIIIIIIIIIIIIIIIIIIIIIIIIIIIIIIIIIIIIIIIIIIIIIIIIIIIIIIIIIIIIIIII

by Neil T. Daniels

AS THE COWRITER, I have pretty much kept myself anonymous. My job was to link the bits and pieces together. To do the research, add the punctuation, and be as descriptive as possible. (A special thanks goes to Jan Russo for believing in the project from the start. Also to Mike Emmerick for his wonderful editing and making sure that it was right. A sincere debt of gratitude to be given to Francine Cherry, who deserves a book of her own.)

I got to call or meet with many of the names Don mentions in the book. No matter how many websites, books, magazines, or newspapers I read, nothing would have been possible without the unparalleled memory of Don Cherry himself. He has a vast diary in that head of his.

Don and I are very similar. I grew up in Pasadena, but not the Pasadena in Don's home state of Texas, instead, Pasadena, *California.* The houses we grew up in have the same description. Like Don finding a golf course to caddie on, I found a neighborhood grocery store to spend my time in.

I want to dedicate this book to a few people of my own: *Tom Joyce,* who took a five-year-old boy under his wing at the store where I spent my childhood. *Ken Preston,* my high school buddy, who has heard and put up with my own rambling stories for over 35 years. *Mort Werner,* whose colors-of-a-peacock helped to brighten and expand a black-and-white mind. *Lee Hale,* who constantly inspires me with all that he has accomplished, and teaches me that it can be done with hard work and talent, but most of all, with caring, kindness, and grace. My six-year-old twins, *Neil and Kelly*, who must think Don is now a relative of theirs, listening to my stories every day. I now view the world through their love-filled eyes. My beautiful wife, *Chris*, who gave me the freedom to work on this project and anything else I attempt to do in life. I am the luckiest man in the world to share life with her.

Finally, my own mother, *Mary Daniels*. I remember as a child catching her one day dancing around the small kitchen of ours. Mom had a spatula in one hand while the radio blasted out a song called "Band of Gold." I asked her who her favorite singer was, and without hesitating, she replied, "Don Cherry!" Mom never changed her answer. When she was diagnosed with cancer, I made her a tape of Don's music to soothe her pain and worries. "Green Green Grass of Home" was the last song my mother heard before her untimely passing. She was not only the greatest mom ever, but my best friend. I miss her very, very much.

I highly suspect that my mother and Don's mother had some sort of hand in bringing us together.

Index

Index